# Constructing Ottoman Beneficence

SUNY series in Near Eastern Studies

# Constructing Ottoman Beneficence

## An Imperial Soup Kitchen in Jerusalem

Amy Singer

State University of New York Press

Published by State University of New York Press, Albany



Printed in the United States of America



For information, address State University of New York Press,
90 State Street, Suite 700, Albany, NY 12207

Production by Kelli Williams
Marketing by Patrick Durocher

**Library of Congress Cataloging-in-Publication Data**

Singer, Amy.
Constructing Ottoman beneficence : an imperial soup kitchen in Jerusalem / Amy Singer.
p. cm. — (SUNY series in Near Eastern studies)
Includes bibliographical references and index.
ISBN 0-7914-5351-0 (hc : alk. paper) — ISBN 0-7914-5352-9 (pbk. : alk. paper)
1. Waqf—Jerusalem—History. 2. Endowments—Jerusalem—History. 3. Turkey—History—Ottoman Empire, 1288–1918—History. I. Title. II. Series.

BP170.25.S56 2002
361.7′5′09569442—dc21 2002024171

10 9 8 7 6 5 4 3 2 1

*To my teachers*

# Contents

# List of Maps and Illustrations

Cover illustration "Die großherrliche Küche," #12 in F. Taeschner, *Alt-Stambuler Hof- und Volksleben, Ein Türkisches Miniaturenalbum aus dem 17. Jahrhundert* (Hannover: Orient-Buchhandlung Heinz Lafaire, 1925, reprinted Osnabrück: Biblio Verlag, 1978). This album includes a rare glimpse of many scenes from everyday life. The illustration depicts the kitchen of a well-to-do notable, probably similar to, though smaller than, that of the Haṣṣeki Sultan ʿimaret. Three, possibly four, stages of food preparation are depicted: preparing the cooking fire with large pieces of wood; cooking soup in a huge cauldron over a blazing fire; carrying the cauldron full of soup, heavy enough to require four men to lift it; and, possibly the head cook, supervising service of soup into bowls. The several smoking chimneys emphasize how much activity such a kitchen generated, with the chimneys in the background suggesting the presence of a baking oven and/or another hearth in an adjacent room. Courtesy of Widener Library, Harvard University. Permission from copyright holder Biblio Verlag (Bissendorf).

Figure 2.1 North façade, an eighteenth-century drawing. 41

Figure 2.2 Doors in the north façade. 42

Figure 2.3 Overall ground plan. 47

Map I.1 The Old City of Jerusalem. 2

Map 2.1 Endowed villages. 51

# Acknowledgments

Philanthropy in all its permutations has grown to be the focus of my research and teaching during the past decade. I am deeply grateful for the extensive financial generosity which has enabled me to complete this book. My research was supported by grants from the Israel Science Foundation founded by the Israel Academy of Sciences and Humanities, the American Research Institute in Turkey, and Tel Aviv University. For their professional help I would like to thank the staffs of the Topkapı Saray Archives and Library, the Başbakanlık Arşivi, Haifa University Library, Tel Aviv University Library, the Jewish National Union Library, Widener Library at Harvard University, the Skilliter Centre for Ottoman Studies (Newnham College, Cambridge), and the Oriental Institute, and Bodleian Libraries at Oxford. A special thanks to Mualla Kalaycıoğlu of the Haseki Hospital Library in Istanbul.

As I worked out an understanding of the Haṣṣeki Sultan ʿimaret, I was fortunate enough to have many thoughtful and articulate interlocutors. Ideas that evolved into this book were born and flourished in conversations, lectures, and seminars with my students and colleagues in the Department of Middle Eastern and African History at Tel Aviv University; at the Center for Middle East Studies at Harvard University; at the Murat Sarıca Seminar, the American Research Institute in Turkey, the Institut Français d'Etudes Anatoliennes and at Bilkent University in Turkey; and at the Middle East Center of St. Antony's College, Oxford. For their insights and assistance, I would like to thank Butrus Abu Manneh, Tülay Artan, Halil Berktay, Hülya

Canbakal, Paul Cobb, Kate Fleet, Jane Hathaway, Halil Inalcık, Cemal Kafadar, Benjamin Lellouch, Yusuf Natsheh, Gülru Necipoğlu, Christoph Neumann, Nicole van Os, Eleanor Robson, Jim Secord, Lucienne Şenocak, Sara Wolper, Lucette Valensi and Dror Ze'evi.

For the past six years, Michael Bonner and Mine Ener have been collaborators on a larger conference and book project about charity and poverty in the Middle East. Working with them has provided a continual source of inspiration and ideas. They and the scholars who convened for four days at the University of Michigan's Center for Middle East and North African Studies in May 2000 under the auspices of an NEH Collaborative Research Grant helped sharpen my thinking and articulate many of the complex issues raised by philanthropy.

Leslie Peirce is my valued *yoldaş* of many years in exploring Turkey and Ottoman history. Together we have discovered and discussed the endless variety of physical, material, and written documents that make the study of Ottoman history so compelling. Miri Shefer and Liat Kozma worked as my research assistants during the years that produced this book. I would like to thank them for their invaluable contribution of enthusiastic and intelligent help with all aspects of the project.

My thanks to Michael Rinella, Kelli Williams, and Patrick Durocher of SUNY Press for their editorial expertise and guidance.

With so much help and encouragement, I would be ungenerous if I did not acknowledge that I failed to heed all the advice given and to incorporate the wealth of suggestions proffered.

Finally, thanks seems a small word to recognize the unwavering companionship David Katz has provided as a partner in this life.

# ABBREVIATIONS

| | |
|---|---|
| *EI* | *Encyclopaedia of Islam* (Leiden: Brill, 1913–1934) |
| *EI*$^{2}$ | *Encyclopaedia of Islam,* 2nd edition (Leiden: Brill, 1960– ) |
| *İA* | *İslam Ansiklopedisi* (Istanbul: Milli Eğitim Bakanlığı, 1949–1986) |
| *IJMES* | *International Journal of Middle Eastern Studies* |
| *İstA* | *Dünden Bugüne İstanbul Ansiklopedisi* (Istanbul: Kultur Bakanlığı ve Tarih Vakfının ortak yayınıdır, 1993–1995) |
| *JAOS* | *Journal of the American Oriental Society* |
| *JESHO* | *Journal of the Economic and Social History of the Orient* |
| JS | Jerusalem *sijill* |
| MD | *mühimme defteri* |
| Pakalın | Mehmet Zeki Pakalın, *Osmanlı Tarih Deyimleri ve Terimleri Sözlüğü* (Istanbul: Milli Eğitim Bakanlığı, 1946–1956) |
| *SEI* | *Shorter Encyclopaedia of Islam* (Leiden: Brill, 1953) |
| TSAD | Topkapı Saray Arşivi, Defter |
| TSAE | Topkapı Saray Arşivi, Evrak |
| TSK | Topkapı Saray Kütüphanesi |
| TTD | *tapu tahrir defteri* |

# Note on Ottoman Turkish and Arabic Transliterations

The use of Ottoman Turkish and Arabic sources has complicated the matter of transliterations in this book, as has the use of scholarly writings based on sources in these languages, as well as Persian or written in English, French, German, Turkish, and Hebrew. I have tried to be systematic but cannot promise that I was entirely successful.

In general, when referring to sources in Ottoman Turkish, I have transliterated into modern Turkish (e.g., *sancak*) but maintaining the use of diacritic marks for words originally from the Arabic (*fakır*). When referring to words in Arabic, and especially the names of villages belonging to the waqf, I have used standard Arabic transliteration as recommended by *IJMES* (Niʿlīn, Yāzūr).

Words that appear in the *Concise Oxford English Dictionary*, such as "kadi," I have written without italics. I have also written the words "waqf," "ʿimaret" and "waqfiyya" without italics as their frequency would make the text look too cluttered if each instance were italicized.

In Turkish words, the following characters are pronounced as indicated:

c = "j" as in jam
ç = "ch" as in church
ğ = soft g, lengthening the sound of the preceding vowel
ı = undotted "i," sounds like the "e" of shovel
ş = "sh" as in ship

# INTRODUCTION

And she also set down the following condition: that each of the righteous men who sojourned in the room should receive a ladle of soup and a loaf of bread at every meal served, and a piece of stew meat on Friday evenings; that the *imam* of the mosque, the clerk of the endowment, and [the employees] of the public kitchen each receive a ladle of soup and two loaves of bread at every meal served, and a piece of stew meat on Friday evenings; and she also established that at every meal served, four hundred persons from among the poor and wretched, weak and needy each receive a loaf of bread and each two a ladle of soup in a bowl between them, and share a piece of stew meat on Friday evenings. Furthermore, it was made a condition that no one other than the aforementioned servants be appointed [to receive] food by claiming a pre-emptive right or by request, and that no one make it a habit to remove food in copper buckets. Such that if by some means someone removed the food designated [for him], let it give him no sustenance.[1]

Hurrem Sultan, wife of the Ottoman Sultan Süleyman I, specified these instructions for the endowment she made in Jerusalem in the years before she died in 1558. Today, in the center of the old walled city, the large and imposing building complex known as the Haṣṣeki Sultan ʿimaret or al-Takiyya still sits just up the hill from the

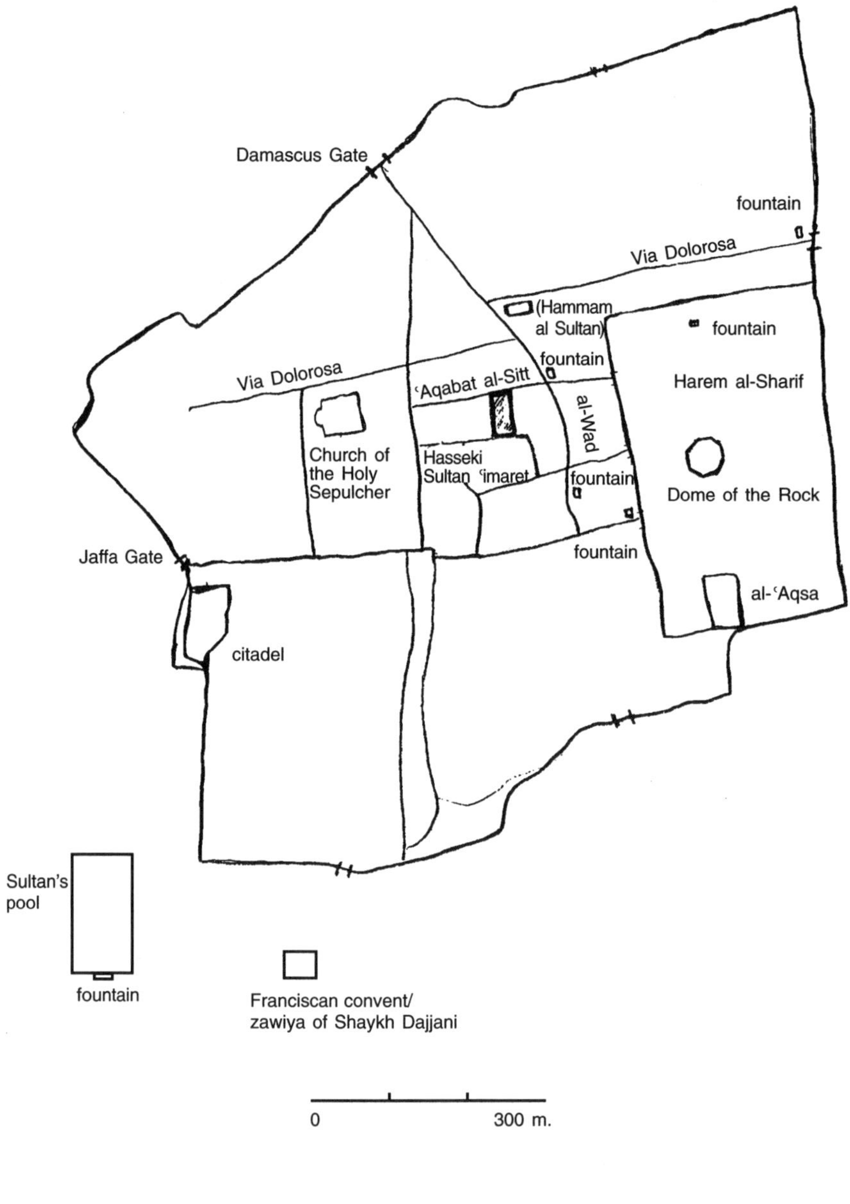


Map I.1 The Old City of Jerusalem, the Haṣṣeki Sultan ʿimaret in the center. Map by the author.

corner where Al-Wād and ʿAqabat al-Takiyya Streets intersect, one block south of the Via Dolorosa. ʿAqabat al-Takiyya (Incline of the Hospice) was known in the past as ʿAqabat al-Sūq (Incline of the Market), for the market that crossed above its steep western incline. Eastward, the street leads briefly down and then up again toward the Ḥaram al-Sharīf, the Noble Sanctuary, from where the Dome of the Rock and the al-Aqṣā mosque dominate the Jerusalem skyline. The street has also been called ʿAqabat al-Sitt (Incline of the Woman), not for Hurrem, but for Ṭunshūq, the Mamluk woman who built the original house on the site at the end of the fourteenth century. From the outside of the building, the worn walls and huge doorways define its circumference much as they did in the sixteenth century. Inside, the agglomeration of structures bears witness to over four centuries of repairs and reconstructions, leaving one to wonder as to the precise contours of the original fourteenth-century house and the later repairs and additions.[2]

Around the year 1550, amidst the din of building and the dusty work of carrying stone, sand, and plaster to make repairs to the existing structure, the identity of the Ottoman imperial patroness was completely unambiguous to Jerusalem's residents. Her agents were already busy supervising renovations.[3] Early in the 1550s, the public kitchen (*ʿimaret*)—the most active facility in the endowment—began to serve rice soup and bulgur (cracked wheat) soup from vast cauldrons to some 500 people, morning and evening. Food continued to be served or distributed there in the succeeding centuries. In 1705, Antoine Morison, a devout French traveler, noted: "Each day, approximately one pound of bread and one bowl of soup, made with olive oil and some vegetables, cooked in cauldrons of remarkable thickness, breadth and depth, are given to each poor person who arrives there."[4] And Ermete Pierotti, a French architect and draughtsman writing 150 years after Morison, found the same scene, if somewhat diminished: "only one cauldron (5 feet in diameter and 4 deep) over a large furnace is in use; four others are seen as a reproach to the managers, who keep them unworked . . . In the one in use a quantity of wheat is boiled, and after being seasoned with good oil, is distributed among the poor, each of whom also receives from two to four loaves."[5] Since the 1920s, the same building has housed the Muslim Vocational Orphanage (*Dār al-Aytām al-Islāmiyya al-Ṣināʿiyya*), although this has not disturbed the distribution of food from the site. UNESCO handed out food there in the 1950s, and today food continues to be served daily to some needy people, while the orphanage remains a vibrant institution. Some current Jerusalem residents remember going to the ʿimaret as children for a bowl of soup early in the morning.[6]

As the consort of Sultan Süleyman I, Hurrem Sultan had made endowments (or had seen them made in her name) in the Ottoman imperial cities of Istanbul, Bursa, and Edirne, as well as in Mecca and Medina, the towns holiest to Muslims. Known in Christian Europe as Roxelana, she was the most powerful woman in the Ottoman empire during the mid-sixteenth century and not an obscure character in the annals of Ottoman history. The endowment in Jerusalem was not as large an undertaking as her Haseki complex in Istanbul, which permanently named an entire quarter in that city.[7] Nor was it as stunning as the double bath she built, which still stands in the center of Istanbul between the Aya Sofya and the Sultan Ahmet mosque (the "Blue mosque"). Hurrem died the year after the Jerusalem ʿimaret was formally established, and it was her final endowment. Collectively, these endowments amplified the traditional idioms of imperial female beneficence, immortalized the memory of Hurrem, and enhanced even further the reputation of her powerful husband.

A pious endowment organized within the context of Muslim law and society is called a *waqf* (pl. *awqāf*). Though waqf-making has no explicit articulation in the *Qur'an*, there are verses that contain repeated admonitions to believers that they be charitable, that they give in addition to the alms (*zakāt*) that were the specific obligation of all Muslims. Evidence of endowments exists from the early records of Islamic history, though they became more prevalent and more popular over time. Endowments existed throughout the Islamic world, serving as the agents of everything from small-scale beneficence to large public welfare projects, building anything from mosques and schools, to roads and bridges, to neighborhood water fountains. Their beneficiaries included, equally, scholars and students, sufi dervishes, indigents and family members. Differences in size and purpose shaped them, as did the skill and sincerity with which they were managed and the effects of their immediate environments.

In Ottoman times, endowments were the ubiquitous formal vehicle of voluntary beneficent action for Muslim men and women who owned property outright, whether in large or small holdings. Members of the Ottoman imperial family were active patrons, and the built testaments of their endowments may be found throughout the towns of the former Ottoman lands. Most often, the creation of imperial endowments included the construction of buildings suitable for providing services in ritual, education, and health. Each huge beneficent complex comprised some combination of separate units: mosque, college, hospital, sufi residence, public kitchen, caravansaray, library, market, bath, and others. They were micro-economies in themselves, with their component structures constituting integrated physical units that took over large blocks of urban space, harnessed extensive urban and rural revenues to support their purposes, and affected large numbers of people both directly and indirectly.

By the time of Hurrem Sultan, the tradition of imperial Ottoman endowment-making was firmly in place, reinforced both by the wealth of the dynasty, the ambitions of prominent individuals, and the expectations of the subject populations. Yet the Ottoman empire was not unique, neither among empires nor among Muslim communities, in engendering an active tradition of endowment-making among the most powerful, prominent, and wealthy of its subjects. Waqf-making evolved under the ʿAbbasids and the states that followed them—Ayyubids, Selçuks, Mamluks and others.

Contemporary observers and historians alike have focused on the charitable and constructive aspects of waqf-making, while at the same time criticizing the more selfish motivations of the founders and the destructive impact on endowed properties. Yet generous acts everywhere are financed by wealth acquired through diverse, sometimes questionable, means and motivated by wide-ranging purposes and ambitions. This is not exceptional. Few forms of charity have ever been pure acts of altruism, and only a very few sponsors appear as utterly selfless patrons. However, the human chronicle of philanthropic endeavors is long and also records great good achieved for individuals and societies. In part, we are here concerned to understand precisely this: how philanthropy is used to achieve various aims. Any close examination of charitable activities affords a surprising range of insights into the character of individuals, societies, and states. The case of imperial charity highlights another means by which rulers used resources, regulated and directed their flow as well as how subjects were managed through the resulting institutions.

Beneficence, philanthropy, and charity will all be used here as synonymous translations of the term *ṣadaqa.* While it may be argued that each has a particular meaning, they all refer basically to doing good voluntarily for some person(s) in need, with need defined by the donor. The mechanisms and structures for organizing charitable endeavors, the motivations expressed and implied in their establishment, the kind of relief distributed, and the beneficiaries selected all continually shape attitudes toward charity, wealth, and the role of the powerful. At the same time, they define poverty, deservedness, and the place of the needy in society. However, this book is not about poverty or the poor *per se.* It is about beneficence, whose recipients include people deemed deserving because of their spiritual, social, or economic status, and these include the poor and weak.

*Ṣadaqa* in Islamic law is distinguished explicitly from *hiba*, gift, because it does not require the contractually binding acts of offer and acceptance (*ijāb wa-qabūl*) between individuals. For the jurists, these and several other conditions had to be met to create a valid gift.[8] In social terms, the distance between charity and gift may in fact be less clear, especially an informal act such as putting money in the hand of a beggar or leaving food at the doorstep of a needy family. Even the large-scale imperial distributions of food through waqfs to be discussed here might seem to share some aspects of gift-giving, particularly as they imply an acceptance not only of food but of sovereignty and a reciprocal gift of loyalty. Yet there is a distinction necessary between gift-giving and the formal endowments that constituted waqfs and created large, ongoing institutions like the Haṣṣeki Sultan ʿimaret. One could begin with the observation that a waqf is a one-time gift whose beneficiaries continue for generations; inevitably, it lacks the quality of a transaction between specific individuals. Gifts and their relationship to beneficence are not the focus of the present study, though they deserve a separate inquiry. A social history of gift-giving does not exist for Islamic or Middle Eastern history.[9]

One pious endowment is examined here in depth. It is true that no one waqf can be singled out as a prototype of endowments, for reasons that become apparent in the following discussions. Yet the Jerusalem waqf of Hurrem Sultan was typical of Ottoman imperial endowments for the way in which it was established and managed. Though large in Jerusalem and Palestine, it was among the smaller of such complexes, and though its provincial location (many days' travel from the imperial capital in Istanbul) might have diminished its status, the special sanctity of Jerusalem compensated somewhat for the intervening distance.

The ʿimaret of Hurrem Sultan first came to my attention because it took over large amounts of revenue produced in the villages of southern Syria that were the subject of a previous study.[10] It was an important new institution, and its affairs and agents quickly permeated the human, built, and cultivated systems of Jerusalem and the surrounding region. Further investigation of the waqf itself has revealed its rich extant historical record, both in the Ottoman archives in Istanbul and in the records of the Muslim judges (*kadi*) of Jerusalem. Moreover, the ʿimaret is a living legacy, continuing to function to the end of the period of Ottoman rule, through the years of the British Mandate, Jordanian sovereignty, and Israeli rule in Jerusalem.

While its longevity is intriguing, neither the continuity of function nor the continuous concentration of historical record is unique to the waqf of Hurrem Sultan. Major monuments like this one had a better chance of surviving intact than smaller endowments, as did their documentation.[11] The records of countless Ottoman endowments of all sizes survive in Turkish archives.[12] Many buildings, too, remain to testify to the beneficence of their long-dead patrons. Like the Haṣṣeki Sultan ʿimaret, one may find them still in use. In addition to the eye-catching mosques, public kitchens, too, still operate—for example, in the complex of Bayezid II in Amasya and in that of Mihrişah Valide Sultan at Eyüp in Istanbul.[13]

Concentrating on one endowment highlights its particular component institutions and explains how they both affected and were shaped by local politics, economics, society, and culture, even during the first years of their existence. The discussion of one waqf is important not only because the complex process of its founding and operations touched numerous aspects of local economy and society, but because the evidence available about this one foundation also compels a reconsideration of certain modern myths and allegations about waqfs. These derive partly from the historiography of the nineteenth- and twentieth-century Middle East and Islamic world, which often sought to blame Muslim institutions for their perceived failure to modernize. In part, too, the endowments and their influence on property relations and agricultural production were distorted (and sometimes demonized) because the sources employed to study them were chiefly normative legal texts or prescriptive foundation documents, and not ongoing records of waqf activities. Deviations from prescribed norms read in written texts led observers who lacked an extensive understanding of the institution to compose severe criticisms of waqfs.[14]

This book focuses on the period and circumstances of the initial founding of the Haṣṣeki Sultan ʿimaret. The volume of documentary material extant on this institution might have been reason enough for this concentration. More importantly, the complex genesis of this endowment merits focused consideration because it opens a window on the entire culture of Ottoman imperial philanthropy. When Hurrem Sultan set about creating the endowment in Jerusalem, she was acting within a framework of traditions, motivations, and circumstances constructed from elements of Ottoman and Islamic history and culture, as well as from the immediate context of the empire in the mid-sixteenth century. The conceptualization of such a foundation came largely from

Istanbul, from the amalgam of forces that constituted the imperial Ottoman world. This book aims to untangle and explicate the social realities, economic pressures, political ambitions, beneficent practices, and spiritual promptings which created a philanthropic endeavor and a uniquely Ottoman institution. A companion purpose is to discover how such an endowment was actually put together and set to work, that is, to understand its physical and functional construction.

Once established, the waqf belonged more and more to Jerusalem culture and society, less and less to the more remote realm of the imperial center. Rather quickly and unsurprisingly, the waqf became an integral element in the landscape of Jerusalem, deeply entangled in the particularities of the city and region, and in the web of relations that brought Ottoman imperial authority face to face (in various guises) with the needs and interests of local Jerusalemites (of all types). As the owner of large agricultural properties in the region, the employer of some fifty persons and the source of regular assistance to a needy population, the waqf was inextricably enmeshed in the economic and social dynamics of Jerusalem. Of course, a continual tension persisted in the character and administration of such an institution, since the Ottoman central administration never relinquished a claim to be responsible for its functioning. The waqf thus remained unmistakably Ottoman, as did a great many Ottoman institutions in their local and provincial incarnations.

Altogether, the purpose of this book is to situate the creation of the Haṣṣeki Sultan ʿimaret at the intersection of several aspects of Ottoman culture and tradition. The arrangement of the chapters is intended to enable readers to consider the ʿimaret in several aspects simultaneously. The ʿimaret is both the concrete example of certain general ideas about waqf-making, the philanthropy of prominent women and Ottoman food-related policies, as well as an object of study in and of itself. Three chapters (1, 3, 5) address general themes of Ottoman history and some theoretical propositions concerning them, providing a frame for the more empirical chapters (2, 4). There is thus an alternating rhythm between the general, imperial context of beneficence and the specific Jerusalem endowment.

First, the ʿimaret was founded in the context of Ottoman endowment-making, which combined Muslim, Byzantine, and earlier traditions of imperial philanthropic endeavors. Chapter 1, "Devote the fruits to pious purposes," provides a basic explication of waqf. The discussion draws a coherent picture of the structural components of endowments, the origins and evolution of waqf-making, and the constellation of motivations that inspired it.[15] It serves as a starting point for discussing endowments in Islamic societies generally, Ottoman society more particularly, and most specifically, the ʿimaret of Hurrem Sultan. In part, its purpose is to introduce a non-specialist to the institution of waqf and provide an historical survey of the activity of waqf-making. At the same time, this chapter raises some of the more problematic questions about the nature of endowments, to which later chapters will suggest some new kinds of answers.

Chapter 2, "A Bowl of Soup and a Loaf of Bread," considers how the endowment came to be, reading the endowment deed as a reflection of the founder's motivations and intentions for the structure and functioning of the waqf's institutions. It thus provides immediate illustration of many issues raised in the first chapter. An initial tour of the buildings and endowed properties, the personnel and beneficiaries, traces the creation of Hurrem's waqf for a few years beyond her death. The chapter explores the spectrum of motivations for establishing the Jerusalem endowment within the contexts of both imperial and local politics and society. It allows us to understand how the ʿimaret was meant to operate before considering how it did work and the significance of its existence both for Jerusalem and for the empire.

Once the reader is familiar with the public kitchen and its inception as both an ideal and a physical institution, the discussion turns to the founder and her importance within the contexts of Ottoman history and the beneficence of women. Waqf-making exemplified the specific role of imperial women as philanthropic agents in Ottoman times, although the highly visible role of imperial or high-ranking women as patrons belonged to numerous traditions. Chapter 3, "Ladies Bountiful," looks closely at these women. It builds on the recent research about Ottoman imperial women and the nature of the power they exercised in the imperial household. This work has demonstrated the extent to which women like Hurrem could be independent agents in their endowment-making, as well as key partners of the sultan in the projects of imperial legitimation and image-building associated with the endowments.[16] In addition, the ties explored here between the Ottoman Hurrem Sultan, the Byzantine Empress Helena, and the Mamluk al-Sitt Ṭunshūq exemplify the dynamic relationship between the Ottoman empire and its various predecessors, both on the imperial level and in specific locations around the empire. The connections between these women open up a further dimension in the present discussion, that of the role of gender in endowment-making, as well as giving a place to individual women in the present story.

The public activism of women in the Ottoman world also had—and has—numerous counterparts in other cultures and periods. Ottoman women participated in a seemingly universal phenomenon: that of women of wealth, rank, and power who realize that power by undertaking large beneficent endeavors, whether for their own sake or as part of a family or communal effort. Women have appeared throughout history as energetic philanthropists in many of the world's cultures and societies. Contemporary newspapers are also replete with examples of wealthy and powerful women, as well as men, giving away some portion of their resources for the benefit of cultural, spiritual, civic, welfare, medical, and educational institutions. As benefactors, these women and men are generally recognized and applauded as exemplary members of society. Yet women have often earned special renown for their beneficent endeavors and their patronage of those needing assistance and relief, through myth and tradition, by virtue of limited public roles available, reinforced by the tendency to view women's options within a narrow spectrum of mostly nurturing stereotypes. One must ask, therefore, whether and how there is a gendering of charitable activity that directs women to that role and shapes their philanthropic choices.

Chapter 3 focuses more closely on Jerusalem, and the focus is maintained in Chapter 4, "Serving Soup in Jerusalem." This detailed chapter is intended to contrast with the more theoretical and idealized formulations of waqf in Chapters 1 and 2 by demonstrating some of the complex realities of managing a waqf day to day, year to year. It complements the preceding discussions of women and Jerusalem, which emphasized the dynamic and organic evolution of the site. While the endowment deed is the point of departure for this discussion, it serves only as a base line against which to consider the waqf in operation. Its managers used the deed as a norm to which they referred in running the place or to which they might be held, but they were obliged by practical considerations and immediate daily needs to make changes in order to adhere as closely as possible to the general purpose of the endowment.

Food and traditions of feeding also influenced the formation of the waqf in Jerusalem and the institution of the Ottoman *aşhane* or "food house."[17] The public kitchen was the focal institution in the Jerusalem endowment, carefully organized and provisioned, scrutinized regularly to try to ensure its proper functioning. In order to understand the imperial concern displayed over one particular kitchen's pots and porridges, Chapter 5, "Feeding Power," picks up many of the specific examples presented in the preceding chapters but examines them in another imperial context, that of food supply and distribution in the Ottoman empire more generally.

The focus on ensuring supplies of basic foodstuffs to its subjects was not unique to the Ottoman empire. Provisioning cities was imperative, including distributing basic sustenance to those who could not feed themselves and stocking provisions against emergency shortages. The stipulations quoted from the endowment deed at the beginning of this introduction all testify to the degree of control over distributions that the Ottomans sought to retain. Moreover, differences in the quantities of food allotted to various groups clearly reflected hierarchies of deservedness as defined from above. Imperial generosity was measured and circumscribed, tuned to the political barometers of cities around the empire, and consciously employed to emphasize Ottoman hegemony. The aggregate effect of all food distribution mechanisms in the Ottoman empire meant that a significant proportion of the urban population was receiving some assistance or subsidy of its daily sustenance. The public kitchen endowed by Hurrem is evaluated in this context, as well as for its impact locally in Jerusalem.

Altogether, the book enables its readers to know intimately one public kitchen while building an explanation of how this particular institution (and, to some extent, this type of institution) existed at the intersection of multiple dimensions of the Ottoman world.

The Ottoman archival collections contain simultaneously a wealth and poverty of sources on this topic. By combining the uniquely rich surviving documentation, the manner and complex process of endowing can be explored not only through the intentions set down in the endowment deed, but also in their execution. Reports from the Topkapı Palace archives, the *mühimme defterleri* (records of imperial orders) and the *kadı sicilleri* (judicial protocols) of Jerusalem together afford a far more explicit understanding of how the properties were reshuffled and revenues apportioned, and the ways in which local concerns affected the seemingly straightforward organization of an imperial endowment. On their own, the physical grandeur and orderliness of the foundation documents (*mülknames*, *waqfiyyas*) and the regular columns of the official registers of expenditures (*muḥasebe defterleri*) belie the more difficult reality of the institution's beginnings and daily operations. The dynamics of transferring the properties, organizing services, and sorting out employees and beneficiaries shed new light on the process of endowment-making, the history of Ottoman Jerusalem, and the nature of Ottoman provincial administration.

These same sources, however, shed little light on events, practices, accidents, or attitudes that were not part of an official record of operations. They are practically mute concerning the perspective of those who ate at the ʿimaret and yield little on that of the employees or the peasants who supplied the bulk of its foodstuffs. The impoverished people who received a measure of sustenance from the vast cauldrons remain largely unknown in the historical record. Nor do we have a clear notion of how people gained the right initially to receive food from the kitchen or an indication of the criteria used to judge poverty or deservedness.

The research of other scholars, such as Suraiya Faroqhi, Miriam Hoexter, and the late Ronald Jennings, has already demonstrated the rich detail available in Ottoman archives about single institutions.[18] There is also a tradition of waqf research that has produced analytic works asking more general questions about waqf; they include the writings of Baer, Barkan, Gerber, and Yediyıldız.[19] These maintain waqf as the focus, the central problematic. Yet waqf is often only one form of many larger categories; for example, it is one kind of property holding, one type of capital investment, one form of patronage, one mode of beneficence. And it is within these multiple, overlapping contexts that I think it is most useful to consider it.

Nonetheless, until now it has rarely been possible to trace out in continuous detail the series of steps by which the revenue sources of an endowment were organized, the buildings prepared, and the whole put to work at its pious purpose. More importantly, it becomes clear through this analysis that waqf-making is a far more complex, varied, and imperfect process in its execution than the more usual descriptions of it indicate, often based on the endowment deed alone. Robert McChesney wrote diachronically about the shrine complex in Balkh and demonstrated how changeable one endowment can be, using a variety of sources. Miriam Hoexter's work on the Awqāf al-Ḥaramayn of Algiers undertook a similar project, though with different kinds of sources and questions.[20] The present study enjoys a denser documentary base from which to discuss a single institution than either of these two. Here, the endowment deeds are only one of several kinds of Ottoman records available. The combination of endowment deeds, property titles, account registers, reports, imperial orders, and local judicial registers supplies abundant sources for a study of the Haṣṣeki Sultan ʿimaret.

Much of the once-absolutist sense of the nature and administration of endowments is contravened by such a close examination, and it further impels us to reconsider some truisms about endowments generally. There is a tendency to understand the process of foundation as one which removed properties from their usual context and to see all operations which sought to return them to the market as aberrant. Any deviation from the original plan of the endowment was blamed on corrupt managers and the flawed nature of waqfs. Careful consideration, however, shows that the original plan of a waqf was more a general outline than a detailed blueprint for all times. As McChesney has noted: "Many authors, whether legal thinkers attempting to formalize the principles of waqf or scholars concerned with waqf as a phenomenon in history, have found it difficult to correlate the idea of the inevitability of change with the legal concept of waqf's immutability."[21]

"Practicing Beneficence," the concluding chapter, assesses to what extent the Jerusalem endowment succeeded in fulfilling its purpose initially. The chapter reflects further on the nature of Ottoman beneficence to examine in what ways it shares traits with beneficence universally and in what ways the particularities of the Ottoman world and Jerusalem make it unique. This study took shape in response to a lacuna on the subject in Ottoman history, both for Ottomanists and for historians generally. Conclusions offered here thus contribute to an overall reconsideration of the meaning and importance of waqfs in Ottoman and Islamic histories. The structure of endowments was an integral aspect of Ottoman institutional history. Beneficence was inextricably woven into the most basic fabric of Ottoman society; the empire was not a welfare state but a welfare society. At the same time, Ottoman imperial modes of beneficence provide an important paradigm for the study of beneficence worldwide.

Beneficence itself is important as a subject of study. The instinct to give is perhaps a shared one, but the articulation of that instinct occurs in culturally specific terms. Empirical studies of charitable endeavors in Europe and the United States exist in large number. The present preoccupation and concern to (re)assess and question the effectiveness of welfare states as agents of beneficence and charitable relief is partly what prompted the present examination of an historical situation. Yet rather than search for "missing" institutions familiar in Western societies, this study emphatically focuses on the Ottoman model to understand its role in Ottoman society.

The historical investigation of beneficence is integral to interpreting any society or culture of the past. To understand the history of beneficence means also to understand how notions of entitlement and obligation evolved in societies, creating the systems, commitments, and ideologies in which we live today. Without an appreciation of the ways in which states and societies develop effective forms of relief for dependent individuals and groups, one can scarcely comprehend much of contemporary political and economic discourse and culture. The same is true of the past.

Chapter One

# "Devote the Fruits to Pious Purposes"

"And those that believe, and do deeds of righteousness—those are the inhabitants of Paradise; there they shall dwell forever." (*Qur'an* II:82)[1]

"The Prophet said: 'When a person dies, his achievement expires, except with regard to three things—ongoing charity (*ṣadaqa jārīya*) or knowledge from which people benefit or a son who prays for him.' "[2]

Endowments exist in myriad forms around the world, created when an individual, an organization, or a political entity sets aside resources and designates the revenues to support a specific purpose. The beneficiaries may be family members, religious institutions, cultural endeavors, health facilities and services, public works, or needy and impoverished people. As a vehicle for philanthropy, endowments belong to a category of human endeavor that existed before the founding of Islam in the early seventh century C.E. and one that remains integral to many human societies today.[3]

No contemporary written documentation or other evidence exists to record the precise inception of endowments in the Muslin world. No one has yet shown definitively the first steps of their development in Islamic law and society, though they clearly belong to the earliest periods of Islamic history. Judgments and claims about waqf origins and evolution thus begin to some extent *in medias res*. Informed speculation, rather than continuous and unequivocal evidence, is the basis for identifying the roots of endowment–making in early Muslin society.[4] According to Islamic tradition, the first waqf was made by the Prophet from the wealth left to him by one of his followers. Alternatively, the first waqf is ascribed to ʿUmar b. al-Khaṭṭāb, who asked the Prophet whether he should give away as charity (*ṣadaqa*) valuable lands he had received. The Prophet told him: *"in shi'ta ḥabbasta aṣlahā wa-taṣaddaqta bihā"* ("If you want, retain the thing itself and devote its fruits to pious purposes.") This ʿUmar did, specifying that the land should never be transferred by sale or inheritance.[5]

The earliest written references to waqf include legal texts and inscriptions from the late eighth and early ninth centuries C.E.[6] By the time these records were made, the works of the jurists recorded not only evolving doctrines but also the disputes among themselves about the nature of waqf and the details of laws applicable to it, indicating that the institution had been in place for some time. More ordered and comprehensive legal works on waqf were produced in the mid-ninth century, by Hilāl al-Ra'y (d. 245/859) and al-Khaṣṣāf (d. 261/874), who were the first to devote whole treatises to the subject.[7]

However it began, waqf-making acquired popularity as the chief vehicle of formal philanthropy throughout the Muslim world. Despite the strict legal constraints surrounding their founding and operation, endowments evolved as enormously flexible and practical institutions. Part of their popularity also derived from the fact that the waqf was not merely a tool of philanthropy, but simultaneously achieved other goals for the founders. Hence waqf has continued to be used until the present in Muslim communities, and in many cases the laws governing waqf-making have today been integrated to national constitutions and legal systems implemented by individual states.[8]

Scholars have pointed to waqf as one instrument that traditionally organized and distributed relief and assistance to the needy and weak in Muslim communities. What gradually has become the responsibility of governments, public agencies, and non-governmental organizations in the modern era was, for the most part, previously undertaken in beneficent endowments constructed by individuals, often from among the wealthy and powerful elites.[9] Much relief was probably also distributed informally within communities, as has often been the case in societies and cultures around the world.[10] Unlike informal assistance, however, waqfs usually generated an inky trail which now lends them disproportionate visibility as historical objects. The historian has a more difficult task to document informal assistance, though it may also be institutionalized as customary distributions of food or money at holidays, or at festivals such as circumcisions, weddings, and funerals.[11]

This chapter examines the components of waqf and surveys the spectrum of motivations attributed to endowment makers. For those with no prior experience or knowledge of Islamic endowments, it is important to understand their basic structure and the relationship among the component parts before embarking on this investigation of Ottoman beneficence. In addition, an examination of the motivations for and purposes served by waqf-making will make it possible to appreciate the popularity of this institution. Fundamental misapprehensions of the nature of waqf's component parts and the motivations for founding waqfs have led to criticism of the institutions based on mistaken assumptions. As a result, endowments and endowment-making have been condemned, at times without really understanding them. Only an understanding of their complex nature and the use of endowments over time enables us to recognize which flaws derive from the institution and which from the particular circumstances in which it was founded or operated.

Understanding the roots of Muslim waqf-making establishes some of the cultural context of the Ottoman practice. Although existing research on waqfs throughout the Muslim world since the rise of Islam is substantial, the chronicle still has vast lacunae. The present chapter is intended to situate Ottoman imperial waqf-making, so as to demonstrate how it belongs to a tradition of imperial Muslim philanthropy while at the same time constituting a particularly Ottoman exercise. The discussion also situates Jerusalem as a long-time focus of Muslim philanthropy and as a part of the Ottoman empire.

## WHAT IS A WAQF?

A waqf is a pious endowment, established according to the stipulations of Islamic law. *Waqf* means, literally, "stopping," and this one word has come to refer to the entire institution of pious endowments in Islamic societies. It is not clear precisely when or why the Arabic roots *w-q-f* and *ḥ-b-s* ("to hold, imprison") were associated with the institution, but "waqf" was in widespread use by the third/ninth century. The basic connotation of these roots—"to bring to a halt; to hinder"—refers to the suspension of transactions imposed on the properties transferred into the endowment for the beneficiaries. If the beneficiary was a structure like a mosque or school, then it, too, was untransferable, the thing itself "halted," its ownership unavailable for sale, surety, mortgage, or legacy.[12]

Men and women, wealthy and humble, established pious foundations throughout the Muslim world. Most of the written evidence for specific endowments documents the more conspicuous actions of wealthy and powerful individuals. Yet waqf-making was restricted only by the requirement that the property endowed be owned outright by the founder and that the founder be of sound mind, adult, and free (*ʿāqil, bāligh, ḥurr*) and unencumbered by unfulfilled liabilities when establishing the endowment.[13]

The multiplicity of functions and relations that construct a waqf have caused the meaning of the word to become less precise and often misleading over time. It has become the shorthand denotation of what is actually a system of relations (or rather, many versions of a basic system) between properties and people, each element having a defined function within the whole. Technically, a waqf comprises the properties or things endowed (*mawqūf*) which produce revenues to support a specific beneficiary *(mawqūf ʿalayhi*). The person establishing the waqf (*wāqif*) may only endow things that he or she possesses entirely and freely (*mülk*). Thus there can be no outstanding claims or liens against the property, and the ownership is of the principal (*aṣl*) and not merely a usufructory right (*taṣarruf, manfaʿa*).

A vast range of immovable properties of varying dimensions may be endowed: whole buildings and single rooms, huge fields and small garden plots, orchards and individual trees, as well as commercial structures like mills, looms, presses, and bath houses. Movable items like *Qur'ans*, carpets, and furnishings for mosques and shrines, as well as weapons and horses for warfare can also be endowed, although some disputes exist among the Muslim schools of law (*madhhabs*) in this respect, as well as changes over time. In the sixteenth and seventeenth centuries, the debate about what could be endowed focused on the cash waqf (*waaf al-nuqūd*), wherein monies endowed to the waqf had to be put to work, earning interest, in order to yield the needed revenues. As the taking of interest (*ribā'*) was forbidden in Islamic law, the cash waqf seemed to constitute a legal impossibility, one that was harshly condemned and debated. Opponents of the practice were very vocal in the sixteenth century, but ultimately failed to halt its widespread use. On the pragmatic side, the chief religious official of the Ottoman empire, Şeyhülislam Ebu's-Suʿud Efendi (d. 1574) allowed cash waqfs because they constituted a popular practice (*taʿāmul* and *taʿāruf*), served the welfare of the people (*istiḥsān*) and had been allowed in some previous judicial rulings. Cash endowments came to provide an important source of credit in Ottoman society.[14] Only in the Arabic-speaking lands of the empire, Muslim before the Ottoman conquest, did the cash waqf not develop extensively.

The beneficiaries of an endowment were institutions such as a mosque (*jāmiʿ, masjid,*), college (*madrasa*) school (*maktab*), sufi residence (*khānqāh, zāwiya, ribāṭ*) public kitchen (*ʿimaret, aşhane, ṭaʿām*), hospital (*bimarhane*) or fountain (*sabīl*). Structures such as bridges, roads, fortresses, and water works might also be maintained by endowments. Individuals could be named beneficiaries, whether relatives of the founder or people unrelated by blood ties. They could be personal dependents or clients, or the functionaries of endowed institutions. For example, salaries for scholar-teachers and students affiliated to a particular *madrasa* were generally funded in this way.[15] Further, a waqf might be set up to assist the pious voluntary poor (in Islamic societies these are often the members of sufi mystical orders), the destitute, travelers, widows, orphans or other people deemed needy, weak, and deserving of assistance.

Beneficiaries were allowed on the condition that they constituted a valid pious purpose. Such purposes were defined in the *Qur'an*, which said: "The freewill offerings (*ṣadaqāt*) are for the poor and needy, those who work to collect them, those whose hearts are brought together, the ransoming of slaves, debtors, in God's way (*fī sabīl Allāh*), and the traveller" (IX:60). *Ṣadaqa* could benefit various members of the wider community of Muslims, including those who themselves collected the alms tax, new converts, captives, or debtors. It could also serve specific individuals, often immediate family members. "Whatsoever good (*khayr*) you expend is for parents and kinsmen, orphans, the needy, and the traveller; and whatever good you may do, God has knowledge of it" (II:215). *Ṣadaqa* and *khayr* are both more general terms than *zakāt*, which refers specifically to obligatory alms. The use of *ṣadaqa* and *zakāt* in the *Qur'an* is not, however, unambiguous. For example, verse IX:60 lists the categories of people eligible to receive alms, yet the comparison with II:215 and other verses shows an overlap between the recipients of alms and voluntary donations, one which existed in practice as well.

Among the earliest reported waqfs were those made *fī sabīl Allāh* (lit. in the path of God, or, for the cause of God). Many purposes might answer this characterization but one of the most important at the time was jihad. Contributions to the military needs of the early Muslim fighters included a range of movable properties such as slaves, horses, and weapons. While they were inherently suited to the purpose, as the principal of a waqf they were ultimately used up and diminished. Over time, too, the importance of these donations for the war effort abated as the first military expansion of the Muslims ended and the fruits of the conquest were used to finance its continuation. By the third century A.H. the *waqf fī sabīl Allāh* was the exception allowed due to tradition, while the more general doctrine of Ḥanafī law had come to restrict endowed property to immovables.[16]

Jews and Christians, too, could establish endowments to support anything that was a pious purpose according to Islamic law, such as a fountain, a public kitchen, or a shelter for the poor; churches and synagogues did not meet this qualification. Under the Ottomans, however, some Christians religious establishments were also supported by waqfs. In many cases, these endowments comprised extensive properties belonging to monasteries, whose tax yields to the state constituted important revenues. Allowing the monastery property to be recorded as waqf by means of legal fictions protected it and was appreciated by the monks, who continued to remit their taxes.[17]

Another fundamental characteristic of a waqf under Ḥanafī law is that it must be made in perpetuity. In fact, the permanence or reversibility of endowments was a point of some disagreement among the schools of law, as was the validity of a temporary waqf. Abū Ḥanīfa (d. 150/767), founder of the Ḥanafī *madhhab*, himself had said that waqfs were only permanent when made as part of the final testament of the founder. Yet according to his student, Abū Yūsuf (d. 182/798), a waqf was irreversible, and this was the practice in the Ottoman empire. To emphasize and notarize this condition, a formal request was usually made to the kadi to annul the waqf at the time of its foundation, whereupon the kadi declared the impossibility of abrogating what was already endowed, citing the opinion of Abū Yūsuf. This latter decision might be appended in writing to the endowment deed itself.[18]

For the waqf to be legal, all parts of an endowment had to be stipulated at the time of its founding, usually in an endowment deed (*waqfiyya*). The revenue-producing properties were alienated permanently as the principal capital for the endowment. The immediate and successive beneficiaries (institutions and/or people) were stipulated along with the condition that when they expired—the building collapsed or the line of people died out—the revenues would devolve upon the poor of Mecca and Medina or of some other place.[19] This condition rested on the assumption that the poor were as enduring as any property (if not more so) and that as long as human beings exist, poor people will be found among them.

A manager (*mutawallī*) also had to be stipulated when the foundation was established, in order to oversee the proper functioning of the endowment and to ensure that the specific terms laid down by the founder were fulfilled. He or she was responsible for ensuring the continuing productivity of the properties for the maximum benefit of the endowment, seeing to their upkeep and good repair and replacing dilapidated or diminished properties with more productive ones. All such changes, however, had to be expressly authorized by the local kadi, who was responsible for the general welfare of individual endowments in his jurisdiction.[20]

A perpetual succession of managers had to be established as well, in keeping with the requirement for the eternal existence of the waqf. They were frequently from the family of the founder. Otherwise, and if the succession expired, the local kadi was responsible *ex officio* to name the most appropriate and able person for the task—at times, himself. The endowment deed might provide for additional staff, depending on the purpose of the endowment. From one endowment to another, the number of people varied with the quantity or size of the beneficiaries and with the extent of the endowed properties to be managed. Waqf employees filled key posts, such as teachers, doctors, accountants, and revenue collectors, as well as auxiliary functions, such as the custodians associated with any building. In larger and smaller endowments alike, the manager might hire additional temporary or permanent staff as needed, for example to carry out structural repairs.

While a written endowment deed is not an absolute requirement for the constitution of a waqf—only a formulaic oral declaration before witnesses is needed—the practice of writing the stipulations of the endowment in ink, occasionally in stone, evolved to a norm.[21] However, deeds vary extensively in their length and detail, leaving broader or more narrow scope for decision-making to the manager and the kadi. In the Ottoman period, the terms of such deeds were often entered in their entirety into the written protocols of the kadi (*sijill*) upon the initial constitution of a waqf; at other times they were recorded or re-registered at a later date (possibly much later), at a moment when it was deemed necessary to confirm the endowment and its properties.[22]

Over time, the literal meaning of waqf and the condition of its perpetuity have perhaps been responsible for overemphasizing the permanency of the revenue-yielding properties as part of any single endowment. The negative picture of waqfs, as well as criticisms of their harmful effects on agrarian practice and property development, seem to have evolved to some extent from a fixation on the supposedly "stopped" aspect of the endowed principal. Assets are described as "frozen" or the word "waqf" is translated with the European term "*mortmain*" ("dead hand") wrongly implying inertia.[23] In practice, properties were not permanently excluded from transactions, but were exchanged out of (*istibdāl*) and purchased for endowments as needed, according to legal procedures that provided for these possibilities. The endurance of the *purpose* of the waqf was supposed to be the aim of the manager, and s/he was obliged to manage it according to the principle of *maṣlaḥa*, the public interest or welfare of the Muslim community.[24] The manager was restricted in this only to the extent that the deed might specifically forbid some action or because some transaction was forbidden in Muslim law. At times, it was in the best interest of the endowment to replace unprofitable properties or to specify some aspect left undefined in the deed. Thus a waqf, founded as a permanent institution under Ḥanafī law, was in fact mutable. Being a legal construct, changes to the components and conditions were permitted only in precise ways, justifiable only in the interests of the waqf itself as interpreted according to ideas of public good. This left substantial leeway for the managers.

## THE ROOTS OF WAQF

The *Qur'an* does not refer specifically to waqf, but rather to alms (*zakāt*) and generally to good works (*ṣadaqa, khayr*). Payment of the alms tax is one of the five basic obligations of the believing Muslim. *Zakāt* is often discussed in the *Qur'an* along with prayer (*ṣalāt*), charitable gifts or voluntary donations (*ṣadaqāt*) and good deeds (*ṣāliḥāt*), those things that help believers gain entrance to Paradise.[25] Waqf is a type of good work, sometimes called *ṣadaqa mawqūfa*.[26]

At the roots of waqf are Muslim religious principles and practices, as well as those of the societies and cultures from which and among which Islam and the first Arab Muslim state evolved. Viewed from a longer perspective, the endowments or foundations of classical Greece and Rome contributed to formulating the practices of the west Asian and Mediterranean regions, though these had been adapted and translated through the media of Byzantine and Zoroastrian society and culture.[27] Islam emerged on the cusp of the Byzantine Christian and Persian Zoroastrian oikoumenes, and there also encountered the social organization and tenets of Judaism in communities scattered throughout the larger political units.

In Judaism, the specific use of a term meaning justice or righteousness (*ṣedaḳâ*) to name obligatory charitable contributions dates at least to the second century C.E.[28] However, no extensive scholarly discussion exists of the Jewish institutions of beneficence and relief in rabbinic times or in premodern Europe, despite the centrality of the religious obligation to charity in Judaism. According to historian Mark R. Cohen, "In-depth probing of the actual lived experience of the poor and of the mechanics of charity seems to have been impeded by idealized assumptions about Jewish generosity and about the universal meritoriousness of the poor, as elaborated in biblical, talmudic, midrashic and medieval sources."[29] With little understanding of the practical applications of *ṣedaḳâ* in the Jewish communities of Arabia, its connection to Muslim *ṣadaqa* or to waqf as it developed among the first Muslims is difficult, if not impossible, to trace. The linguistic similarity, however, suggests the possibility of some influence from Jewish to Muslim thought and practice. The early Muslim community included many Jews, and close contacts continued with the Jewish communities in Arabia.[30]

Byzantine traditions probably played some role in configuring ideas and forms of Muslim charity, though again, the paths and modes of influence between Byzantine Christian and early Muslim culture are not always obvious or directly traceable. Byzantine beneficent foundations were plentiful and proximate for the first Muslims in Arabia, Syria, and Egypt. Byzantine Christian practices in these conquered areas, like Jewish ones, may well have been absorbed into the evolving Muslim Arab culture, converted along with people to whom they were familiar. Byzantine notions and forms of charity themselves developed from the impact of Christian ideas of charity on the existing Roman practice of consecrating property for religious purposes (*res sacrae*) and Roman forms of public assistance. This was especially evident in the imperial and Christian city of Constantinople from the time of Constantine I (d. 337). There, and eventually in many parts of the Byzantine empire, beneficent institutions intended for the needy public were set up with imperial funds to be run by the Church authorities.[31]

New formulations of charitable assistance emerged as a recognizable and particular aspect of Byzantine society between the fourth and sixth centuries. By the seventh century, Byzantine society had evolved a highly articulate spectrum of charitable institutions for the separate care of orphans, widows, travelers, lepers, the hungry, the aged, and the sick. These were in addition to or integrated with the numerous monasteries found in both towns and isolated wildernesses all over the empire. Support for these institutions came from donations by the Church, the Byzantine state, and private individuals of greater or lesser stature. Numerous institutions were established by the Byzantine emperors, as well as their mothers, sisters, wives, and daughters. Private donations might subsequently be enlarged by imperial support to ensure the survival of an institution.[32]

Zoroastrian traditions of endowment-making in the pre-Islamic Sassanian empire also possessed features that had counterparts in Muslim waqf. These included the basic structure of an irrevocably endowed principal whose fruits maintained its own existence. Like waqfs, the Zoroastrian foundations could support a range of endeavors defined as "for the soul" (of the founder) or "for pious purposes": religious ritual, public works, or the family of the founder.[33]

While the evolution of Byzantine Christian charitable philosophy and practice has been more thoroughly investigated and rests on a broader base of concrete evidence than Jewish, Zoroastrian, or ancient Arabian, there is ultimately no persuasive reason to prefer it to the others among possible cultural antecedents. Muslim religion and society first evolved in a region obviously replete with charitable traditions and examples. It is not necessary to sort out the proportionate contribution of each religion or culture to what became the practice of endowment-making in Islam.[34] It would have been strange had this new faith emerged with no explicit practices of or ideology about "charity."

What is salient is that the Muslims articulated the principle and obligation of beneficent giving into their religious and moral philosophy, generating concrete mechanisms that were both adapted from the spectrum of practices they observed and created in forms particular to the interpretation of Islamic law and culture of their time.[35] Whatever practices and ideas existed among those who became the first Muslims, whether borrowed or invented, they supported the tenets of the new faith and became anchored in its evolving legal codes. These, in turn, constrained and shaped the actions of Muslims. As the Muslim communities and state had needs of their own, which were a combination of the political, social, and spiritual, the institutions and practices they produced became a way of defining themselves, particularizing themselves among the other existing states and communities. That their practices were similar to or echoed ideas found in other contemporary cultures—irrespective of their origins—may have contributed in some measure to the appeal and spread of Islam.

Realization of charitable goals and obligations was inscribed and articulated in the idiom of the new religion. Obligatory alms-giving was a tax owed to God but intended as a practice among people. As the Muslim state consolidated itself, it began enforcing payment of the alms tax, which had previously been initiated by each individual. With increasing demands for funds, the state soon imposed other taxes as well. These increased, while the concomitant willingness of Muslims to pay *zakāt* in addition declined.[36] Ultimately, waqf seems to have eclipsed *zakāt* in material and social importance. *Zakāt*, however, "continued as the main justification for a Muslim government's various urban taxes or as a ritualized form of personal charity but no longer as the material foundation for most specifically Islamic concerns."[37] The historian Marshall Hodgson tied the decline of *zakāt* to that of the caliphal state. This strong, centralized political unit of the early Muslim era gave way to a period in which numerous *amirs* (princes) gained greater power over smaller units, acquiring land grants (*iqta*ʿ) from the state treasury with which to support themselves.

It is perhaps this diminishing return from *zakāt*, coupled with the ever-present exhortation to be beneficent, which led to the increased popularity of a waqf, a means to fulfill the demand to be charitable while reserving the possibility of benefit to the donor. As historians have pointed out, charity in Islam is an obligation which constitutes a divinely sanctioned claim by the poor against the rich. Providing for one's family was also an obligation. Waqf offered a versatile and attractive means to fulfill both obligations.[38]

Once established, the form and practice of waqf did not remain fixed. Just as the basic idea and structure of pious endowments coalesced in the early Islamic community from several influences, so did the practice of waqf-making and it continued to evolve in different ways, based on the experiences and needs of different Muslim communities.[39] The absence of any mention of waqf in the *Qur'an* may have allowed for additional flexibility in the evolution of the law as well as the practice.

## WHY FOUND A WAQF?

By their nature, waqfs are conceived first and foremost to be pious acts, inspired by religious belief, aspirations to attaining Paradise, and the obligation of giving charity. In their execution, however, waqfs are legal entities, shaped by economic and fiscal constraints. They existed in different cultural contexts, employed for political and social goals, as tools of financial ambition as well as the means to legitimacy and status. Waqf-making clearly increased in popularity over time, certainly among rulers and notability, and apparently among people of more modest means as well. The preference for waqfs as a form of beneficence over the obligatory alms tax was due partly to the fact that founding a waqf could accomplish several purposes simultaneously. For all people, waqfs were the means of performing an act pleasing to God and contributing to the community. They could serve to protect personal wealth, provide for the founder's family, and distribute inheritance in shares different from those prescribed in Islamic law. For the members of an imperial household and other wealthy individuals, waqfs were also a convenient tool of patronage, used to broadcast power and to legitimize and strengthen sovereignty.

An examination of these varied motivations makes clear how versatile an institution a waqf was for its founders. Thus the following discussion considers the multiple uses of waqfs and how their ability to serve many motivations also engendered severe criticism.

From the richest to the poorest of people who chose to endow their property, the declared purpose in doing so was to bring the founder closer to God (*qurba*) and to obtain a place in Paradise.[40] "[Hurrem Sultan] having seen and beheld these endless graces and boundless favours bestowed on her, and out of gratefulness therefor and in compliance with the noble content of the holy verse: 'Do good, as Allah has done good unto you,' unlocked the cupboards of favours and gifts . . ."[41] As here, a religious motivation for making waqfs is the one most consistently articulated in the endowment deeds; the *Qur'an* promises rewards from Allah for generous gifts and beneficent acts. Beneficence brings spiritual benefit and is also a means of atoning for sin.[42] "Take of their wealth a freewill offering (*ṣadaqa*), to purify them and to cleanse them thereby, and pray for them" (IX:103).

The teachings of the *Qur'an* encourage generous and benevolent actions: "True piety is this: to believe in God, and the Last Day, the angels, the Book, and the Prophets, to give of one's substance, however cherished, to kinsmen, and orphans, the needy, the traveller, beggars and to ransom the slave, to perform the prayer, to pay the alms" (II:177). "Surely those, the men and the women, who make freewill offerings and have lent to God a good loan, it shall be multiplied for them, and theirs shall be a generous wage" (LVII:18). Beyond announcing individual generosity, these endowments also form part of the calculations of mortals against the possibility of Paradise after death. Their actions do not derive from a pure and simple altruism. For those who believe in a state of being beyond death and a final day of reckoning, the charitable actions of a lifetime are an investment in eternity.

Motivations other than the spiritual aspiration for *qurba,* the goal of Paradise, and the humanistic aim of providing financial support for people and institutions certainly informed waqf-making. These attendant motivations, however, must be discovered largely through circumstantial or indirect evidence, as the endowment deeds announced only the piety and beneficence of the founder. Endowments served as vehicles for political legitimation, social status, and patronage of all types, from the level of the personal to the imperial. They also contributed to developing population centers—urban and rural—by providing the necessary infrastructure in the form of market space, inns, and baths, as well as key social and cultural facilities like mosques, schools, and public kitchens.[43] Hodgson and others have emphasized the evolving relationship between waqf-founding and political legitimation, increasingly exploited from the tenth and eleventh centuries.[44] Concomitant to a fragmentation of political authority in the central Islamic lands was the rise of an international order of scholars (*ʿulamā*) educated in the growing number of *madrasas*. The foreign-born *amirs* who ruled various principalities became patrons of the scholars, endowing *madrasas* for them and in return gaining support in their own political contests. The distribution of salaried positions in waqf-supported institutions as a form of patronage was thus used to attract and maintain loyal supporters among the respected men of learning who served as the spiritual and intellectual guides of the polity.

Such patronage was also integral to the re-establishment of Sunni orthodoxy after the conquest of the Fatimid Shiʿite state in Egypt (969–1171), since the proliferation of mosques and colleges was intended to promote Sunni scholars to prominence, ultimately at the expense of Shiʿite scholars. The Zengid, Ayyubid, and then Mamluk *amirs* who succeeded the Fatimids, along with their households, endowed colleges and tombs, especially in Damascus, Aleppo, and Cairo, and reinforced existing endowments. In this way, they could control the appointments affiliated to these institutions and establish an economic hold on the local religious elites whose support, in turn, was an integral element of their legitimacy.[45] During their long reign, the Mamluk sultans expanded significantly the number of positions to be filled by scholars, students, *imams*, sufis, and other personnel, as well as their own power as distributors of those positions.[46] Widespread Ottoman endowment of mosques and colleges, as well as support for sufi institutions, was part of their own anti-Shiʿite drive against the Safavids from the early sixteenth century.

In Rūm Selçuk Anatolia, an offshoot of the Great Selçuk empire, the symbiotic relationship between the scholars and *amirs* was perpetuated by territorial expansion in the twelfth and thirteenth centuries.[47] Here the sultans set up endowments not only for the scholars but to benefit merchants (and, by extension, the treasury) in the form of numerous large caravansarays which punctuated the major trading routes across Anatolia, providing lodging, food, and security for those on the roads.[48]

One result of this patronage of the *ʿulamā* was to provide them with a measure of economic independence, as they received stipends—sometimes enormous ones—from the endowments.[49] While individual fortunes fluctuated, the scholars as a class in the Sunni world of the Middle East and North Africa seem to have maintained a large measure of economic independence and standing, up until the nineteenth-century reforms. At that time, widespread changes in the administration of endowments and the creation of government-run and sponsored schools undermined the intellectual authority, financial control, and steady income formerly enjoyed by the scholars.[50]

For the Ottomans, waqf-making was a key tool in colonization and settlement in newly conquered areas. Maintaining the practices of the Selçuks and *beys* (the local rulers), the Ottoman sultans recognized existing endowments and established many new ones to support a familiar roster of beneficent institutions and public works. However, under imperial Ottoman patronage, in many cases the individual buildings also gradually became integrated to larger, more ordered complexes.[51] Each building of the complex housed the services and functions obviously associated to it: prayer and ritual, instruction, lodging, food distribution, medical care, etc. Numerous examples of these exist, from the somewhat scattered agglomeration of the Muradiye (Murad II, 1421–1451) in Bursa, to the oft-cited grandeur of the Süleymaniye (Süleyman I, 1520–1566) in Istanbul, with its orderly, rectangular arrangement of buildings. Clearly, only people controlling enormous resources could establish and endow such complexes.

The capital to fund the original construction of the endowed components was largely derived from the spoils of war, regular and plentiful, at least through the mid-sixteenth century. Sultans incorporated substantial rural properties into their endowments, both proximate to and remote from the sites of the institutions themselves. Urban complexes, in addition to their rural holdings, were supported by commercial and service structures often newly constructed in the vicinity of the complex. Rents from these markets, bath houses, industrial and residential structures sustained the waqfs. Altogether, the physical expansion, newly created jobs and commercial possibilities fostered the growth of towns and neighborhoods in cities in Anatolia, the Balkans, and the Arab provinces, contributing to a sense of prosperity and expanding Ottoman power.

Outside the cities, the establishment of sufi residences paralleled the use of endowed urban complexes as a typical Ottoman instrument of colonization. A rural residence became the nucleus of settlement, as the lands endowed to it were brought under cultivation, improved so as to support its expanding functions. It served not only as a site of ritual but also as a guest house and public kitchen. In many instances in the Balkans and Western Anatolia, the *zaviye*s were Muslim outposts in a predominantly Christian area and so functioned to further the process of Islamization and Ottomanization.[52]

Bursa, Edirne, and Istanbul, the imperial capitals, show best the effects of sultanic waqf-making, how the endowing of large complexes furthered urbanization and the growth of cities. Istanbul is the exceptional case because of its size and long-term status as capital. From the time of the conquest in 1453, each sultan added endowed structures to the cityscape, often a complex bearing his name or that of a member of the imperial household. They, together with the viziers and other prominent people, also contributed to the settlement and expansion of Istanbul. Neighborhoods throughout the city still bear the names of these donors: Fatih, Süleymaniye, Sultanahmet, Haseki, Kocamustafapaşa, Mahmutpaşa and others.[53]

Under the Ottomans, much of the rural property endowed for imperial waqfs belonged to the treasury (*miri*). This practice was acceptable so long as the sultan had added to that treasury with his victories and was essentially funding his endowments from his private share of the spoils. The Ottoman historian Muṣṭafa ʿAli, writing later in the sixteenth century, explained:

> As long as the glorious sultans, the Alexander-like kings, have not enriched themselves with the spoils of the Holy War and have not become owners of lands through the gains of campaigns of the Faith, it is not appropriate that they undertake to build soup kitchens (*ʿamāyir*) for the poor and hospitals or to repair libraries and higher *medreses* or, in general, to construct establishments of charity (*xayrāt u meberrāt*), and it is seriously not right to spend and waste the means of the public treasury on unnecessary projects. For, the Divine Laws do not permit the building of charitable establishments with the means of the public treasury, neither do they allow the foundation of mosques and *medreses* that are not needed. Unless a sultan, after conducting a victorious campaign, decides to spend the booty he has made on pious deeds (*xayrāt u ḥasenāt*) rather than on his personal pleasures, and engages to prove this by the erection of [public] buildings.[54]

Süleyman and his predecessors had contributed extensively to the treasury by virtue of their military successes. As a result, they employed their winnings in monumental beneficent works, using treasury funds and imperial lands for waqfs. A later sultan like Aḥmed I who had no conquests was criticized for his expenditures on the Blue Mosque. Moreover, the practice of distributing *miri* lands itself came under fire and ultimately became the basis for confiscating some waqfs in the nineteenth century.

Critics of waqf have launched skeptical and moralizing barbs especially against the motivations of those who set up waqfs to benefit themselves and their families. They emphasized how easily waqf could be used to circumvent the rules of inheritance, dictated by Islamic law and incumbent upon the estate of a deceased person. Whether intending to exclude potential heirs, include those left out or shift the portions due each one, a person could fix waqf terms while still alive and feel some security that they could not be tampered with after his or her death.[55] In his recent thesis, Hennigan suggests that the early popularity of waqf evolved alongside restrictions placed on bequests which made the rigid prescriptions of inheritance law more unavoidable. A waqf enabled the founder to ensure that property was not parcellized at all, or else only according to his or her precise wishes.[56] Moreover, there is a clear Qur'anic sanction for beneficent giving aimed at the members of one's own family. It is not difficult to understand how this could evolve to become an important category of endowments, nor to see why it was criticized as self-interested and lacking true beneficent motivation.

Waqfs made for the benefit of founders and their families could either name them as beneficiaries, establish successive family members in (paying) positions such as that of manager of the waqf, or both. Under the Ottomans, properties endowed for the benefit of founders' families were made on lands, some of which had been given as imperial grants (*temlik*) or usurped from the pool of state properties distributed either as revenue sources (*tımar*) or auctioned as tax farms (*iltizam*). The net effect was income lost to the imperial treasury, a phenomenon noted and criticized by memorialists such as the seventeenth-century Koçu Bey. The latter equated the proliferation of waqfs with the decline of revenues to the state treasury and the attendant weakening of the army. Not only were the lands withdrawn from the imperial domain, but, it was claimed, they were untended and so unproductive generally.[57] This kind of critique was repeated regularly, but rarely substantiated.

A waqf created to benefit the founder and his or her family was also a protective shield against imperial confiscation. Waqfs were popular among the notables and functionaries, a means to safeguard the wealth they accrued while in service. A fall from imperial favor or death under any circumstances could entail the confiscation of property. While these men made many endowments that benefited the public, such as schools and sufi residences, they also made waqfs whose beneficiaries were their own relations. With the principal alienated to God or the community, the property could not, in theory, be confiscated. When various rulers did attempt to confiscate endowed properties from the waqfs, the ensuing outcry caused widespread discontent. Bayezid II, for example, was compelled to reverse the confiscations of his father, Meḥmed II, in the face of threats from the leading religious figures and notables who had suffered as a result.[58]

The distinction between so-called "family" or "private" (*ahlī, dhurrī*) and "charitable" or "public" waqfs (*khayrī*) is more misleading than instructive. Koçu Bey was one voice among the critics of "family" endowments, which were deemed corrupt on several grounds: they did not benefit the poor or the public; they worked to circumvent normal inheritance divisions; and they facilitated the usurpation of state property, often acquired as revenue grants or tax farms and not as freehold. Yet it is impossible to confirm or deny the altruistic motives of any founder, given the nature of the evidence. The division into two categories has allowed for a condemnation of the so-called family endowment as a self-interested undertaking, as compared to charitable endeavors, despite the fact that the "charitable" endowment of a wealthy person might establish the management of it as a well-paid position to be filled by family members.

Critics of family endowments forget that they are one means to fulfill the Qur'anic obligation to care for family members.[59] Moreover, the usurpation of state property, which was not trivial, was paralleled by the outright grant of state properties. Sultans gave properties, either as a form of largess or under duress, but they did cede them. Finally, even endowments that named family members as initial beneficiaries also stipulated that needy people would benefit when there was no more family to enjoy the endowment. In the premodern world of disaster, disease, and generally shorter life spans, a line of beneficiaries might expire within a generation or two. The subsequent and ultimate beneficiaries were generally the local indigents, the pious poor, or the poor of some holy place like Mecca, Medina, or Jerusalem. Thus all endowments were essentially "*khayrī*."[60]

As with most endeavors, the motivations for making any endowment appear to include layers of intentions and constellations of causes. A tenth-century story illustrates how impossible it is to separate "good" from "bad" motivations and questions the relevance of doing so:

> . . . al-Munajjim [a tax collector] . . . used to be praised for establishing pious endowments in his district, for repairing the local irrigation system, and for giving alms to the appropriate people. Privately, al-Munajjim said that he did these things for God; but, he added, if he had done them for appearances, that would be good too, and why shouldn't the local people keep up appearances (*riyā'an*) by a matching hypocritical pretense that they believed in the high-minded motives of the benefactor? Nowadays, he complained, if a man is munificent (*jawād*) they say his is "making commerce with his munificence" (*mutājirun bi-jūdihī*) and consider him a miser.[61]

Al-Munajjim suggests that no one can know the true motives of a person's good works. Perhaps, too, neither donors nor their potential beneficiaries are capable of purely generous acts, the donors in their giving, the local people in appreciative acceptance of the beneficence extended to them. Yet the result to the beneficiaries is likely the same and so they might as well allow the donor his praise.

This disjuncture between the donor and recipient permeates beneficent action. In theory, the donor aids the recipient materially while the beneficiary enables the donor to benefit spiritually or socially, even to redress the balance of his life's bad actions by accepting the *ṣadaqa.* Thus between them there is a jointly beneficial exchange. In practice, the separate motivations of donors and recipients—except the most pious and selfless among them—determine that two largely distinct spheres of action are brought into proximity and made interdependent.

## THE OTTOMANS

By the time the Turkic predecessors of the Ottomans in Anatolia initiated the second great encounter of Muslims and Byzantine Christians, both the Byzantine and Muslim practices of making beneficent endowments had evolved. The Turks who entered Anatolia after the Battle of Manzikert in 1071 met a different Byzantine empire than the one which was defeated and pushed back during the first century of Islam. It was weaker, fighting challenges from within and without with diminishing success. As they moved into and colonized Anatolia, the Selçuks and then the Ottomans took over Byzantine settled spaces, reshaping them. They co-opted not only the sources of support for beneficent and charitable undertakings but also the endowed Christian institutions themselves.[62]

Over the centuries, Byzantine Christian charity had become more associated to the monasteries than the churches, and the ideology of beneficence and attitudes to the poor had become more selective and discriminatory.[63] During the long conquest of Anatolia, the wide-scale Turkish confiscation of Church and monastic properties worked to undermine the economic basis and financial resources of these Byzantine institutions. Greatly impoverished, the Church, centered on Constantinople, could no longer afford to sustain its extensive system of judicial administration, social services, and spiritual guidance. At the same time, the Rūm Selçuk state in Anatolia fostered widespread endowment initiatives.[64] Much property captured from the Byzantines was endowed by the Anatolian Selçuks to support mosques, caravansarays, colleges, ʿimarets and other institutions. These reflected and bolstered the prosperity and strength of the subsequent Turkic principalities as they formed in Anatolia. Out of economic and social necessity, some Christians may have turned to those Muslim institutions offering public support that had replaced the defunct Christian agents.[65]

The question of Byzantine influence in shaping Ottoman practices has long been debated, rarely dispassionately.[66] Given the limited quantity and particular quality of sources for the era of Byzantine contacts and interactions with Turks in Anatolia and the Balkans, discussions about influence and borrowing remain partly conjectural and imperfectly substantiated. The Turks came to Anatolia with their own cultural practices, administrative forms, military know-how, and economic systems. These were, by turns (and with some contradictions), Central Asian, nomadic, Persian, Muslim, and settled in origin. The process of amalgamation in which they now engaged had been repeated frequently as Muslims conquered new lands. Once again, as with the initial evolution of waqf-making in Arabia, existing practices were assimilated by the Turkish Muslims as they became culturally and politically predominant in Anatolia, incorporated so as to create something particularly Ottoman.

After the Mongol invasion and the general Selçuk collapse in the mid-thirteenth century, Anatolia was fragmented into small *beyliks* or principalities. Waqfs of the former Rūm Selçuk sultans were preserved, while the *beys* continued to make endowments, often smaller shrines and ceremonial sites for local sufis who provided them with the kind of support sultans sought from the scholars, but at a lower price. The size and type of these endowments reflected the more modest revenues of the local rulers, as well as their more circumscribed status and aspirations.[67] By the early fourteenth century, the Ottomans were one of the principalities, based in the northwest corner of Anatolia.

The immediate context for the founding of the Haṣṣeki Sulṭan ʿimaret, and for this investigation of it, was the Ottoman empire of the mid-sixteenth century. After 250 years of dynastic continuity, the Ottoman state had grown from one among a cluster of Anatolian principalities to the premier Muslim state, a world power straddling Asia, Africa, and Europe. While the pace of conquest would diminish during his reign, Süleyman I ("the Lawgiver" among the Ottomans, "the Magnificent" in Christian Europe) still led successful offensive campaigns. The territorial gains, annual levies, and booty continued to fund large endowments supporting public benefit and social welfare, in addition to the principal expenditures on campaigns and the court.

Süleyman's forty-six year rule (1520–1566) was also the period in which the huge territorial gains of his father, Selim I (1512–1520), were consolidated. Selim had added much of eastern Anatolia, western Iran, and all of the Arabic-speaking provinces comprising the former Mamluk empire to the Ottoman domains. The territories acquired doubled the size of the empire, made it strategically predominant in the Eastern Mediterranean, bolstered the imperial economy by adding agricultural resources and profitable trade routes, shifted the population balance to become emphatically Muslim, and placed the Ottomans in control of the holiest sites of Islam: Mecca and Medina, Jerusalem and Hebron.

Waqf-making by Süleyman and his household—his mother, wife, daughter and son-in-law—continued in by-now-familiar forms, aiming at a conventional variety of imperial purposes. These contributed to the physical, economic, and social well-being of Ottoman subjects, expanding religious, educational, and social services, as well as displaying dynastic power. They aimed also at affirming and increasing imperial prestige, emphasizing the strength of the empire to those living both inside and outside its domains. For Muslims everywhere, the endowments of Süleyman's era served to enhance his position as premier ruler of the Muslim world and guardian of the Holy Cities. Süleyman was also characterized and presented as the model of the just ruler, codifier of imperial law (*ḳanun*) in harmony with the *sharīʿa*. It was this identity which was most obviously promoted after about 1550.[68]

Like their predecessors, the Ottomans continued to make waqfs in favor of religious and social services, although their preferred forms and objects of support changed to reflect the character of their enterprise and the availability of funds. Where the Ottomans differed from the Mamluks and Selçuks was in the matter of succession to the throne, and this had important implications for waqf administration. Ottoman succession went to one prince only, and for a long while from the late fifteenth to the early seventeenth century, all other princes were eliminated. There was thus no challenge to the reigning sultan from within the family. This meant that Ottoman territory was never divided as a result of the death of the sultan, nor was succession the result of a contest between commanders. Thus, the ruler was not competing with the families of previous or future rulers to control the resources of their endowments. The endowments were part of the general capital of the entire family, and it behooved the reigning Ottoman to look after the waqfs of his ancestors since their condition was a reflection on him as well. At the same time, however, each sultan was in part a competitor with his predecessors in the contest to earn a reputation as a successful ruler, to leave his mark on the empire. This more subtle, ongoing rivalry also inspired waqf-making.

While in practical terms it was only the sultan, his household, and a few powerful and solvent individuals who could afford to endow large complexes, it would also have been unsuitable for others to set up anything but more modest imitations. Imperial waqfs were intended to be an expression of imperial beneficence and imperial capacity. Among members of his own household, the sultan could control this closely, since their endowments were made from properties deeded to them for this purpose. Among the notability, one assumes there were some self-imposed limits as well as the practical, financial ones.

There was, too, a crucial difference between the endowments of the imperial family and those of their viziers and other high-ranking officials. The officials, as private individuals, generally assigned the management of their waqfs to members of their families or households. Only when the family and household descendents were extinct did the management pass to some state official, often the holder of the highest-ranking position in the professional hierarchy to which the founder had belonged. Sultans and members of the imperial family, on the other hand, conferred the management of their endowments on Ottoman officials directly. There was no material benefit to the imperial family from the waqfs. Unlike other waqf founders and the sultans of other empires before them, the Ottoman dynasty benefited largely in non-material ways from their endowments. *Qurba*, prestige, legitimacy, and patronage were their rewards. The viziers and other officials, by retaining management in family hands, were more typical of most other waqf founders, where the endowment only came into "public" hands once the family was extinguished.[69]

In the sixteenth century the imperial Ottoman endowments most often named as their managers a member of the Ottoman military-administrative hierarchy, sometimes one of the ranking palace staff. The general inspector (*nazır*) of the imperial waqfs was initially the chief white eunuch of the palace (*babüsseʿadet ağası*). After 1591, this responsibility was taken over by the chief black eunuch (*darüsseʿadet ağası*), who headed the eunuchs of the imperial harem. It was the *nazır* who appointed the managers of the imperial endowments, and this authority carried with it enormous prestige, power, and the possibility of financial benefit.[70]

Imperial waqf-making was part of the institutional canon of Ottoman imperial identity. The consolidation of Ottoman imperial identity was also reflected in the canonization of aesthetic forms. Easily recognizable, these aesthetic conventions were the material counterpart to the standard titulature employed to evoke the power and character of the sultan.[71] They both reflected the melding of religious, spiritual, and imperial political elements in that identity and successfully announced the sovereignty of the sultan in his realms. The Süleymaniye complex (*külliye*) is perhaps the emblem of this phenomenon. Its domed prominence on the Istanbul skyline proclaimed Süleyman's stature to anyone in the city or approaching it. The complex included all the major components of such constructions: a mosque for prayer, colleges for teaching and study, a hospital for the physically and mentally ill, a public kitchen to feed people, tombs for the founder and his wife, together with commercial structures and agricultural properties to fund its operations.[72]

The ʿimaret endowed by Hurrem Sultan—the focus of this study—was a product of imperial Ottoman culture, yet it was established in Jerusalem, a provincial town. By the mid-sixteenth century, Jerusalem was enjoying some benefits from the Ottoman rule that began in 1516. In the broadest perspective, the city profited from the imposition of orderly rule, with a new imperial capital far to the north in Istanbul and the provincial capital in Damascus. Jerusalem was now part of the vast Ottoman economy, whose local impact included a relatively thriving and secure trading network, with increased attention and resources devoted to the pilgrimage caravans bound for Mecca and Medina. Muslim pilgrims sometimes detoured to Jerusalem on the way to or from the Hijaz or made a separate trip to the city. Christian and Jewish pilgrims came as well, and the fees paid on their entry to the city and the Church of the Holy Sepulcher contributed something to the city's income.[73]

At the same time, Süleyman invested considerable money and energy in restoring the defense and water supply systems of Jerusalem. These improvements were supplemented by the indirect effects of the salaries paid to local labor and the purchases from local suppliers.

However, while the city benefited from these investments, the Ottomans could not alter its character. Basically, Jerusalem was a holy city, a destination for pilgrims. With little industry or economic advantage as counterweight to its location on a mountain at the edge of the desert, the city remained dependent for survival on the fees it could charge visitors and the money they spent on food, lodging, services, and souvenirs, as well as the generosity of patrons of all types.

A foundation like the ʿimaret was intended to provide food as assistance to a variety of people. Like other beneficent endowments of the time, it was intended to aid, not to cure, the weak and impoverished among those who ate there, as well as to recompense the employees and to give strangers their due welcome. Unlike many large imperial complexes, the public kitchen was the principle feature of Hurrem's complex. In this it also differed from the other endowments already extant in Jerusalem. Over hundreds of years, Muslim rulers had contributed mosques, colleges and sufi residences to the cityscape of Jerusalem. The Dome of the Rock and al-Aqṣā were the focal prayer sites, with the schools and residences ringing them on three sides around the perimeter of the Ḥaram al-Sharīf. Prayer, the study of Qur'an, tradition, and law, and the hosting of pilgrims, sufis, and scholars were the chief activities supported by those who made endowments. Thus while Hurrem's public kitchen was fairly typical of Ottoman endeavors, it was rather unique in Jerusalem. There were numerous waqfs which supported the distribution of food to students or sufis or guests. But at the time it was founded, there appears to have been only one such kitchen in operation in Jerusalem, and no other similar institutions are known to have been established subsequently.

The above sketch situates the Haṣṣeki Sultan ʿimaret in the historical stream of waqf-making. By the time it was established in Jerusalem, the practice of waqf-making had long been embedded in Muslim culture, continued by Ottomans in the tradition of their Selçuk, Mamluk and Byzantine predecessors. Waqf-making was easily intelligible to the subjects of the empire, and the large Ottoman endowments were self-evident in the meaning they broadcast to those who encountered them. Hurrem's endowment was thus part of an established culture of imperial beneficence, integral to the identity of the Ottoman empire and its rulers. The spectrum of possible motivations, together with the choice of waqf as a means to achieve or promote these aims, are inextricably part of this culture. By combining the attainment of individual goals, elite status aims, and social and economic relief into a single mechanism, waqfs became extremely powerful and popular instruments. The effects were not unlike those of some large philanthropic foundations today.

Chapter Two

# A Bowl of Soup and a Loaf of Bread

"Whoever gives one dirham of *ṣadaḳa* in Jerusalem (*Bayt al-Makdis*) gains his ransom from hellfire, and whoever gives a loaf of bread there is like one who has given [the weight of] the earth's mountains in gold."[1]

"As children we looked in awe at the huge cooking pot and at the high chimneys and the main dome over the kitchen. The people of Jerusalem used to have soup instead of breakfast, mainly because of poverty. But some families used to send their children to get soup as a blessing (*baraka*) and for the distinct taste of the soup, which one couldn't get in regular home cooking. That soup was often sweetened with sugar, and some would add to it lard and nuts. A group of well-off Old City merchants would sometimes send someone to fetch some of this soup for them because of its taste and because they believed there was a blessing in eating it. Thus soup in Jerusalem, like the meal (*simat*) of Ibrahim al-Khalil [in Hebron], was not for the poor only, but also for the rich and for anyone who wanted to taste."[2]

Traditions and practices of imperial waqf-making shaped the context in which Hurrem Sultan established her Jerusalem endowment. The same considerations persuaded many people, including other members of the imperial household, to make endowments in cities throughout the Ottoman empire. The Haṣṣeki Sultan ʿimaret in Jerusalem thus belonged to a large class of imperial endowments. Having reconstructed the general cultural inducements behind Hurrem's action in Jerusalem, it is now instructive to consider the immediate manner and motivations for founding this one particular complex.

Each waqf was born of its own proximate circumstances, and the Jerusalem ʿimaret was no exception. It was a particular institution, established for specific reasons, within a unique congeries of circumstances, having its own individual characteristics and conditions. Personal, local, and imperial politics configured the choice of sites, institutions, and language of the founding. And even the most formulaic and standard of actions and documents reveal themselves to be carefully tuned to imperial needs and the mood of the moment.

Continual repairs and additions made to its component structures over 450 years have reconfigured the internal space of the Haṣṣeki Sultan ʿimaret to keep it alive and serviceable today. As a result, the original interior organization of the complex as constituted by Hurrem Sultan and the builders who worked for her is not clearly evident. No archaeological excavation has been made, nor is one likely soon, since the space is still in use as an orphanage, vocational school, and public kitchen. The loss to scholarship is a gain for humanity. Thus we can only speculate (though within some clearly defined limits) on the precise layout of the buildings and the spatial experience of the employees, temporary residents, the poor and the pious, and anyone else who received food from the public kitchen at the time of its founding.

The entrances to the complex, devoid of the inscriptions that probably crowned them, were the large, impressive portals that remain today on the north and south façades. One cannot be sure how the flow of human traffic was regulated as people came to receive and consume their meals. If the kitchen is today more or less in the same location as it was then, the central northern door, opening onto the internal courtyard, provided a more direct access to it and to what may have been the refectory.

The endowment deed (*waqfiyya*) must be one focal document of study for any waqf, a starting point. Therein, the founder prescribed the details of property, purpose, expenditure, office, and remuneration which the endowment was to support, in theory, for eternity. It thus provides one view of the motivations and concrete specifications of the founder. More often than not, foundation deeds have been the single source for the study of any one waqf, with additional information gleaned sparsely, if at all, from historical chronicles, legal records,

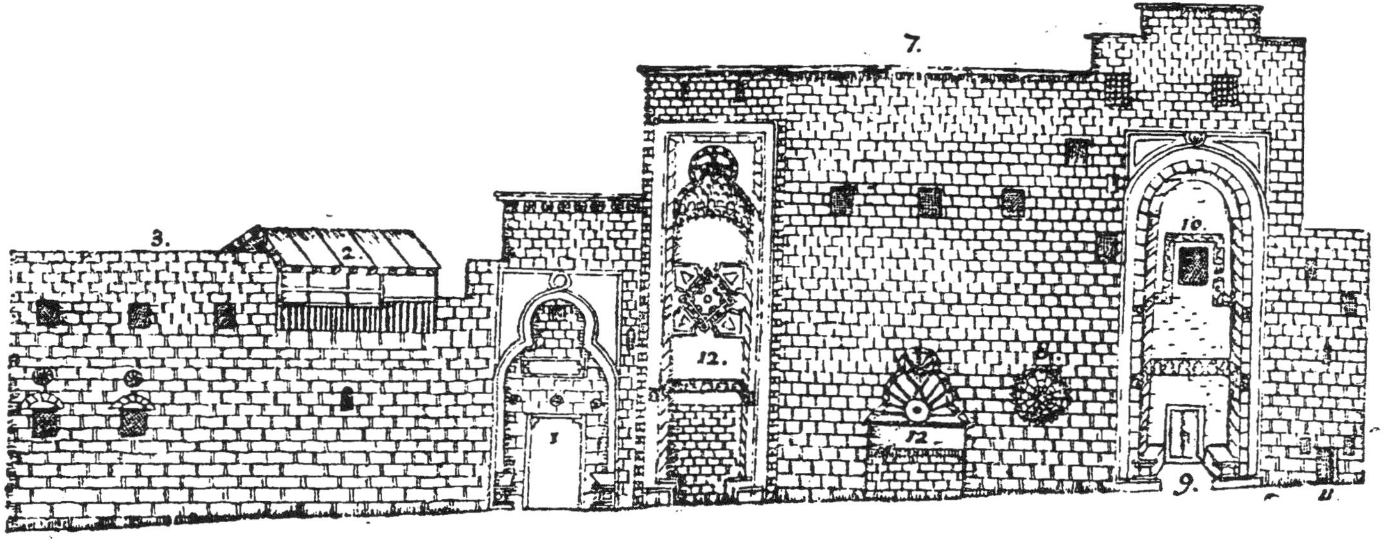


Figure 2.1 North façade, an eighteenth-century drawing. 1) main door of the ʿimaret, 2) veranda where the Ottoman officials and notables meet for conversation, 3) oven, 7) a small cloister giving access to the cellar having an air-hole at no. 8, 9) door leading to the courtyard and the private rooms on the upper floor, 10) window with an Arabic inscription incised on its frame, 11) tailor shop, 12) two walled-up doors. Fr. Elzear Horn, *Ichnographiae Monumentorum Terrae Sanctae (1724–44)*, ed. E. Hoade (Jerusalem: The Franciscan Press, 1962), 192. Illustration courtesy of Widener Library, Harvard University. Permission from copyright holder The Franciscan Printing Press, Jerusalem.

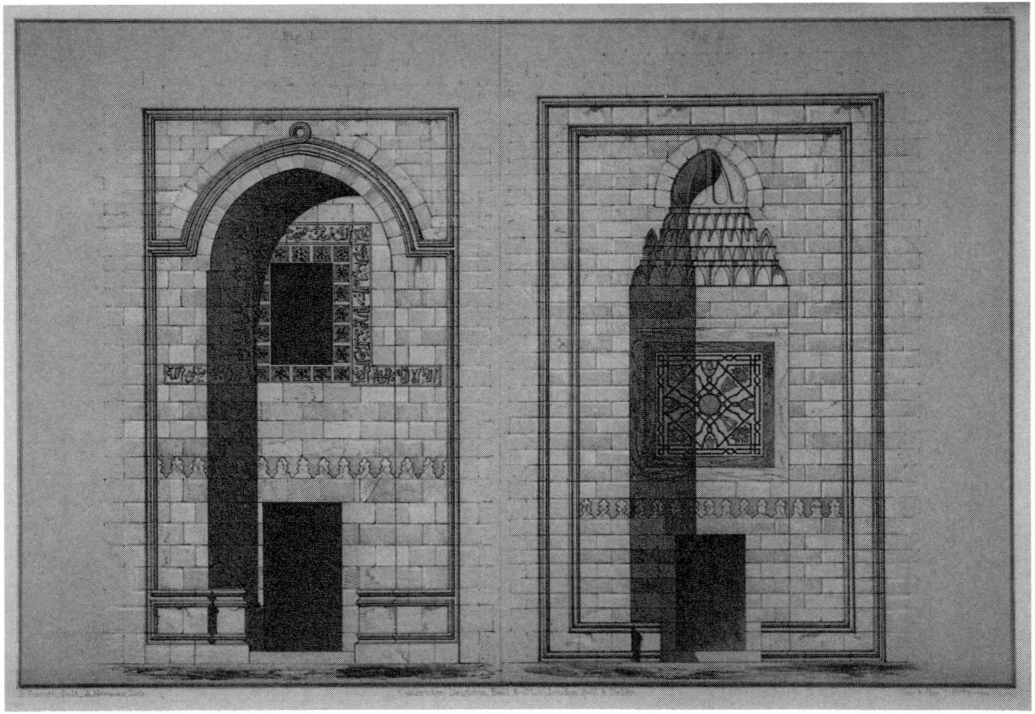

Figure 2.2 Doors in the north façade, nineteenth-century drawing. Both doors belong to the original house of al-Sitt Ṭunshūq. The doorway which appears as bricked up in the eighteenth-century drawing here seems to be open. Ermete Pierotti, *Jerusalem Explored* (London: Bell and Daldy, 1864), Illustration #43. Courtesy of Widener Library, Harvard University. This work is in the public domain.

or other occasional sources. However, these deeds were prescriptive, and misleading in their clarity. In setting down the founder's intentions and instructions, they captured a single point in conceptual time and space. The imperial moment of endowment was thus recorded for each specific institution as it was established.

Yet even at that moment, the endowment as conceived was already altered. The concrete mechanics of erecting the buildings and initiating operations translated the composite of general intentions and motivations discussed in the first chapter into a functioning institution. The linkage of motive, intent, and realization is imperative for understanding how quotidien constraints and impulses worked to reconfigure the "nobly constructed" and well-intentioned designs of imperial charity. The realities of local conditions and demands—economics, politics, personal rivalries, topography, and culture—came into play to shape the endowment into something that could work in and for the local environment. In part, the deed itself anticipated this by leaving many details unspecified. In part, the reshaping was another manifestation of the endless negotiations between Ottoman imperial projects and politics and the local people of the various provinces who were the engines of their realization. In between the sultan and his tax-paying subjects was the army of administrators, soldiers, and scholars who translated, implemented, adapted, and negotiated the connection between Istanbul and the rest of the empire.[3]

Establishing an endowment entailed a series of legal and organizational actions. These were common to a greater or lesser degree for most endowments. Yet, for one as large as the Jerusalem foundation (which, while being the largest in Ottoman Palestine, was far from being the largest waqf established by the Ottomans), the procedures for creating the end purpose were complex and time-consuming. Here, and in many instances, this meant building or repairing structures, both the revenue-consuming properties in which various services were provided (e.g., mosque, kitchen, caravansaray), as well as those generating revenues for them, such as shops, baths, mills, or workshop–factories.

This chapter tours the components of the Jerusalem ʿimaret in order to explicate how, in concrete terms, a waqf comes to be. Despite the numerous texts of endowment deeds available, nowhere has this process been carefully examined in empirical as opposed to theoretical or idealized terms.[4] In doing so, the reader becomes familiar with one impressive beneficent undertaking, while gaining a clear sense of the process of endowment-making.

## THE WRITTEN RECORD

The stipulation and construction of the institutions in Jerusalem—mosque, caravansaray, and kitchen buildings—was fairly straightforward. By comparison, organizing the properties intended to provide revenues for the ʿimaret, including the construction of the double bath (*çift ḥamam*), was a more complicated undertaking. The process lasted almost a decade and left behind not a paper trail but rather a superhighway of documentation. The quantity of paper is in itself indicative of the care and precision involved in property transactions. And, the superior material and aesthetic qualities of some of the documents reveal much about imperial Ottoman culture and Süleyman's own reign.

Although the ʿimaret was physically remote, its manifestation in Istanbul took the form of a spectacular series of documents drawn up to record the transfer of property from the sultan to his consort. Before Hurrem could endow any properties, she had to receive full title to them from Süleyman. Between the years 1550–1557, Süleyman issued ten title deeds (*mülkname*), transferring to Hurrem specific properties which she then endowed for the ʿimaret. These title deeds defined the properties and their expected revenues. The documents themselves constitute some of the most beautiful from Süleyman's time. Each is a parchment 2–3 meters in length, headed by a large, highly embellished *tuğra* (the stylized signature of the sultan). The writing then continues in varied combinations of black, gold, and lapis blue ink. In comparison with their physical magnificence, however, the contents are rather humble.[5] The material splendor of these documents reflected the symbolic importance of such transactions between Süleyman and Hurrem, providing the exquisite wrapping for what was a mundane list of unexceptional properties. They were thus, like the luxurious clothes and tableware of the imperial palaces, "containers commensurate with the recipient's ranks or status."[6]

While the title deeds documented Hurrem's ownership of the properties, the waqfiyya recorded the actual transfer of the properties to the waqf. Two versions exist of the waqfiyya for the Haṣṣeki Sultan ʿimaret. The earlier is in Ottoman Turkish, dated 30 Cemaziülevvel 959/24 May 1552, while the later is in Arabic, dated Awāsiṭ Shaʿbān 964/9–18 June 1557.[7] Perhaps the Turkish came to its present home in Jerusalem with the first administrators as a reference to guide them before the later deed was drawn up. Or, the earlier waqfiyya may have been a draft made in Ottoman Turkish to enable Hurrem herself to read it.[8] In fact, she stipulated that she would serve as co-administrator during her lifetime, a role she actually filled to some extent if the documents regarding managerial issues were intended for her. There seems some merit in the belief that the waqfiyya was written for Hurrem to read or have read to her, since it is in Turkish and does not lack any of the expansive and intricate formulae of a final document. Had the Turkish been a draft, such as the entries one sees in the *mühimme defterleri,* it needed to include only the purely informational elements, without all the ceremonial and rhetorical flourishes.[9] In fact, the Arabic text contains a shorter laudatory description of Hurrem than that in the Turkish text.

Nonetheless, the titles, the calligraphy, and the inclusion of the formal legal elements in this Turkish waqfiyya, including the kadi's formal validation of the endowment in the face of the *pro forma* attempt to revoke it, all suggest that it represented the endowment as originally conceived. A second deed probably became necessary with the numerous, rapid changes that took place in the endowed properties. The Arabic version was also the more aesthetically elaborate and ornate of the two documents, suggesting that it was a final presentation copy, after organization and construction of the waqf had been completed. Notably, however, neither waqfiyya approaches the dramatic beauty of the title deeds.

The linguistic chronology of these deeds is curious. In fact, Süleyman issued an order on 16 Safer 960/1 February 1553 that all the waqfiyyas and related documents stored in the imperial treasury and the imperial mint, which were written in Arabic as had been customary, were to be translated into Turkish. This order was addressed to Alâüddin Efendi, one of the teachers in Hurrem's *medrese* in Istanbul.[10] Thus one might have expected to find the *later* version of the deed written in Turkish and the *earlier* in Arabic, but this is not the case. If other versions existed, they have not yet come to light. That Hurrem's deed was already written in Turkish perhaps bears witness to her own status and that of imperial women, showing how they were accommodated.[11]

The waqfiyya, whether Turkish or Arabic, can be divided into several parts.[12] A long introductory section replete with praises to Allah and his prophet Muḥammad (1–2) is followed by Süleyman's formal signature (*tuğra*) (3) and the confirmation and witnessing of the document by Caʿfer b. ʿAli, chief judge (*kaziʿasker*) of the Anadolu province. It continued with reflections on the nature of human existence, the beneficence of God and laudatory descriptions of Hurrem and Süleyman (5–12). Several pages more were devoted to extolling Hurrem's beneficence and her motivations (12–17). Only then did the physical and operational details of the Jerusalem endowment begin.

First, Hurrem appointed a supervisor (18–19). Then followed a list of the buildings to be constructed (20–23) together with the revenue-generating properties to be endowed for the waqf (24–28). After the properties came a list of the functionaries of the waqf (29–45) along with their duties and their salaries in coin. The deed then set down recipes for the daily soups, bread, and special dishes for feast days which were to be prepared and served in the kitchen. Specific quantities of soup and bread were stipulated for each category of people expected to eat there (45–52). Finally, instructions for bookkeeping and management were given, and the document was concluded and dated (53–54).

## INSTITUTIONS OF THE ENDOWMENT (*AL-MAWQŪF ʿALAYHI*)[13]

Compared with the huge imperial complexes of Istanbul, Bursa, or Edirne, the Haṣṣeki Sultan ʿimaret was a modest structure. Yet in the city space of Jerusalem the complex was of outstanding proportions. This resulted as much from its physical situation as from its real size. The buildings stand on the uphill slope of ʿAqabat al-Sitt, a little ways above where this street meets the north-south course of al-Wād Street, away from the Mamluk *madrasas* and other monumental structures on or near the Ḥaram al-Sharīf.

Its components, as stipulated in the endowment deed, included: a mosque (*mescid*) and fifty-five rooms (*ḥücerat*) to which were connected an ʿimaret. This latter comprised a walled enclosure (*maḥuṭa*) and numerous roofed structures including a kitchen (*maṭbah*), baking oven (*furun*), cellar (*kilar*), granary (*enbar*) woodshed (*maḥṭab*), refectory (*me'kel*), toilets (*kanaf*), caravansaray (*han*) and stable (*ıṣṭabl*).[14]

When the Ottomans took over the residence of the Mamluk al Sitt Ṭunshūq al-Muẓaffariyya, built at the end of the fourteenth century, the existing multi-storied structure already included several large halls, numerous rooms, and an internal water source.[15] They enlarged the complex to the east and the south; it was transformed by the addition of cooking facilities and a large water fountain to fulfill its new role. Judging from the early expenditure registers for the waqfs, Ṭunshūq's house itself was in need of basic repairs by the mid-sixteenth century. The earthquake that rocked Jerusalem in 1546 may have damaged it, in addition to the usual wear and tear of time. Some of the material for the repairs—inscribed and sculpted stones—was taken from the nearby Ashrafiyya *madrasa*, which had been partially demolished in the same earthquake.[16]

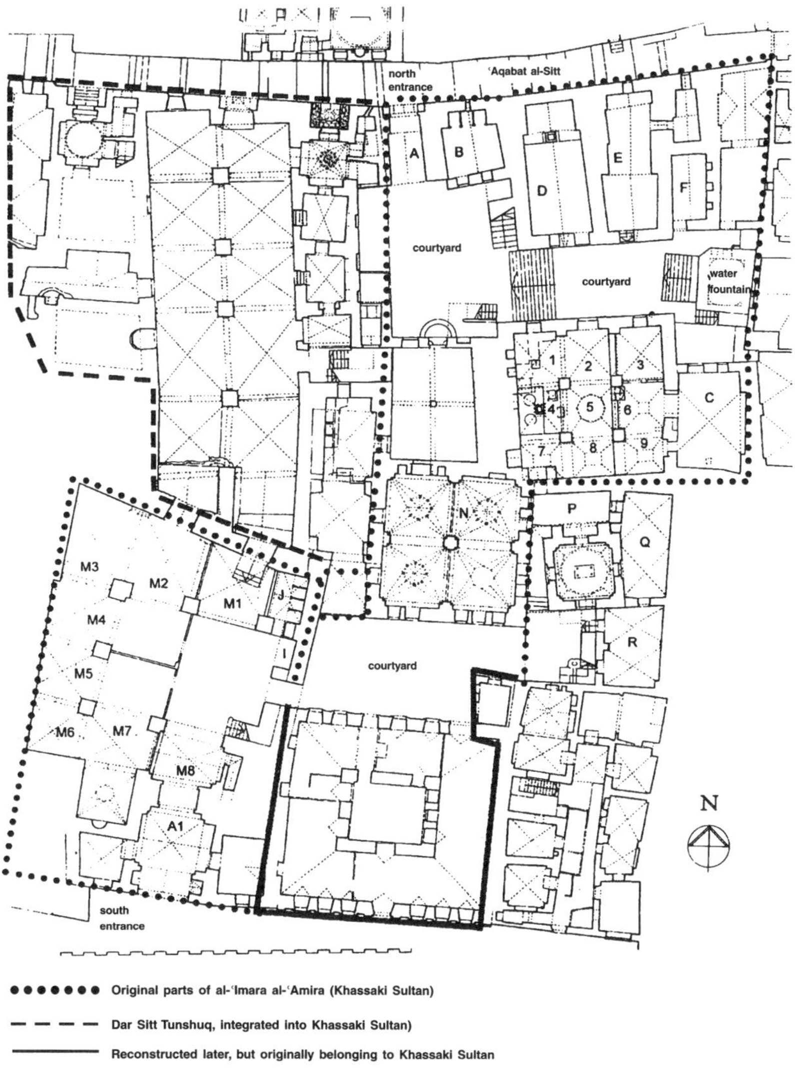


Figure 2.3 Overall ground plan. A) north entryway, B) room, 1–6) original kitchen, 7–9) extension of kitchen (mid-sixteenth century), C) storeroom (*kilar*), D) bakery, E) rectangular hall, F) large room, N) hall with four bays, possibly the original mosque or refectory?, P) rectangular room, Q) storeroom, R) storeroom (both Q & R of later construction), A1) south entryway, M1–M8) bays of the caravansaray, I) recess, J) rectangular room. Reconstructions and additions have altered or masked some of the original configurations of the buildings in the complex. In Sylvia Auld and Robert Hillenbrand, eds., *Ottoman Jerusalem. The Living City: 1517–1917* (London: Altajir World of Islam Trust, 2000), 772, figure 15.1. Permission from copyright holder the Altajir World of Islam Trust. (Printed labels on the plan added by the author).

Somewhat surprisingly, Hurrem's endowment was an active enterprise even before the official date of its founding. There was general repair work under way and the kitchen was operative before the necessary construction was finished, a fact which supports the speculation that Hurrem was not investing in an entirely new institution in Jerusalem. Conceivably, her endowment served to ensure and expand the functions of some existing institution which was either insufficient to the needs of the city, or had been weakened to the point where it required a significant investment to re-establish its operations.

Of all the buildings set up by the endowment, the kitchen was the focus of activity. The mosque was not a Friday mosque (*jāmiʿ*) to attract large numbers of people; it was probably for the use of those who lived in the rooms, the temporary occupants of the caravansaray, the functionaries of the ʿimaret and residents of the immediate quarter of the city. In any case, the main Friday prayer was conducted on the Ḥaram. No schools were initially established in this complex, which might have drawn people in or filled the mosque with students to study and pray. Jerusalem certainly did not lack for schools; the Mamluks had lined the north and west sides of the Ḥaram al-Sharīf with *madrasa*s, as well as some of the streets leading to it from the west. Yet the city was not a prestigious center of learning to compare or compete with Cairo, Damascus, or afterwards, Istanbul. Sufis and pilgrims could appeal to the many residences endowed over the years that also served food. Little is known of the rooms or the caravansaray. Presumably the latter offered free room and board to merchants, pilgrims and other travelers for the traditional three-day period of hospitality. It is possible that after this people could remain as paying boarders in the rooms, though there is no specific evidence for this.[17]

## ENDOWED PROPERTIES (*AL-MAWQŪF*)[18]

Hurrem received assets in the districts of Jerusalem, Gaza, Nablus, and Trablus (Tripoli). The first two title deeds predated the waqfiyyas and both referred, with minor variations, to the village of Amyūn in the Kūra subdistrict (*naḥiye*) of the province (*beylerbeylik*) of Trablus.[19] The waqfiyya, however, included not only Amyūn but additional properties in and around the city of Trablus for which no title deeds were found: the caravansaray of Shaykh Ṭutmāj and shops near it; a plot of land; a vaulted market, the Qayṣariyya al-Ifrānj;[20] the Saʿdiyya and ʿAwāmīd soap factories; the four Ṭayṭariyya water mills in the village of Rash-ḥīn; the four Ra'iyya water mills in the village of Bistānīn; and the three Ṣahyūn windmills. When villages were endowed, the percentage of their revenues formerly paid in taxes was redirected to the waqf. The waqfiyya specified exactly which taxes and fees were part of the endowment. As for industrial properties, such as mills or a bath house, they could either be run by the endowment personnel, so that the income reverted directly to the waqf, or their operation could be leased by the waqf to a second party, in which case the waqf received its own revenues in the form of rent.

One year after the first title deed was issued, Hurrem received additional revenue sources for the waqf: two other soap factories in Trablus, the taxes levied there on tobacco and firewood, the village of Ludd and the Qayqaba farm (*mezraʿa*) in the district of Gaza, and the village of Jīb in the district of Jerusalem.[21] Jīb, in this regard, presented an interesting case, since its revenues were already endowed. The agricultural revenues of Jīb belonged entirely to the endowment of the Mamluk Sultan Īnāl (r. 1453–61) in Egypt. In addition, three tribes of the Hutaym confederation of Bedouin were listed as affiliated with the village. The taxes they paid were in the form of sheep and goats—twenty-seven head per tribe per year. Because these levies were the only unendowed revenues in the village, the Ottomans appropriated them for the waqf. They also designated the *ʿöşr* (tithe) and *rüsum-i ʿörfiyye* (customary levies) of Jīb, formerly earmarked for military revenue assignment (*tımar*), to become part of the waqf.[22] In this way, they managed to extract revenues from villages whose principal agricultural revenues were otherwise untouchable because they were endowed. There were many such places in the former Mamluk lands.

Villages that were part of the endowments for the shrines and monuments of the Ḥaramayn al-Sharīfayn (the two noble shrines of Mecca and Medina), the endowments of the Dome of the Rock in Jerusalem, the Mosque of Ibrahim in Hebron, and large imperial Ottoman endowments (including the ʿimaret), were exempt (*serbest*) from other taxes, according to stipulations found in various Ottoman codes.[23] Peasants living in these villages thus enjoyed a privileged status in principle, free from the visits of tax collectors and revenue holders other than those of the waqf. They were free, too, from extraordinary levies. Villages belonging to endowments established for other purposes, however, including those preserved from the Mamluk era, did not enjoy similar exemptions.

After the first addition to the waqf, eighteen months elapsed before another property change was made. During this period, the bulk of the operating revenues for the endowment came from the properties in the province of Trablus, some 300 kilometers to the north of Jerusalem. Then, between August 1556 and June 1557, in the year before the final Arabic waqfiyya was drawn up, three more title deeds were issued.[24] All the properties in them came from areas closer to Jerusalem. Most were part of an exchange for already-endowed properties. The income from the lease (*muḳaṭaʿa*) of the Trablus soap factories had proved unreliable, while repairs to the factories themselves were a constant burden. The distance from Jerusalem to Trablus must have complicated the supervision of operations and the ability to ensure a fair return from the tenants. In addition, the roads to and from Trablus were not secure, so that a sizable delegation with a military escort was regularly required to make the trip in order to collect endowment monies.[25] Thus it is not entirely surprising to find that several of the properties—the Saʿdiyya and ʿAwāmīd soap factories and the Ṣaḥyūn windmills—did not appear in the waqfiyya of 1557. In their place, twenty villages in the districts of Jerusalem and Gaza were added to the endowment. Closer at hand and more easily accessible, their addition to the waqf facilitated matters for the revenue collectors.[26]

Discussions of properties and transfers make it clear that the manager began collecting endowment revenues as soon as the title deeds were issued but before the waqfiyya was drawn up. Evidently Hurrem's intentions and those of Süleyman in giving her the property were anticipated by the manager. While the collections may demonstrate great efficiency on the part of the manager, or his eagerness to please, the bookkeeping of revenues whose claimants were changing could not have been simple. In principle, the title deed only established ownership over the property, while the waqfiyya created the endowment. The first manager of the ʿimaret was from the pool of military administrators who lived on their appointments to larger (*zeʿamet*) or smaller (*tımar*) revenue grants. His jumping the gun on collecting revenues may have reflected competition for revenues among the men of this class.

In the district of Jerusalem itself the new properties included Jericho (Rīḥā) and the nearby farm of Ra's al-Diq, the villages of Bayt Jālā, Jufnā al-Naṣārā, Bayt Kisā, Bayt Liqyā, and Buqayʿat al-Ḍān. From the district of Gaza: Niʿlīn, Yahūdiyya, ʿAnāba, Ranṭiyya, Jindās, Kharbatā, Bir Māʿīn, Bayt Shannā, Bayt Dajjān, Safariyya, Subtāra, Yāzūr, and the farm of Kansa. In the district of Nablus, the village of Qāqūn, as well as taxes levied on the Ḥaythana al-Jammāsīn tribe in the farm of Khashāna were also added.[27]

Several more changes were made ten months later, just before the waqfiyya was issued. The village of Jufnā al-Naṣārā was not meant to be part of the endowment at all, but had been written by mistake instead of Bayt Laḥm (Bethlehem) and two plots of land (*ḳiṭaʿ-i arż*)—Ra's al-Ḥaniyya and Khillat al-Jawz—belonging to the nearby village

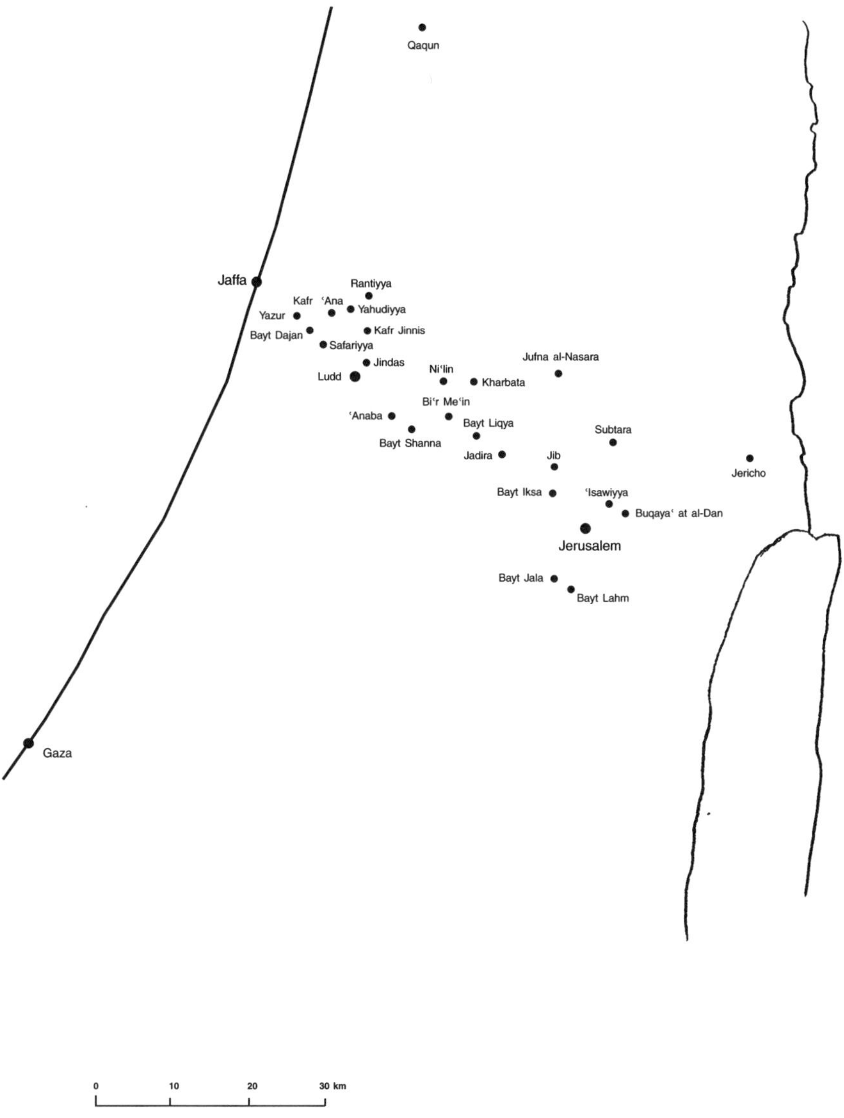


Map 2.1 Endowed villages in the *sancaks* of Jerusalem and Gaza (by Muḥarrem 972/August 1564). Note the relative concentration of the villages to the west of Jerusalem, from the city towards the coast. Map by the author.

of Bayt Jālā.[28] Other lands belonging to villages already listed had been left out of the list entirely: the plot of Buqayʿat al-ʿArnīn belonging to Buqayʿat al-Ḍān, the farms of Bayt Nūshif and Rukūbīs belonging to Bayt Liqyā, the farm of Kharrūba belonging to Bayt Kisā and the farm of Dayr Sallām belonging to Qāqūn. Finally, the title deed added to the endowment the poll tax (*cizye*) on 131 Christians in Bayt Jālā and 91 in Bayt Laḥm, which had previously been part of the revenues of the imperial domain (*haṣṣ-i ṣahi*).[29]

Perhaps to obviate any confusion after so much transferring of properties, an enormous summary title deed was drawn up simultaneous to the issuing of the Arabic waqfiyya. It reiterated the properties, their former holders and how much each property was expected to yield according to the most recent revenue survey. Both the title deed and the waqfiyya bear the same date: mid-Shaʿbān 964/9–18 June 1557, although for legal reasons the title deed preceded the waqfiyya. In fact, the title deed was clearly issued first during this ten-day period, because further changes to the endowed properties listed in it were then recorded in the waqfiyya. The village of Jericho, which had headed the long summary list, did not appear in the waqfiyya at all, nor did the nearby farm of Ra's al-Diq. Moreover, several properties were included for which no title deeds were found: the villages of Kafr ʿAnā and Kafr Jinnis, and the farm of Kafr Ṭab, all in the district of Gaza. Altogether, their revenues matched, and even surpassed, those that had been expected from the expunged Jericho.[30] The title deed and waqfiyya reflect an exchange transaction at the eleventh hour.

Jericho is an extreme example of the problems encountered in organizing endowment properties. Entries for Jericho in the Ottoman survey register of 952/1545 recorded its tax revenues as 19000 akçes, and this was the figure then expected as endowment revenues in the title deed dated 963/1556.[31] The survey listed these revenues as income of the imperial domain. In the next survey (dated 967/1560), they were listed as belonging to the endowment, even though the Arabic waqfiyya had been issued in 965/1557 *without* including Jericho. The survey information was thus out of date by the time it was "published" in Istanbul.[32] A subsequent note in the margin of the survey, undated, said that other properties had been exchanged for Jericho and that the village was no longer part of the endowment.[33] By the time a copy of this survey register was made in 1589, another note had been appended to explain that Jericho and Ra's al-Diq had been removed from the endowment properties and transferred to the governor's domain (*haṣṣ-i mir-i liva*).[34]

A marginal note also appeared alongside the village of Jīb in the 967/1560 survey, listing three Bedouin tribes. Their task was to transport threshed grain from Jericho and other endowment villages to the ʿimaret in Jerusalem. For this the tribes received no fee; in addition they were each expected to bring twenty-seven head of sheep and goats as was customary (*ʿadet diye*). These eighty-one head were valued at 30 *akçe* apiece, for a total of 2430 *akçe*.[35] The note in the survey was clearly out of date in referring to Jericho as part of the waqf, though quite probably the tribes continued to be responsible for transporting and delivering the grain from that village and others to Jerusalem.[36]

These exchanges of waqf properties are important evidence for different aspects of Ottoman administration and endowment management. First, the ease with which they can be traced today exemplifies Ottoman record-making in this period. Second, the persistence of changes is yet another indication that records, especially survey records, were no better than snapshots of one particular instant and must be used accordingly, since they could not keep up with the monthly or yearly changes in landholding and revenue use. Third, the widespread use of exchange demonstrates how flexible a waqf could be and also had to be concerning its endowed properties. The fact that waqf properties were readily and, here, frequently exchanged suggests that they were treated as economic and commercial commodities. The symbolic and religious aspects of the endowment were embodied in the services it offered and the buildings or institutions supported by the properties. The revenue-yielding properties themselves were mere instruments for these aims. Yet this does not mean that they could be transferred at will; their connection to the waqf dictated that defined legal procedures be followed with the approval of the kadi in order to effect any such changes. These procedures existed and were readily invoked. Thus the immediate equation of property transfer from an endowment with corrupt management of that endowment is an incorrect assumption.[37]

The final property originally endowed by Hurrem Sultan was a double bath around the corner from the ʿimaret itself, inside the city. It sat on the Via Dolorosa, just east of al-Wād Street, between what are now the third and fourth stations of the Cross.[38] The bath was an entirely new building, constructed especially for the endowment, increasing the facilities available in the city for routine hygiene and ritual cleansing.[39] Once built, the operation of the bath was leased out, with the rental fee constituting revenues for the waqf. However, construction took some time, and, as is not unheard of, went over budget, so that initially the bath came under the "expenditures" (*ihracat*) heading of the waqf accounts and not that of "revenues" (*maḥṣulat*). Meanwhile, this project, together with the repairs and improvements made on Ṭunshūq's house, provided employment for both skilled and unskilled workmen in the city.

The initial endowment process ended with the issuing of the Arabic waqfiyya in 1557. However, two years after Hurrem's death in 1558, Süleyman added properties to the original endowment to honor her memory. This act was inscribed in another waqfiyya dated to the end of Shawwāl 967/15–23 July 1560.[40] The new properties, located in northern Syria, included the village of Ḥārā in Sidon province and the farms of Ṣūfiyya, Jalyūba, and al-Kanīsa. Curiously, the additional properties were already referred to as part of the endowment a year prior to the date of the title deed and the waqfiyya, though the fact is said not to be commonly known.[41] The amount added to the endowment revenues was not very large—approximately 9300 *akçe*s annually—yet the gesture by Süleyman was an important token of his esteem and Hurrem's status.

In fine-tuning the list of properties to support the endowment, concerns for reliable and easily accessible income prompted exchanges. Jericho was a steep climb down to the Jordan River valley and back up to Jerusalem, and the city of Trablus was several days' journey to the north. Transport of goods was expensive and the roads were not completely secure. There were of course endowed properties located hundreds and thousands of miles away from the institutions they supported, most importantly for the Ḥaramayn al-Sharīfayn endowments in Mecca and Medina. The properties contributing revenues to the numerous institutions there were spread over the length and breadth of the Islamic world.[42] While proximity was preferable, it was not mandatory for endowed properties. The prestige and strength of an institution might compensate for the distance of its supporting properties in maintaining a sufficiently effective administration of their revenues.

## PERSONNEL[43]

All activities of the waqf were supervised from Istanbul. The chief white eunuch at the Topkapı Palace (*babüsse'adet ağası*), served as supervisor (*naẓır*) of the endowment *ex officio*. While he had no specific day-to-day tasks regarding the endowment, he did have ultimate responsibility for its proper functioning. Regular accounts of income and expenditure were forwarded to the palace for inspection, presumably the reason they reside in its archives today.[44] At the time of the founding of the 'imaret, the chief white eunuch was Ca'fer Ağa, who died in Zu'l-hicce 964/October 1557, just after it was formally established.[45] In the deeds he was called the absolute representative (*vekil-i muṭlaḳ*) of Hurrem in matters concerning the waqf. The supervisor received no salary or direct remuneration from the budget of the waqf. This being said, surplus revenues were to be forwarded to him (potentially, though not legitimately, an important source of supplementary income), and he probably controlled the appointment of the manager, an important means for dispensing patronage.

In Jerusalem, thirty-seven people were listed as part of the endowment staff in 1552; by 1557 their number had grown to forty-nine. Each had a specific title, function, salary, and daily portion from the food cooked in the kitchen. Together, they were supposed to ensure the proper upkeep and functioning of the endowment buildings and services, as well as the fiscal administration of the endowment properties. Most of the personnel were in one way or another associated with the kitchen, reinforcing the impression that its operations were the focus of activities, whether or not this was the original intention of the founder.

The general manager of the complex in Jerusalem was the *mütevelli*, who was assisted by a secretary (*katip*) and revenue collector (*cabi*). Between 1552 and 1557, the number of revenue collectors increased from one to five, in order to handle the work resulting from the addition of properties to the endowment. For the mosque, one man—Sunni and Ḥanafī—was appointed as *imam* and *mü'ezzin*. This combination of functions, along with the scant mention of the mosque itself in records related to the endowment, reflects its relative unimportance.

The director of the ʿimaret (*şeyh*) was in charge of organizing the chores associated with preparing meals. The number of people required and the specification of their tasks elucidate the ways in which food was prepared, the division of labor, and the relative value of each task in this period. In consultation with the *şeyh* and the manager, the expenditures agent (*vekil-i harc*) bought necessary supplies for the ʿimaret. A granary keeper (*enbari*) and pantry keeper (*kilari*) supervised the stocks of foodstuffs, all of which were meticulously recorded by another secretary (*katip*) appointed solely for this task. The kitchen proper was staffed by a chief cook (*re'is aşcı*), his associate, and an apprentice (*şakird*); a chief baker (*re'is ḫubbaz*), his associate and three apprentices; two inspectors (*naḳib*) for the bread and the other foods; and one person to pound the wheat, along with two others to wash and clean the wheat and rice.[46] In addition, there was a person to transport the wheat to the mill for grinding and to bring back the flour; a head miller and two associates to work the mills; and a person to carry water from the courtyard for kitchen use and also to sprinkle water on the ground (presumably to reduce dust, as is common in the region even today). The scullery staff comprised two dishwashers for the pots and kettles (*ḳab ḳacaḳ yumaḳ içün*). Two *çanaḳcı* were also listed who looked after the cups and bowls of the ʿimaret.[47] Five more people had joined the kitchen staff by 1557: two more associate bakers; two additional people to prepare wheat and rice for cooking; and another *çanaḳcı*.

For the general welfare and custodial care of the endowment, a guardian of the mosque and rooms (*ḳayyım ve çırakcı*) lit and doused the candles, opened and shut the doors, and swept; one person looked after all aspects of the caravansaray; there was a doorkeeper (*ḳapıcı*) of the kitchen and refectory and another person (*ferraş*) to sweep out the kitchen, refectory, and ʿimaret, as well as take out the garbage; and a person to light the lamps and candles (the ones not in the mosque and rooms). A master repairman (*ustaz meremmetçi*) was provided for in the Turkish waqfiyya, but by the time the Arabic text was drawn up five years later, he had metamorphosed into a staff of four: a combined carpenter-builder-stone cutter (*najjār wa-bannā' wa-ḥajjār*); a repair man for the double bath; a man to attend to the water channels (*qanāwātī*) leading to the baths and everywhere else in the ʿimaret; and a cashier or money changer (*ṣayrafī*).[48]

This was the staff of the endowment. It is hard to know whether it was considered a good place to work, although the ʿimaret did seem to offer some attractive terms to its employees. The positions there included two meals a day along with the salary, with special dishes for festivals. Work was steady year-round, not dependent on seasons or military successes, though vulnerable should the ʿimaret cease functioning, as happened occasionally. On the other hand, the work was demanding and unrelenting, as anyone who has cooked for or cleaned up after large numbers of diners will recognize.

The list of ʿimaret employees in Jerusalem was completely standard, familiar from the waqfiyyas of numerous other ʿimarets like those of the Süleymaniye or Fatih complexes in Istanbul or that of Bayezid II in Edirne. These, however, employed six cooks and six bakers each, along with larger staffs of wheat and rice sifters, servers, and dishwashers.[49] Small staffs, more comparable to those of the Jerusalem ʿimaret, were found at the Muradiye in Edirne or the complex of Selim II in Karapınar.[50] Of course, all these staffs bore only faint resemblance to that of the imperial kitchens in Topkapı Palace, the "top of the food chain." There, separate kitchens served distinct groups among the palace residents and staff, with one kitchen dedicated solely to the production of sweets (*ḥelvahane*). In the second half of the sixteenth century, sixty cooks and 200 other servants worked in these kitchens.[51]

One question which arises concerning the permanent positions in this or any other foundation is what they actually entailed, whether they were full- or part-time and whether the titles implied real tasks or simply sinecures. During the initial period which is the focus here, the reports and expense registers clearly indicate that the ʿimaret was a functioning kitchen, serving large quantities of food to many people regularly. Over time, however, it is unclear what happened to the large staff and how much food continued to be cooked on site. By the mid-nineteenth century, the staff was smaller, and much food was in fact distributed in bulk as basic supplies, to be taken home and prepared there.[52] Quite possibly, some amount of cooked food continued to be prepared for distribution from the ʿimaret, even if most beneficiaries received raw materials. That this is the case is suggested by the fact that even today, when the place serves chiefly as an orphanage and vocational training facility, meat with rice and vegetable soup is cooked and distributed to needy people on Tuesdays and every day during Ramadan.[53]

Curiously, a *subaşı* was appointed for the villages of the waqf, yet he was not listed among the staff in the waqfiyya itself. *Subaşıs* were soldiers who carried out various police functions, both in the city and throughout the district of Jerusalem, helping to keep the peace and serving as agents of the kadi. They were paid salaries, but might also lease revenue-collection rights from other Ottoman officials. The *subaşı* of the ʿimaret villages had no authority to collect revenues, since the ʿimaret had its own revenue collectors. Moreover, his salary was not part of the endowment expenditures (at least not obviously), despite the fact that the position seems to have become permanent, one of the various *subaşı* appointments in the district. This suggests that keeping the peace and ensuring that the villagers kept to their agricultural obligations were the jurisdiction of local Ottoman officials, no matter what the status of the villages.[54] Appointing a *subaşı* specifically for these villages also indicates that they were recognized as a unit, despite the fact that they were not located all together, not even all in the same districts.

During times of hardship, particularly during the winter, a butcher was appointed to the ʿimaret to ensure a regular supply of meat. Butchers not only slaughtered animals but were often responsible for maintaining contacts with the villagers and bedouin who supplied the animals and for ensuring their arrival in the city. Because none was listed in the waqfiyya, the appointment of a butcher was a more complex undertaking than hiring another kitchen hand, requiring imperial approval. It seems to have become imperative for the kitchen, and a butcher was authorized under Süleyman, and then again under Sultans Selim II and Murad III.[55] The presence of two butchers in the provincial ʿimaret in Karapınar suggests that this position may have been created frequently for these large kitchens. Although there are no butchers listed in the waqfiyyas for any of the large ʿimarets in Bursa, Edirne, and Istanbul, they may well have been appointed subsequently. These ʿimarets needed large quantities of meat. In Istanbul, they competed with the palaces for regular supplies and confronted more difficulties than in Jerusalem, since the distinction and distance between urban and rural was greater in the metropolis than in the province. The task of supplying meat on a large scale was not one eagerly sought, however, as the risk and expense anywhere meant a huge outlay for an uncertain return.[56]

## SOUP

Precise directions for the preparation and distribution of food were included in the waqfiyyas, an indication of what were typical and basic dishes at the time, as well as the appropriate distinctions among people of different classes. The Jerusalem ʿimaret was not the only one to have instructions for food preparation written down in this way, and the recipes in Jerusalem were similar to those stipulated for public kitchens elsewhere in the empire. Variations depended on the founder of the endowment, the clientele, and the agricultural produce available locally. The attention given to food supply, preparation, and distribution was continual, as reflected in the repeated reports on the kitchen's operations and the problems it encountered.[57]

The waqfiyyas make no mention of the specific equipment required to prepare and serve the food and to maintain the buildings. Yet by implication from the tasks listed, all manner of spoons, ladles, pots, buckets, bowls, knives, brooms, and other implements were necessary. Pack beasts were either kept or leased for hauling grain to the mill and back, and their fodder is usually listed in the expense registers. The copper cauldrons and bowls used to cook and serve food also had to be retinned (*kalaylatma*) regularly, to prevent the poisoning of the diners.[58] The cauldrons (*ḳazgan*) in which the daily soups were prepared repeatedly impressed visitors to the Jerusalem ʿimaret over the centuries. Whether these are the ones (two enormous and one large) now in the Ḥaram al-Sharīf museum in Jerusalem is uncertain, but they must have been comparable. Other, similar Ottoman cauldrons can be seen in the kitchens at the Topkapı Palace in Istanbul and various ethnographic museums throughout Turkey. While huge pots were needed for cooking the daily soups, preparation of special dishes for Friday and Ramadan evenings required something smaller, like the third pot in the Jerusalem museum.[59] Perhaps it was possible to cook the more liquid soups in larger containers, whereas the drier rich dishes could not be properly prepared if the pot was too big.

The standard daily menu consisted of two soups (*çorba*), cooked and served, morning and evening, with bread. Plain loaves (*fodula*) baked from flour, salt, and water weighed a standard 90 *dirhems* after baking.[60] Bulgur (or burghul, cracked wheat) soup was the evening meal, made with clarified butter, chick peas, onions, salt, and cumin. Mornings, the soup was rice with clarified butter, chick peas, onions, salt, and, according to the season, squash, yogurt, lemon, or pepper for additional flavor. While simple, the soups, together with the bread, offered a sound composite of basic nutrients—protein, carbohydrates, vitamins, fat, etc.[61] However, it is impossible to say that they provided sufficient nourishment because there is no indication of how much water went into the soups, nor how large the portions actually were. These two soups were common fare in ʿimarets, whether in Istanbul, Edirne, Konya, Damascus, Ergene, or Bolayır.[62] At the Süleymaniye, one might find spinach, carrots, or parsley mixed with the rice soup, while at Fatih there could be chard.[63] The ʿimaret at Dil, near Yalova on the south coast of the Marmara Sea, appears somewhat exceptional in that it served meat every day as part of the standard fare, not reserved for special guests. Soup was both a real and symbolic dish. It represented the most basic form of nourishment, the minimal meal of subsistence, and the food to which even the poor could aspire daily. In a memo she sent to the grand vizier in the mid-seventeenth century, *valide* Ṭurhan Sultan complained: "There is not enough firewood in the Old Palace to boil soup!"[64]

Elsewhere only higher-ranking visitors received better than the familiar soup. At Fatih, special guests or travelers were treated to a mutton-enriched dish (*dane*), a stew (*yahni*), and bread. Should the rank of the diner make it fitting, he was to be served a rice dish sweetened with honey and saffron (*zerde*) as well, or sometimes a rice stew with plums and other fruits (*ekşi aşı*). Members of the class of descendents of the Prophet (*eşraf*) were especially treated to a breakfast including sheep's trotters (*paça*), squash, honey, and jam.[65] Instructions to the director of the Süleymaniye ʿimaret explicitly enjoined him to welcome travelers better than any place else, and although *dane* and *zerde* were served to this group daily, no fancy breakfasts were on offer.[66] However, visitors of rank could presumably request special dishes from the prepared foods vendors at their own expense.[67] At the Selimiye ʿimaret in Karapınar, separate feasts (*ziyafet*) were budgeted for governors and other high-ranking travelers on the Anatolian highway between the capital and farther provinces.[68] Absent, too, at the Jerusalem ʿimaret was the offer of honey to arriving travelers. This was the practice at the Süleymaniye and at Fatih, where bread and honey were budgeted daily for this purpose.[69] Honey is a rich natural source of energy, pure sugar quickly absorbed into the body and thus ideal for weary travelers. Its absence in Jerusalem might have derived from the relatively small number or lower station of the travelers arriving at its door or was perhaps due to the limited budget.

On special days, however, richer dishes were served to everyone. These festivals included Friday nights (the night between Thursday and Friday), the nights of Ramadan, the nights of 'Aşure, Mevlud, Regaib, Berat, the sacrifice festival (*kurban bayramı/'id al-aḍḥa*) and the end of Ramadan (*şeker bayramı/'id al-fıṭr*).[70] At such times bread was served as usual, but the regular evening wheat soup was replaced by *dane* and *zerde.* These two dishes were both ceremonial staples, expected and so placed on every table, no matter the rank of the guest. For example, they appeared on the tables of rich and poor alike at the circumcision feast of Süleyman's sons, the Princes Bayezid and Cihangir, in 1539.[71]

The 1557 waqfiyya for the 'imaret also stipulated that four cauldrons (*ḳazgan*) full of soup (*maraq*) made "with all the necessary ingredients" (*al-ma'rūf bi-jumla ḥawā'ijihi wa-lawāzimihi*) should be prepared for the day of 'Aşure. Although no specific ingredients were listed, this rich pudding, traditional for the occasion, was made with wheat, rice, apricots, almonds, grapes, plums, chick peas, and fat in the Süleymaniye 'imaret. The recipe was probably similar in Jerusalem, though local custom and availability varied the particular dried fruits and nuts added.[72]

Precise quantities of each ingredient to be used were listed in the waqfiyya, along with the quantity of firewood budgeted for cooking each meal. However, no amount of water was stipulated, and as the size of the cauldrons used is now uncertain (although they were certainly huge), the total amount of soup cannot be easily calculated. One should note, too, that it is the very elasticity of soup that makes it such an appropriate dish for a public kitchen. When pressed, the cooks could easily increase the quantity of soup to feed more people. In doing so, the nutritional value of the soup (and the taste) was diminished. Yet the chief objective in serving soup was not always to furnish a caloric minimum. Rather, the act of distribution in and of itself had greater symbolic import. Obviously it was preferable that the soup remain edible so as not to elicit critiques like that of Muṣṭafa 'Ali, who described the fare served in Istanbul 'imarets in his day:

> their bread has become black as the earth and looks like a lump of dry clay, their soup has turned into dishwater, their rice and puddings into vomited matter, most of their stewed meat (*yakhnī*) is made of the meat of emaciated sheep that were slaughtered after having died. . . . The *medrese* students who are assigned food there . . . come solely to meet their colleagues; they pour their soup to the dogs, and they themselves stay hungry and withdraw after for a while having filled their air with the hullabaloo of the metal soup bowls.[73]

In such a situation, even the symbolic effect of the distribution was undermined.

Leaving little to chance or the discretion of the manager, the waqfiyya also specified exactly how much food comprised an individual portion at meals. The manager, agent, and revenue collectors were notably absent from the list of food recipients. All the other staff, those working daily at the ʿimaret, each received one ladle of soup and two loaves of bread, with one piece of meat each served from the *dane* on special evenings. Each of the people living in the rooms received a ladle of soup and one loaf of bread per meal, and on special evenings a piece of the meat as well. Finally, the 400 "poor and needy, weak and destitute" each received one ladle of soup in a bowl for every two persons and one loaf of bread per person; every two shared a single piece of meat on special evenings.[74]

Meal service in the Jerusalem ʿimaret was not unique in being circumscribed with rules of order. Everywhere, set quantities of ingredients, fixed by weight or monetary value, were used in daily preparations of food and bread. The prescribed distribution of food also varied in quality. As noted above, in some places distinguished guests received more food and choicer dishes, such as they might eat at their own table at home. This was not a corruption of the intended function of a public kitchen but part of the implicit purpose for which it was established: to host people in a manner commensurate to their rank, within the limits prescribed by the means of the local endowment. At the Fatih and Süleymaniye ʿimarets, special 'tables' (*sofra*) were laid for these guests, at which they enjoyed their meals. The Süleymaniye assigned separate dining areas for the guests, who ate in the *tabhane,* as distinguished from the refectory (*me'kel*) where everyone else received food. In Jerusalem, the refectory served for all who ate there. Thus, alongside the quality of food, the place and circumstance in which one ate marked the status of the diner as well.

The fare described in the ʿimarets may be taken to represent the point of departure for all cooking in its composition. Depending on class and location, more varieties of meat, bread, vegetables, fruits, and delicacies were available, and the size of portions or amount laid out on the table changed. Another factor distinguishing between the fare of the poor, the working people, the notability, and the imperial hierarchy were the vessels used to serve food. These varied from the simple bowls of the ʿimaret to the delicate and decorated dishes of the Ottoman elites.[75]

Two further factors refined the demarcation of class or group boundaries among the ʿimaret clients: the quantity of food served and the order in which people ate. In Jerusalem, the quantity of soup varied between one half and one whole ladle, while people received either one or two loaves (*fodula*) of bread. A definite hierarchy existed, but it was not nearly as extensive as that described by the crowd fed at the Fatih ʿimaret. There, the students and staff of the prestigious Seman schools received one ladle of stew and two loaves of bread, while the school tutors (*muid*) got twice this amount of soup. Students and staff from other, dependent schools seem to have received one ladle apiece, while 600 more students (*softe*), apparently less advanced or worthy, shared 300 servings among them with one loaf of bread each. Among the staff of the Fatih, the secretary of the waqf, the expenditures agent, his secretary, and the ʿimaret director received two ladles apiece of soup, while everyone else who worked in the complex received only one. Whatever was left was distributed to the poor, with no serving size stipulated.[76]

Again, here, a clearer picture emerges of whom these ʿimarets were intended to feed. Travelers, officials on the move, religious students and teachers, and also, but far from exclusively, the poor. Notably, no military personnel were mentioned; they had their own barracks and camps. Yet the population fed by each ʿimaret also varied with the character of its locale. Jerusalem had far more pilgrims than Istanbul, many fewer religious students. In Damascus, the *han* of Murad Çelebi, which seems to have functioned much like an ʿimaret, served *dane* and *zerde* twice a week during the four months during which pilgrims passed through the city on their way to and from the *ḥajj*.[77]

Any institution had to be sensitive to its immediate environs, as a story from Konya illustrates further. After the ʿimaret of Selim II was built, the kadi of Konya sent a request to the sultan that the dervishes in the *zaviye* of Celaluddin Rumi, which was very nearby, as well as some of the other neighbors, be included in the daily food distributions. Apparently, the smell of cooking food from the ʿimaret was quite overwhelming, particularly as these people lacked the means to obtain sufficient food regularly for themselves. Twenty-five people were thus added to the roster of diners, and the ʿimaret's budget was increased to reflect this.[78]

The order in which people ate also signified. At Fatih, the esteemed guests ate first, then the Seman population, followed by that of other schools, the staff, and finally, perhaps, the poor. At the Süleymaniye, too, learned men came first. The order of service may have been similar in every ʿimaret but was also determined by the size of the refectory. In Jerusalem, people ate in shifts with a differentiation among the poor as to the order in which they ate. The first to eat were the employees of the ʿimaret and the mosque, after whom came the residents of the fifty-five rooms, followed by the servants of the place. Finally, the poor were admitted in shifts because the refectory could not hold them all at once: the poor among the learned, and then the other poor people, and finally the women.[79] This order matched the distinctions in quantities of food distributed.[80]

The quantity of food as well as the order of receipt both articulate a hierarchy of deservedness at work in the ʿimaret. While the list of recipients included many different people, they were sorted into categories according to how much food they received and in what order. Those who worked at the ʿimaret received the most, the residents somewhat less. Labor was recompensed with food, workers recognized as more deserving and needy than residents or guests. The last group, the poor, received half the ration of the residents. They were lower in status, closer to the margins of subsistence, and the ʿimaret was not the place to revise the social order. Among the poor, a hierarchy was marked only by the order in which they ate, not the quantity they received. Yet the question arises: what happened to those served last when the food ran out? Were they turned away hungry? At the Jerusalem ʿimaret, these would be the women. Although they are not specifically mentioned, one might guess that small children accompanied some women, with older male children accompanying men, earlier. Thus, among those at the bottom of the list, women and small children occupied the least secure place, their chances of eating more precarious. Of course, they were better off than those who could not gain admission to the place at all.

Altogether, the ʿimaret kitchen was intended to feed the occupants of the fifty-five rooms and the caravansaray, the functionaries of the endowment, and 400 "poor and needy" persons,[81] a total of some 500 persons twice daily. In anticipation of problems supervising distribution and controlling crowds, the waqfiyya explicitly dictated that no food was to be given to anyone who came from outside by means of special intervention or petition, nor could anyone remove food in a bucket.[82] These restrictions presumably enabled the director of the ʿimaret to keep closer count and control over the numbers and identities of those who came to eat, as well as to ensure that the quantities of food cooked were sufficient for the obligations fixed by the deeds. People could not simply drop by to pick up food, but had to have some established or justified relationship to the ʿimaret. It must have been an obvious temptation for some to try to save food or get more than their allotment, in order to remove it for a later time or to share with those not admitted. The Süleymaniye had a similar restriction, but qualified it in the case of learned, indigent, or sick people who had no food assignment at the ʿimaret as part of a position there. Food could be taken to them.[83]

To discover just who ate at the Jerusalem ʿimaret, aside from the personnel, is not easy for this period. Interpolating from later periods as well as other ʿimarets, it is possible that visiting officials and passing merchants were among the residents of the caravansaray and rooms. One might wonder whether the ʿimaret fare served them was supplemented by their own purchases in the market of ready-made foods and whether they also enjoyed the hospitality of local merchants and dignitaries. Seemingly full of details, the waqfiyya omits to describe how the people affiliated to the endowment were to be selected, appointees as well as beneficiaries. Only the overseer in Istanbul was clearly identified. He chose the manager, and presumably the manager selected the employees in Jerusalem, with the assistance and recommendations of the director of the ʿimaret. The kadi of Jerusalem was supposed to verify that appropriate people were appointed.

Finally, nowhere is there a clue as to the identity of the 400 "poor and pious" people who received daily rations, how they were to be recognized on a daily basis when they presented themselves at mealtimes, or whether they were even a fixed group. In later years, it became part of the kadi's duty to determine who had the right to eat at the ʿimaret, and it seems that this right was attached to the possession of a bowl.[84] The ʿimaret was not explicitly attached to any institution like a school or dervish residence. The ambiguity of the word *faḳir/fuḳarā* allows for the possibility of many different kinds of 'poor' people: indigents, pious paupers, sufis, widows, orphans, students, pilgrims, people down on their luck, the sick or handicapped, etc. One might assume tentatively that the group which ate at the ʿimaret included them all.

Examining ʿimaret waqfiyyas leaves many questions unanswered. However, despite the various admonitions to take good care of all who arrived, the institutions were clearly not public kitchens bearing the legend, "let all who are hungry come and eat." They had limited, if impressive, resources as well as predetermined obligations to specific groups of people. Therefore, the access to food and the quantity and quality of food distributed were rigorously defined in each case. For some travelers, even the time of day was important: if someone arrived before the noon prayer at the Sultan Selim ʿimaret in Konya, he could eat that day; if not, he was entered only in the next day's roster.[85] At the İsmail Bey ʿimaret in Kastamonu, latecomers were offered a snack of honey, walnuts, cheese and similar raw foods to tide them over until the morning meal.

## WHY JERUSALEM?

Many factors conspired to induce Hurrem Sultan to found the waqf in Jerusalem. The immediate and specific motivations for establishing the ʿimaret were probably an amalgam of the pious and political. Clearly, the endowment deeds were limited by tradition and formula to expressing only the more pious and beneficent inspirations. To date, no other immediate contemporary impulse or inducement for the founding of the Haṣṣeki Sultan waqf in Jerusalem can be recovered. Halil Inalcik has suggested that the residents of Jerusalem sent an appeal for the construction of some kind of public facility.[86] If they did, their appeal may have been linked to the destruction suffered in the city from the enormous earthquake that struck all of southern Syria in 1546, causing much structural damage in Jerusalem and elsewhere.[87]

The impetus to found the ʿimaret may have derived also from an upsurge in the town's population under the Ottomans, due to a combination of natural growth, migration, and the increased numbers of pilgrims after the Ottoman conquest. The registered population of Jerusalem had almost doubled between the years 945/1538–39 and 961/1553–54, from approximately 7600 to 13,500. Projected tax revenues from Christian pilgrims visiting the Church of the Holy Sepulcher rose by 50 percent from 80,000 to 120,000 *akçe* in the same period, suggesting a significant increase in their numbers as well. One obvious consequence of this expansion was the need to ensure a larger steady supply of food to the town, both for purchase and for beneficent and symbolic distribution.[88]

Considered from the vantage of Istanbul, Hurrem and/or Süleyman may have chosen Jerusalem as the site for a new waqf because it was one obvious place for the preeminent Muslim ruler to establish an endowment. Despite the easy conquest of the city, the Ottomans had to work to insert themselves into the built fabric of the over-memorialized space.[89] Süleyman had already funded extensive constructions and endowments in other cities of the empire, including Mecca and Medina. He was building a large complex in Damascus in the mid-1550s in addition to the one set up by Selim I, including a large ʿimaret that distributed food, mostly to *ḥajj* pilgrims.[90] This ʿimaret was completed just as work began on the Haṣṣeki Sultan complex. During the first half of Süleyman's reign, he invested great effort and expense in restoring the fortifications and water supply system in Jerusalem, repairing the external city walls and the network of aqueduct and pipes that supplied water from springs south of the city to supplement the insufficient wells and rainwater cisterns within the walls. In addition, he built public fountains and funded repairs to the Dome of the Rock and al-Aqṣā mosque.[91] All this activity served equally aspects of Süleyman's domestic and foreign policies, reminding all and sundry that the ruler of the Muslim world would protect and enhance the places holy to Islam. The improvement of security and facilities in Jerusalem would be noted equally by Muslim and Christian pilgrims, who would take home news of the impressive new constructions. Rulers in Europe could hardly fail to note the symbolic and strategic fortifications of the Christian holy city by the man so persistently threatening their Eastern frontiers.

From a more local perspective, one can compare Jerusalem with Hebron, the holy city to the south which had perhaps the most long-established and renowned endowment for feeding the pilgrims who arrived at its shrines. The *simāṭ al-Khalīl,* the table of Abraham, was hundreds of years old; its endowed properties were registered and confirmed in the Ottoman surveys of the area at the time of the conquest. Perhaps the presence of this kitchen made the absence of a comparable institution in Jerusalem more obvious. The numerous Mamluk *madrasa*s in Jerusalem made some provisions for their students and staffs, and the many hospices and inns took care of other travelers. Yet all these were apparently insufficient and may also have ignored entire categories of people in the city, notably local indigents and Ottoman travelers.

Once Jerusalem was selected, the choice of the site within the city was not haphazard. It must have been a practical one, in part: Jerusalem, though not entirely built-up, certainly afforded few open building sites, fewer close by the Ḥaram al-Sharīf. An existing site and available building provided a ready-made foundation and initial source of building materials, reducing the expenses entailed in constructing a new foundation. As will be discussed further in Chapter 3, the choice may also have devolved from the previous affiliation of one or more pious women to the site. Ṭunshūq's house may have been a conscious choice on Hurrem's part, in which she built on the *baraka* (blessing, beneficent force) of the previous owner in organizing her own charitable institution.

On a more personal level, Hurrem's age may have been a factor in the decision to found this particular complex. She was ill in the years that the ʿimaret was being founded, although perhaps not as early as 1549 when the first repair work began. By the time the final deed was made in 1557, however, she was ailing and perhaps anticipating her death.[92] Thus this ʿimaret was obviously her last major beneficent undertaking, the last in a succession of pious deeds aimed at procuring the founder a place in Paradise.

As might be expected, the waqfiyya for the Jerusalem complex dwelt emphatically on Hurrem's piety and renown as a generous patroness of works benefiting the Muslims. Much of the initial portion of the deed was woven from standard phraseology and formulae applied to waqf founders and imperial women. Hurrem was described as

> ʿĀ'isha of the age and Fāṭima of the time, the origin of the best of the blooming sultanate and the shell of the pearls of the glittering caliphate, surrounded by all kinds of favors of the protecting King, mother of the Prince Meḥmed son of the most felicitous and great sultan . . .[93]

The explicit characterizations of Hurrem's person and attitudes convey a sense of her as generous, beneficent, and—no less important—a successful bearer of sons. This form of naming provided the entirely standard vehicle for referring to a woman without mentioning her personal name. Yet in this document, the way in which Hurrem was named had a more explicit political purpose, despite its formulaic appearance. Examining the titles given Hurrem reveals a more subtle layer of the waqfiyya text and adds complexity to the whole deciphering of endowment deeds and their functions.

Hurrem was called the source of both sultanate and caliphate, underlining her role in ensuring the continuation of the Ottoman dynasty, whose head now combined both roles.[94] While these were standard kinds of metaphors, it is unclear whether "source" simply acknowledges her as the mother of the sultan's sons, or was intended more specifically to imply her to be the mother of the next sultan. It would have been curious for Hurrem to be identified as mother of the heir in the Turkish waqfiyya from 1552. At the time, the heir apparent was Prince Muṣṭafa, son of Mahidevran, Süleyman's favorite before

Hurrem. Muṣṭafa was accused of treachery against Süleyman and executed in 1553, widely thought to be the victim of Hurrem's ambitions for herself and her own sons. In the text, then, either formulae had won out over precision in calling Hurrem "origin," (*maṭlaʿ*)[95] or else it was really the "handwriting on the wall" for Muṣṭafa.[96]

In addition, the son mentioned was Prince Meḥmed, who had died in 1542, a decade before the waqfiyya was composed. Neither Bayezid nor Selim, the living sons of Hurrem, was mentioned, although they were soon to be open rivals to succeed Süleyman. Another son, Cihangir, was much beloved by Süleyman but unable to inherit the throne as he had a physical deformity.[97] By naming Hurrem as mother of the deceased Meḥmed, the text then appears to display a tactical neutrality both with regard to Muṣṭafa and his supposed inheritance, as well as in the face of a brewing rivalry between her own sons. At the same time, it may articulate an honest expression of Hurrem's continuing grief for Meḥmed, in whose memory Süleyman had erected the great Şehzade complex on Istanbul's main axis.[98]

By the time the Arabic waqfiyya was drawn up in 1557, Muṣṭafa was dead, but Hurrem was still called mother of Meḥmed. By the time Süleyman added to the endowment in 1560 after Hurrem's death, the additional waqfiyya identified her as mother of Prince Selim. Although Bayezid was still alive, he had been accused of rebellion in 1559 and would be executed in 1561. Here, too, it would seem that the formulae of the waqfiyya were tailored to current political circumstances and used to indicate the imperial position in their regard. Yet one final and confounding twist in this puzzle is provided by the title deeds. Dated between 21 Receb 957/5 August 1550 and the beginning of Şevval 967/25 July–3 August 1560, *all* of them name Hurrem as the mother of Selim, although Muṣṭafa and Bayezid were still alive. There is no reason to think Selim was a secret favorite; in fact, once Muṣṭafa had been executed, Bayezid was reputed the preferred heir to Süleyman.[99] Is it conceivable that the title deeds in their highly decorated form were only made at a much later date, perhaps based on earlier draft versions?

Clearly, the texts of these deeds were not simply composites of formulaic titles pasted to the front of a legal record of property rights. Instead the formulae were used to signal relative positionings within the royal household and political changes in the offing, as well as to broadcast imperial preferences to those who read them or heard them discussed. While some unanswered questions remain here, it bears mention nonetheless that the stock phrases of official documents should not be automatically dismissed as lacking historical significance.

Altogether, the images of Hurrem and Süleyman interwoven in the texts of the waqfiyyas reflect a conscious articulation and reinforcement of imperial policy, ideology, and image-making. The mention of Prince Meḥmed in both versions was the expository occasion for a long digression on the glories and renown of his father, longer than the paean to his mother. Süleyman was hailed as *sulṭan* and *imam*, with great stress on his role as upholder of Islam and the *sharīʿa*. Despite being a waqfiyya of Hurrem's endowment, the text is emphatically about Süleyman. The beneficent image of Süleyman was well-developed by the 1550s, and the text contains the standard characterizations which the building activities of husband and wife sought to legitimate and amplify.

In its timing and location, the establishment of the Haṣṣeki Sultan ʿimaret in Jerusalem looks like part of a tandem effort. It took place simultaneously with the planning and construction of the great Süleymaniye complex in Istanbul. Although mere coincidence is a possible explanation for the timing of the two endowments, it is more persuasive to see Hurrem's effort as a conscious counterpoint and echo to Süleyman's own, both to his previous endeavors in Jerusalem and the ongoing ones in Istanbul and Damascus. The written, verbal articulation in the waqfiyya of Hurrem's supporting and necessary role in perpetuating the dynasty and caliphate would have been available to a limited audience. By contrast, the universally known existence of her several sons and her pious endowments visible in key cities throughout the empire were the physical reminders to all and sundry in the empire of her collaboration in Süleyman's own magnificence, munificence, and piety. Specifically, the Süleymaniye and the Jerusalem complexes were each a continuation of their founder's previous projects and culminating monuments for Süleyman and Hurrem. The Süleymaniye was his crowning building achievement; Hurrem died in 1558, the year after the final waqfiyya for her ʿimaret was issued.

The Haṣṣeki Sultan ʿimaret had another audience as well, as did the Süleymaniye. No visitor to Istanbul could miss or be unimpressed by the vast dimensions of the mosque dome and auxiliary buildings, situated prominently on a hill, dominating the skyline of the city. It would be difficult not to make the obvious comparison to that other, Christian, dome on the same skyline, the Aya Sofya. While the Aya Sofya is no less impressive in its dimensions, the size and integrity of the Süleymaniye complex create a far more expansive monument than the church-made-mosque with its mismatched minarets attached awkwardly at the corners.

In Jerusalem, the ʿimaret was less prominent in the skyline, and without a dome. However, its bulk could not be ignored, made more prominent by its elevation opposite the Ḥaram, and by the continual traffic it created around it. It also sat far closer to the Church of the Holy

Sepulcher than any other large Muslim institution. Both monuments, therefore, not only reinforced the role and status claimed by the sultan vis-à-vis his own subjects, but also conveyed to local and foreign Christians the power and preeminence of the Muslims in these formerly Christian sites. Byzantium and Jerusalem were now emphatically Istanbul/Islambol and al-Quds al-Sharīf.[100]

Given the multifaceted motivations discussed for establishing the ʿimaret, it is important to note that this philanthropic endeavor was probably inspired at least as much by imperial exigencies as by the specific needs of the city of Jerusalem. No doubt the piety of Süleyman and Hurrem was a factor in their choice to make endowments at all. His imperial position imposed further obligations. Yet as donors, they shaped their beneficent projects to serve an array of political and social purposes. In this, they resembled the founders of other endowments who utilized waqfs to safeguard private fortunes or control their devolution. They also resembled philanthropists generally, whose decisions to make large grants are rarely driven only by the desire to "do good."

Chapter Three

# Ladies Bountiful

"And whosoever does deeds of righteousness, be it male or female, believing—they shall enter Paradise, and not be wronged a single date-spot." (*Qur'an* IV:124)

" . . . and her name, Mother of Exiles . . .
"Give me your tired, your poor,
your huddled masses yearning to breathe free,
Send these, the wretched refuse of your teeming shore
the homeless, tempest-tost to me." (E. Lazarus)[1]

Imperial, notable, and wealthy women are recorded in many cultures and eras as compassionate benefactors, ladies bountiful dispensing succor to the weak and indigent, the sick and misfortunate. In Ottoman Turkish, they were given titles like *saḥibet el-hayrat ve'l-ḥüsenat,* mistress of good works and pious deeds.[2] Three women—two Muslim and one Christian—are associated with the site of the Haṣṣeki Sultan ʿimaret in Jerusalem. They are the Mamluk al-Sitt Ṭunshūq al-Muẓaffariyya, the Ottoman Hurrem Sultan, and the Byzantine Empress Helena.[3] Only two of them—Ṭunshūq and Hurrem, both Muslim—had a documented connection to the place during their lifetimes. Yet it was Hurrem and Helena who became bound, even confused, in the Jerusalem landscape. This chapter explores how each of the three women became linked with the place, and so, with the institution and each other. In order to understand the connection between them, the discussion will also consider women as philanthropists in the Ottoman world specifically and in Islamic societies.

Traditions existed in Islamic, Byzantine, and Turkic cultures about the generosity and activism of important women; all of these contributed to the imperial Ottoman culture in which Hurrem Sultan founded her waqf. The Byzantine tradition of women's beneficent activism was recorded in chronicles and was evident through its physical presence in Anatolia, the Balkans, and Christian historical sites such as those in Jerusalem. Patronage of charitable foundations in the Byzantine world was probably one influential component shaping Ottoman waqf-making culture. The empresses and princesses of Byzantium also must have been unacknowledged among the influences on Ottoman women, yet one can only infer the connections between the philanthropic undertakings of imperial Byzantine and Ottoman women. A link between the Empress Helena and the Ottoman Hurrem certainly developed in later centuries, and the mingling of the two women's careers and reputations provides a fascinating confusion of cultural and confessional borrowing and memorializing. No evidence contemporary to its founding identifies the specific site of Hurrem's endowment with Helena. With the exception of the monumental Church of the Holy Sepulcher, very few of Helena's charitable establishments in and around Jerusalem can be precisely located, though she had a reputation as an active and generous patron.

A prominent role for imperial women in endowment-making certainly followed from the traditions of women's leadership roles in politics, war, and governance among the Turkic ancestors of the Ottomans. In story, they had ridden into battle beside the men, and the image of the Princess Salçan saving Prince Kan Turalı (more than once!) is a vibrant one.[4] Yet the fighting women celebrated in the tales of the legendary poet Dede Korkut were a long-dead fantasy by the time of Hurrem. By the sixteenth century, women of the Ottoman imperial household had little contact with arms and battles, and were not formally part of government. Their political involvements were played out now on the household battlefield, one no less complex and dangerous than that where armed soldiers faced each other. Publicly, these women expended their energies in other arenas, philanthropy being a key one and not necessarily apolitical. In this, Hurrem rivalled her Muslim paradigms and surpassed the Ottoman women who preceded and followed her (though she would not know this). Consciously, it seems, she was the most active and visible Ottoman patroness ever, and this in itself was testimony to the unique position and power she achieved.

Beneficence was a prominent form of activism for women in the Ottoman empire. At the same time, their beneficence is one quality repeatedly singled out for praise.[5] Within their own spheres of public activity, therefore, beneficence holds an important place. Yet it does not follow that beneficence was effected primarily by women or that it was even a privileged arena of women. One suspects, too, that the reputation of women for philanthropic activity is partly a selective emphasis of historical recording, meant to reinforce an ideal stereotype present in more than one culture. Such an ideal preserves an acceptable image of female behavior and then serves as a role model for women to follow in future, capturing a particular judgment about the proper and possible channels for women's activism. Why this should be so is not clear, nor is the stereotype necessarily universal. Yet the obvious biological role of women as mothers probably contributes not a little to assumptions that they are naturally fit for and prone to nursing and nurturing weak or dependent beings of all types. Iconic figures such as the Christian Virgin Mary replicate the image endlessly. Among her numerous personae, she is cast as *mater dolorosa,* the mother of sorrows, whose tears have the power to purify and mend. She is also looked to as a source of fertility and a powerful intercessor.[6]

Men were surely not absent or invisible as the providers of assistance and support, nor were they less involved than women in such activities. The huge complexes built by successive sultans are an obvious testament to their philanthropy. Yet, one must ask whether the beneficent role of the imperial Ottoman women was particularized in some way by their being women. Were there differences between the endowments of imperial men and women, and if so, to what may they be attributed? The chapter concludes with a discussion of this question.

## THE CONFLATED TRADITIONS: HURREM-HELENA

The person responsible for the distinctive exterior of the ʿimaret was al-Sitt Ṭunshūq. Toward the end of the fourteenth century, she built a house (*dār al-kubrā*) which forms part of the building currently standing on the site in Jerusalem. Across the street she built her tomb (d. 800/1398), and in the Mamilla cemetery west of the city walls she had a dome built over the tomb of her brother Bahādir. The scant reports of her life indicate that Ṭunshūq (perhaps Ṭunsūq) may have been born in Central Asia and from there was either brought to Egypt as a slave convert or else escaped to Jerusalem from eastern Iran when the Muẓaffarid dynasty (1313–93) was defeated by Tamerlane. She was noted for her piety and her support of the Qalandariyya sufis in Jerusalem.[7] Ṭunshūq's tomb across the street from the house, if not the house itself, recorded her name in the topography of Jerusalem.

When Hurrem took over the site, the building there was not in good condition. She and the men in charge of the endowment locally invested significant sums to repair and enlarge it. Hurrem was proving quite concretely the strength of the Ottoman-Muslim rulers as she (re)created an imposing building. It was an echo of what the Ottoman sultans had achieved in Constantinople since 1453, rebuilding and transforming the once-glorious Byzantine capital. The ʿimaret was part of an ongoing effort by Hurrem and Süleyman to enhance Ottoman prestige and legitimation. It appears to have been pointedly directed against the Christian presence and traditions in Jerusalem. The ʿimaret is located at the western edge of the clustered Muslim foundations, which tend to hug the periphery of the Temple Mount when they are not right on it. It is extremely close to, if not actually within, the perimeter of the Christian quarter and a short block south of the Via Dolorosa as it heads uphill toward the Church of the Holy Sepulcher. In fact, the ʿimaret is approximately midway between the key Muslim and Christian shrines, some 600 feet from each one, in the zone of transition from Muslim to Christian areas of the city. Not only was the ʿimaret physically imposing, but the kitchen there undertook immediately to feed approximately 500 persons twice a day, and when more than expected arrived to receive food, they were not turned away. The capacities of Ottoman beneficence were thus announced to the entire local population, from a site especially close to the Christian residents.

The takeover of the site was thus part of the Ottoman colonization of Jerusalem. Other takeovers occurred as well, like the eviction of the Franciscans from their building on Mt. Zion and the installation there of the local sufi Shaykh Aḥmad al-Dajjānī and his followers.[8] Dajjānī's people were added to the list of those who were to be fed daily from the ʿimaret's cauldrons. Together, the dervish residence and the Haṣṣeki Sultan ʿimaret constituted two prominent and newly Ottomanized sites. Both sit high up, and—in the days before television antennas and the construction of taller buildings—they commanded vistas over the city. While the initial Ottoman capture of Jerusalem in 1516 was bloodless, the city still had to be conquered. The construction of the Haṣṣeki Sultan ʿimaret was but one maneuver in this effort.

A message about Ottoman superiority was clearly aimed at the local Muslim and non-Muslim communities, as well as the pilgrims arriving continually in Jerusalem.[9] The Ottomans had ousted the Mamluks. In addition, the message to the Christians included a reminder of the Muslim reconquest of the city from the Crusaders. Hurrem's act takes on added significance when it is placed alongside the reconstruction of the city wall, the restoration of the water supply system, the construction of new fountains throughout the city, and generally improved security conditions. Between them, she and Süleyman had emphasized Ottoman superiority over all rulers in the recent and remote past, and had seen to the basic needs of the city.

Numerous sources, but all composed after the founding of the ʿimaret, attribute the original foundation on Hurrem's site to Helena. This connection may have evolved with the increasing numbers of Christian pilgrims and tourists who came to Jerusalem after the Ottoman conquest. Their intense scrutiny of Christian sites and traditions seems to have discovered the link between Helena and Hurrem. No concrete tie existed, however. Unlike the clearly demonstrable connection between Ṭunshūq and Hurrem in the Mamluk palace, links between Helena and the site remain undocumented. They were imagined and reconstructed by Christians during a period when they had lost control of the city, and were a means by which they could reassert some memory of a glorious past.

Nonetheless, the connection between the two women is important to examine because it both reinforces and undermines the propagandistic aspect of Hurrem's foundation within the larger enterprise of Ottoman colonization in Jerusalem. Notably, the subsequent attention paid to the ʿimaret was at times deflected from Hurrem to Helena, along with the praise and respect it was intended to evoke. A brief mention of "St. Hellena's Hospital, where there are seven great caldrons, in which she used to have Provisions dressed for the Poor . . ." comes in the letter of an English traveler from 1669. Here, it is the huge cauldrons which identify the building as Hurrem's ʿimaret.[10] In 1705, Morison recorded his recent voyage to Jerusalem, noting as follows:

> The hospital, which Saint Helena had built and founded in Jerusalem, still exists, not in the good conditions which she established there to ease the pain of the poor, but in those which mark the disproportion between Christian charity and Turkish compassion. Each day, approximately one pound of bread and one bowl of soup, made with olive oil and some vegetables, are given to each poor person who shows up . . . The Turks recognize, according to a continuous tradition among them, that they owe this hospital and the assets allocated for it to a powerful Christian woman. They are just enough not to deprive poor Christians who come there, and these latter

> receive the same amount as the Muslims, but as they go there only rarely the director of the place is not bothered by them. The building is very solid, large and worthy of the magnificence of the great princess who had it built . . .[11]

These descriptions, dated some 100–150 years after Hurrem's endowment was made, demonstrate how Christian tradition had assigned Hurrem's building and the original charitable impulse for its founding to the most prominent Christian patroness associated with Jerusalem. Hurrem is entirely absent here. Very much present, however, is the comparison between Christian and Muslim beneficence. Morison relates that the Muslims in charge of the soup kitchen continued to prepare and distribute food, but at some lower standard than that intended by the (Christian) founder. He does not deny Muslim charity, but makes clear he understands it as inferior to Christian and somehow beholden to its example. Yet Morison himself notes that the kitchen served food to Christians and Muslims alike in equal quantities. This detail is itself remarkable. Christians were not specifically included nor excluded in the waqfiyya stipulations.

From the mid-nineteenth century, an account given by William Bartlett, an English topographical draughtsman who traveled repeatedly in the Middle East, shows that the conflation of traditions regarding the origins of the ʿimaret continued. He describes:

> . . . the charitable foundation called the Tekeeyeh, popularly called the Hospice of St. Helena. The façade of this building is a handsome specimen of Saracenic architecture, but it has fallen greatly to decay in almost every respect . . . Food however, is still distributed there daily to the poor, and strangers go to see the huge caldrons of the kitchen. The food consists only of a kind of gruel, made of flour, water, and oil, without salt; but enough is prepared to supply twice a-day the servants of the Haram, the Tartar and the Indian houses for Moslem pilgrims, besides any poor who may ask for it.[12]

Here again, Hurrem is not mentioned at all, though it is clear from the name that the building still held a dual identity and that the clientele of the soup kitchen was mostly Muslim. When he wrote, Bartlett could report that the building was called "Tekeeyeh" in Jerusalem, but "popularly" called after Helena. The original benefactor, he indicated, was Muslim, as attested by the "Saracenic character of the architecture," and he identified her as Ṭunshūq, basing himself on Mujīr al-Dīn, the early sixteenth-century historian of Jerusalem and the only historian to have anything at all to say about her.[13]

As these accounts fail to mention Hurrem, one might wonder if her endowment was, in fact, the place intended in the references to Helena's building. However, Hurrem was not altogether invisible to Christians in Jerusalem. The roughly contemporary account of one P. Gérardy Saintine (1860) makes clear that Hurrem was still acknowledged by some as the founder of the ʿimaret.

> This is the *tekkié* of Hasseki Sultan, known among the Christians by the name of the Hospital of St. Helena . . . This charitable foundation was intended to welcome Muslim pilgrims too poor to sustain themselves, and each morning to distribute to the local indigents of Jerusalem bread and rice prepared primarily for them in enormous cauldrons still visible there. This Hasseki Sultan, a privileged queen, so generous in her charity, could be no other for Christians than that magnificent queen, the mother of Constantine, Saint Helena, whose memory evokes for them a time of unlimited beneficence.[14]

Saintine's perceptive observation is important in emphasizing that the only conceivable patron of the ʿimaret was Helena, since in Christian eyes her beneficence was the epitome, unmatched. Moreover, he shows here how thick was the veil of legend and belief through which many Christians "saw" Jerusalem in general.

Finally, the lengthy, detailed, and illustrated account given by Ermete Pierotti, dated only a few years after that of Bartlett, makes the identification between Helena and Hurrem certain. Moreover, Pierotti's declared purpose in composing his wonderfully illustrated description of Jerusalem, after eight years' residence and employ there, was to correct the accounts replete with myth of travelers of a more religious frame of mind as well as writings of people who never went to the city at all. He depicts:

> . . . a building (several centuries old), of Saracenic architecture, having doorways elegantly ornamented with arabesques and mosaics, and with white, red, and black stones found in Palestine. . . . This is considered, by the Christians, to be the hospital built by the Empress Helena; and it is said by tradition to have been erected before the church of the Resurrection, in order to accommodate the labourers engaged upon it, and to have been afterwards devoted to the reception of poor

> pilgrims. I admit the truth of the tradition, but not that the present building is of that date, for it is entirely Saracenic work. The Mohammedans call it Tekhiyeh el-Khasseki-Sultane (Convent of the favourite Sultana), and from documents which they possess in the Mehkemeh [the kadi's court] concerning the registers of landed property, it is clear that it was built by the Sultana Rossellane, the favourite consort of Solyman the Magnificent, who established there a hospice for the poor and the pilgrims. . . . This charitable foundation is still daily at work, but on a reduced scale, owing to its diminished income. I think, then, that this charity may have been commenced by S. Helena (whence its name); then continued by the Latins after her death, and during the Crusades; and kept up by the Mohammedans after their conquest of Jerusalem, till it was finally enlarged and enriched by Rossellane; who also built large rooms there, and resided in it herself to minister to the poor and destitute; as is stated in the Mohammedan traditions, and in the chronicles preserved in the mosque Kubbet es-Sakharah. . . . As this building is assigned to S. Helena by the Christians, so also are the caldrons. What excellent brass they must be to have lasted in use from A.D. 326 to the present time![15]

Pierotti definitively linked the hospital of Helena and the ʿimaret of Hurrem Sultan in his version of the history and chronology of the enterprise. He, too, described a large building where numerous poor people—Muslims and Christians—received a daily portion of bread and soup, cooked in famously large cauldrons. So many of the elements are similar in the descriptions—perhaps most importantly the physical site—that there can be little doubt that the earlier ones also referred to Hurrem's foundation. Yet Pierotti, while not minimizing Hurrem's role in restoring and enlarging the ʿimaret, still accepted Helena as the original patron.

In one respect, Pierotti added an obvious conflation of the Christian and Muslim traditions, that of the imperial physical presence. Setting aside a discussion of what Helena did or did not find or build during her stay in the city, there seems to be no question of the veracity of her visit to Jerusalem from Byzantium. Hurrem, on the other hand, almost certainly never visited the city. No such visit is recorded in any source, and in general, she rarely left Istanbul. The only Ottoman sultan to visit Jerusalem in the sixteenth century was Selim I, at the time of the conquest.[16] As for Hurrem personally caring for the poor, this is more a Christian than a Muslim stereotype of humility and beneficence, one which highlights the individual confrontation of the benefactor and the needy person. Regarding public kitchens in Ottoman times, the ideal seems to apply to men rather than women: Orham Gazi (r. 1326–62), the second Ottoman sultan, was credited with lighting the first hearth fires at the first ʿimaret in Iznik.[17] Actions in public were the domain of men from the imperial household, not women. Beneficent as they might be, it was their gifts and not their persons which were chiefly on view.

How then did these three women come to associate themselves or to be identified with this one place, if we assume that Helena, Ṭunshūq and Hurrem all were involved with it? Further, why should they have done so? Within the broad context of Byzantine traditions of charity and benevolence, a construction by Helena was certainly plausible, whether or not it ever existed and whether or not Pierotti was correct that the original building was erected to house the workmen building the Church of the Holy Sepulcher. The building of a beneficent woman, housing workers embarked on a holy task, surely was a blessed enterprise. Helena's motive for choosing the site is a complete mystery, though its relative proximity to the Church of the Holy Sepulcher would have sufficed. One wonders whether there were traditions regarding the site prior to her visit to Jerusalem.

Morison also characterized the founder of the building as "that august founder," as well as "a powerful Christian woman."[18] He was referring to Helena, but Hurrem might qualify equally as an "august founder." Moreover, she was born a Christian, possibly the daughter of a priest, and was converted to Islam about the time she was brought into Süleyman's harem, though we know nothing of her memories or childhood traditions.[19] Outwardly, she was a pious and generous benefactor of Muslim institutions. Her Christian origins were not in the least exceptional in her time, and seem to have been widely known both inside and outside the Ottoman empire. This may have made it easier for her foundation to be appropriated to Christian traditions in Jerusalem. On the other hand, a tradition of Helena's association to the site may have made it more appealing to Hurrem as the location for her own foundation. In this manner she both continued the work of a prominent and generous woman, while usurping her position in space and memory.

But what of the Mamluk Ṭunshūq, whose large house interrupted a direct link between Helena and Hurrem? Nothing can be said about Ṭunshūq's residence, and whether or not it housed public charitable services. Very likely, the kitchen of a wealthy woman such as Ṭunshūq sustained many people within the household and distributed leftovers or handouts to misfortunates and indigents in the quarter. The connection to the Qalandariyya sufis who met there may imply that the house or tomb across the way was used as a ritual site; sufi ceremonies could include the preparation and distribution of food, and their residences housed sufis as well as hosting guests of all sorts.[20]

As implied above, the amalgamation and assimilation of broad traditions of charity and benevolence imply that the shifting attribution of the ʿimaret site from Christian to Muslim, or vice versa, occurred with little resistance. In fact, a natural evolution of multiple traditions on a shared site seems to have taken place. The consecutive association of three women to one site suggests that there was something attractive in this succession, as though one improved her standing by affiliation to the other. The sociologist Maurice Halbwachs, in his work on memory and the legendary topography of the Holy Land, suggests three ways in which groups of people organize memories about places, events, and other people. In connection with the present discussion, his first way offers some insight:

> Let us first call attention to numerous instances where several events have been located in the same place, without there being any necessary tie between them, as if a place, already consecrated by some memory, attracted others because of it, as if memories heeded some kind of gregarious instinct.[21]

The location of the ʿimaret was charged with precedent; it attracted a particular kind of pious endeavor and preserved the tradition of one. The figure of the beneficent woman, dispensing sustenance to those in need, is a recurrent motif across cultures and time. How natural that two imperial benefactors should thus become confounded in space via the house of a third wealthy woman in the recounting of their patronage.

Admiration and emulation were not, however, the only possible motives for successive displays of beneficence. The usurpations of the Jerusalem site by one woman from another could easily stem from a more aggressive impetus. Christians and Muslims did not always dwell harmoniously together in Jerusalem. Much of the history of the city is taken up by the military conquests: Arabs from Byzantines, Crusaders from Arabs, Ṣalāḥ al-Dīn from the Crusaders, Ottomans from Mamluks, British from Ottomans, Jordanians from British, and Israelis from Jordanians. Or, read another way: the city passed from Christians to Muslims to Christians to Muslims to Muslims to Christians to Muslims to Jews. Throughout the centuries, while political control over the city changed hands, the Jewish, Christian, and Muslim residents have continually competed with each other and among themselves in their sects and denominations for control over various shared holy sites and for space—vertical and horizontal—in Jerusalem.[22] The shifting attributions of the Helena/Hurrem foundation may be interpreted as calculated attempts to assert superiority and gain legitimation by the Christian and Muslim communities.[23]

If Helena actually constructed a building on this site, she perhaps did so because the site already had a structure associated with pious good works, even those of a woman. One nineteenth-century account asserts that the Helena associated with the place is not Byzantine at all, but in fact one Queen Helena of Adiabène (d. 50 C.E.), queen mother of a vassal state of the Parthian empire, whom the first-century C.E. historian Josephus described as living in the same area of the city. She and her entire family had converted to Judaism, and she was famous for her generosity to the Jews and the Jewish Temple in Jerusalem.[24] Christian Helena would then be taking over a site with Jewish associations. When Ṭunshūq built her house, the newer Helenaic tradition may have been alive, and so she displaced a Christian paradigm. Hurrem, thereafter, could have known of the connections of both Helena and Ṭunshūq to the site, now replacing Mamluk with Ottoman.

## BENEFICENCE AND WOMEN IN ISLAMIC HISTORY

### *Early examples*

Hurrem's actions belonged to a longer tradition of Muslim beneficence, and her endowment deed invoked numerous pious Muslim women. Within the Arab-Muslim tradition, examples begin with the family of the Prophet Muḥammad. In elaborating her virtues, Hurrem's waqfiyya calls her the "ʿĀʾisha of the time, Fāṭima of the age," comparing her to the favorite wife of the Prophet and his daughter.[25] Rābiʿa (d. 801), a renowned mystic and saint,[26] and Zubayda (d. 831), wife of the famously generous caliph Hārūn al-Rashīd (d. 809), are mentioned as paradigmatic women in the additional deed made for Hurrem by Süleyman shortly after her death. Deeds of other Ottoman women also mention Khadīja, Muḥammad's first wife, whose tomb in Mecca was restored by Süleyman.[27] Not surprisingly, the deeds of their endowments cite only beneficent *Muslim* women as paradigmatic benefactors.

Traditions about the earliest period of Islam recall the beneficence of Muḥammad's wives. For example, Zaynab bt. Khuzayma al-Hilāliyya was known as "mother of the poor" (*umm al-masākīn*). Another Zaynab, bt. Jaḥsh, was also famously generous, known as "the refuge of the poor." Ā'isha was evoked frequently in later eras, although her charitable acts were not necessarily more extensive than those of her co-wives; she became an individual example of a collective attribute. Also, she was said to live in poverty, having given away her wealth.[28] Fāṭima was evoked as the epitome of daughter, wife, and mother for her devotion to her father Muḥammad, her husband 'Ali, and her martyred sons Ḥasan and Ḥusayn.[29] Whether these women were historically important as benefactors, they took on that quality as one of their chief characteristics in historical memory. For this they were cited as exemplary to the women of Hurrem's time and continue today to be paradigms for the correct comportment—variously interpreted—of women.

The beneficent actions of prominent Muslim women, as with those of men, are known from biographical dictionaries, chronicles, and endowment deeds. While there are altogether fewer documented examples of women founding waqfs, many individuals emerge from the biographical literature as beneficent patrons among imperial or powerful women in the Islamic world prior to Ottoman times. Women were partners in dynastic endeavors. They supported building, artistic production, and good works to the extent allowed by their personalities and pockets. Those of fantastic wealth and superior generosity have become immortalized as paradigms for later generations. Yet biographical dictionaries do not record all people—far from it. Each treats a category of people—scholars, rulers, artists—and generally the most prominent of that group. Many secondary figures escape mention. Women in general appear less frequently in biographical dictionaries.[30] Alongside them, others may have followed their lead in less extravagant fashion, unrecorded heroines of local history or simply the mothers, wives, sisters, and daughters of rich men or provincial officials. Beneficence was not predicated on wealth; as noted above, it was practiced in obligatory and voluntary forms by Muslims of every class and category.

Zubayda, also cited as a paradigm for Hurrem, was responsible for a large number of public works, among them hospices and additions to the water supply system all along the pilgrimage route from Iraq to Mecca, as well as in the holy city itself, where she passed many months. Although she spent vast sums on her own wardrobe and in support of artistic production, Zubayda's pious incentive seems to have derived from her own experience as a devout woman who made the *ḥajj* more than once and as the wife of a powerful and generous ruler. An already-entrenched tradition of Muslims as contributors to the welfare of Mecca and Medina reinforced Zubayda's personal inspiration. Making the pilgrimage was an important public venture for many imperial Muslim women. They could go without their husbands and used the unique occasion to distribute assistance of all types, including the formal endowment of institutions. Donations of cash, distributions of food, and subsidizing or assuming the costs of the pilgrimage for others were among the acts of beneficence performed by these women. For Hurrem, who barely left Istanbul, Mecca and Medina were nonetheless the sites of important donations. She constructed an ʿimaret in each city, and the water works of Zubayda were extensively repaired. Peçevi, the seventeenth-century Ottoman historian, lists this latter under the good works of Hurrem, though he also attributes the endeavor to Süleyman.[31]

Zubayda remains the paradigmatic figure of her era, but her mother-in-law Khayzurān (d. 789) also expended great sums on luxury as well as beneficent works. These two women stand out vividly because of the size, not the type, of their expenditures, since Hārūn himself patronized endeavors similar to theirs.[32] Other pairs of imperial women include Asma (d. 1087) and her daughter-in-law Arwa (r. 1099–1138) in the Yemen,[33] as well as Hurrem and her daughter Mihrimah (d. 1578). Because each of these pairs was outstanding, they earned at least some lines in a chronicle. The continuity of action over generations emphasizes that beneficent work was typical, perhaps learned through experience in the world of imperial women. As mothers, wives, and daughters of powerful and wealthy men, they had the means to act as patrons and were expected to initiate appropriate projects.

### *The Byzantine factor*

Hurrem's beneficent works also echoed those of Byzantine women. As discussed above, Helena, mother of the Byzantine emperor Constantine I, is a key figure for both the Byzantine case and for the specific subject of this study. Helena's patronage was an important model for other Byzantine women, who were confined, as historian Judith Herrin says, to four model roles of action: martyr, dedicated virgin, patroness, and leading figure by virtue of wealth.[34] As a royal woman, Helena combined patronage and access to wealth in an active career of charitable good works. In the year 313 she converted to Christianity. The traditional account of her life tells that while on a pilgrimage to Jerusalem in 326, she found a relic of the True Cross on which Jesus was crucified and thus identified the site of his burial; on this place the Church of the Holy Sepulcher was erected. Sometime after her death, Helena was canonized, and St. Helena has been credited over time with the founding of numerous pious and charitable establishments in Jerusalem and in the region around the city, all typical of the works of Byzantine imperial donors: hospitals, hospices for travelers, homes for the aged, monasteries, and others.[35] In addition to the undertakings ascribed to her, Helena clearly set the tone for the imperial and wealthy women of the fourth and fifth centuries.

The fourth-century reign of Constantine himself signalled the changing form of public beneficence in the Byzantine empire, as emperors subsequently became active as patrons of large public institutions established to support those in need.[36] After Helena, a succession of women affiliated to the imperial family consolidated the role of women as partners in the imperial dominion, among them the empress Eudocia (d. 404), her daughter Pulcheria (d. 453), and another Eudocia (d. 460). Establishing the form and fact of female power, these women invested large sums in numerous and prominent philanthropic works. With regard to Flaccilla (d. 397), wife of Emperor Theodosius the Great, the fourth-century historian of the Christian Church, Eusebius, notes what is true for all of these women: that they were able to undertake beneficent works on such a scale only because of their access to imperial wealth. In Constantinople itself, as well as throughout the empire, they established hospitals, monasteries, churches, poor kitchens, and refuges for the pious, the pilgrims, and the poor.[37] Jerusalem was a special focus for these endeavors, partly in the wake of Helena's personal example and partly due to its obvious importance for devout Christians.

How Byzantine traditions in general entered the Ottoman world is not always certain. Most importantly with regard to philanthropy, the Byzantine practices that the Ottomans encountered were not entirely unfamiliar. There were at least four spheres in which Byzantine and Ottoman women met one another, in which Byzantine women could have contributed to Ottoman imperial culture.

***In space.*** Ottoman women lived in buildings, towns, and regions of Anatolia, the Balkans, and the Arab provinces which had previously been Byzantine. Byzantine women established numerous pious foundations throughout these regions, some of which survived in name or in actuality to Ottoman times.

***In time.*** Turkic peoples migrated into Byzantine Anatolia beginning from the late eleventh century, as a result of which various syncretic practices developed.[38] The Ottoman and Byzantine states coexisted for some 150 years, from around 1300 until the capture of

Constantinople in 1453 and Trabzon in 1461. There was thus a long period of interaction between them.

***In tradition and myth.*** The reputation of Byzantine empresses and princesses for philanthropic works was well-established in Byzantine culture, recorded in oral and written traditions. They may have been talked about by local residents where the Ottomans conquered, so that the generosities of the previous rulers were repeated from person to person and reached the ears of the ruler and his household.

***In person.*** Almost from the earliest appearance of the Ottomans, reports existed of their marriages with Byzantine princesses, the taking captive of Byzantine women, and the purchase of Christian slave girls.

Most of these modes of transmission were indirect and gradual. However, some practices may also have entered directly, carried by the Byzantine and other Christian women who were brides or captive concubines not only of the Ottomans, but of the Muslim rulers who preceded them and were their contemporaries in Anatolia. At least thirty-four princesses from Byzantine, Trapezuntine, and Serbian courts married Mongol, Turkish, and Turkmen princes and sultans between 1297 and 1461. Most of the Ottoman marriages of the fourteenth century were to Christian women. Among the more prominent early Ottoman patronesses were Nilüfer, Asporça and Theodora, three Christian wives of Orhan, Gülçiçek, wife of Murad I (r. 1362–89) and mother of Bayezid I (r. 1389–1402).[39]

Among the imperial wives of the sultans, however, those daughters of rival and subdued Muslim beys were left childless and without philanthropic edifices to perpetuate their names or memories. The absence of both acted as a blatant declaration of their powerlessness and that of their families. On the other hand, the Christian wives, the imperial concubines who bore children, and the princesses—daughters and sisters of the sultans—were the imperial women who established endowments.[40] From the middle of the fourteenth century, however, the number of marriages to Christian women declined. The old practice seems to have ended with the marriage of Murad II (r. 1421–51) to Mara, daughter of the Serb ruler. In the time of Meḥmed II (r. 1451–81), two Byzantine princesses captured with the fall of Trabzon were brought into the imperial harem and married out from there.[41] More and more, the Christian princesses were replaced by slave concubines. Yet these girls, too, often entered the Ottoman harem from a Christian milieu, raised to be familiar with the basic Christian exhortations to charity.

A Christian woman entering a Muslim household would know of the beneficent actions of other Christian women and presumably have been educated to undertake such projects herself, especially the daughter of a wealthy or noble family. In her new home she would then have encountered traditions similar (though not identical) to the ones she left behind with regard to beneficence, although now articulated in the principles of *zakāt* and *ṣadaqa* and reinforced by Qur'anic verses and *ḥadīth*. The actions prompted by these principles were remarkably similar to those of Christian notable women, with mosques and sufi residences replacing churches and monasteries. Examining the early imperial household, it seems likely that the education of Byzantine girls shaped their future roles as benevolent patronesses. When circumstances dictated their marriage to Muslim men—whether or not they themselves converted—there was no reason for them necessarily to abandon their earlier socialization. In fact, the familiar presence of beneficent activities may have given them a comfortable point of entry to their new environment.

### *Turco-Mongol heritage*

A Turco-Mongol context also existed for Hurrem's charitable undertaking, an additional component in the heredity of Ottoman imperial women's beneficence. Turco-Mongol traditions that infused the Selçuks and other dynasties of Central Asian origin promoted a political and even military role, as well as a beneficent one for women.[42] These are wonderfully illustrated in the verses of the poet and bard Dede Korkut. In them, both men and women recounted their generous deeds in the same formulaic language:

> I sent water into the parched channels,
> I gave the black-garbed dervishes the promised offerings,
> When I saw the hungry I fed them,
> When I saw the naked I clothed them.[43]

At the same time, a prince could dream of a bride who would be his partner in every way:

> Father [said Kan Turalı] you talk of getting me married, but how can there be a girl fit for me? Before I rise to my feet she must rise, before I mount my well-trained horse she must be on horseback, before I reach the bloody infidels' land she must already have got there and brought me back some heads.[44]

From among the Great Selçuks and others who preceded the Ottomans, several prominent women were remembered for their beneficent works, though the historical record omits any account of heroics. Among her endeavors, Arslan Khatun, wife of one Kāykūyid of Yazd in the eleventh century, supported two communal meals (*shīlān*) each day, one for the notability and one for the general public. A certain Zāhida Khatun, who ruled Fars after her husband was killed in 1146–47, used all her jewelry and cash to endow the school she built in Shiraz. Several women of the ruling class in Kirmān were noted for their endowments, including Qutlugh Terken, who ruled from 1257–82 and converted land to waqf. She established foundations not only for the poor but for the needy members of notable families as well. This is an interesting comment on definitions of deservedness; the needy could include those who belonged by birth to a more well-off condition as well as people absolutely impoverished. The deservedness of these "shamefaced poor" derived from the change in their circumstances, and not their condition per se. Similar concepts of poverty existed in early modern Europe as well.[45]

In Ayyubid Damascus (1174–1260), almost half the patrons from the ruling family were women. For the most part, their endowments supported colleges, sufi residences, and tombs.[46] In Ayyubid Aleppo, the most prominent woman patron was Ḍayfa Khātūn, wife of the thirteenth-century ruler al-Ẓāhir Ghāzī. Her endowments there were typical of the women of her time and station: a mausoleum for herself and other members of her family was combined with a college and a sufi residence, for use by sufi women as well as men.[47]

Among the Rūm Selçuks, immediate Muslim predecessors of the Ottomans in Anatolia, Mahperi Hatun, wife of Sultan 'Alaeddin Kayḳubad I (r. 1219–37), founded a large mosque complex including college, bath, and her tomb in Kayseri, as well as five caravansarays.[48] The daughters of Kayḳubad I also endowed a college and their tombs in Kayseri.[49] While a tomb structure may not appear beneficent but rather self-serving, it is important to note that the tombs were built in conjunction with other institutions, like colleges, which did serve a larger population. Moreover, such endowed tombs could include salaries for *Qur'an* readers to recite verses for the soul of the departed founder, as well as distributions of food. Mausolea were the most prevalent institution endowed for or by women in pre-Ottoman Anatolia, whereas in the Ottoman era, endowments seem to have been established for a broader spectrum of beneficiaries.[50]

Women of the ruling Mamluk household, too, were active patrons. Petry attributes this to the more egalitarian and integrated roles for women in the Central Asian traditions of the Qipjak and Circassian Mamluks dominant in Cairo.[51] Behrens-Abouseif qualifies the case of

Mamluk women to a certain extent, pointing out that their endowments were often the work of their husbands and sons. In this there is nothing particularly Mamluk: the patronage of women has generally been a result of men's actions in their names or of monies they acquired from men, usually their fathers and husbands. What is noteworthy is that men were moved to associate women to their philanthropic works, whether as a gesture of homage, a means to make the patronage appear more broadly generated, or in some way to infuse their deeds with a female piety and beneficent hand. Women's beneficence took other forms, too, especially donations and generous acts during the pilgrimage to Mecca, an event which became the embodiment of imperial women's piety under the Mamluks.[52]

The preeminent Mamluk woman was Shajarat al-Durr (d. 1257) who built mausolea for her husband and for herself, setting a precedent for Mamluk men and women to construct tombs as major endowed edifices in Cairo.[53] In general, the endowments of Mamluk women were similar to those of Mamluk men—mosques, colleges, sufi residences—although never as large as the buildings of the sultan. Petry gives examples of several royal women prominent for their patronage and managerial skills. Among them was Mughul, wife of Sultan Çaḳmaḳ (r. 1439–53). She established a *madrasa* and gave to support the poor in Jerusalem, while also being appointed as manager of the endowments of Çaḳmaḳ himself, her father, and her brother.[54]

Sabra, too, considers women as the benefactors of the poor, but sees their actions as part of efforts to safeguard properties from confiscation. More notably, he identifies institutions endowed specifically *for* women in Mamluk Cairo, especially for unmarried women, single, divorced, or widowed. These institutions were rare, and, furthermore, residence in them may not have been voluntary; rather, they existed to control as well as protect unattached women.[55]

### *The Ottomans*

Ottoman women, unlike their Mamluk counterparts but similar to their Selçuk predecessors in Anatolia, were part of a single dynastic enterprise. The Selçuk sultans, however, carved their empire into shares for their sons, who then fought among themselves for the supreme office. The Ottomans, by and large, avoided these disputes of succession and confiscations, so that the dynastic enterprise became a more unified and coherent undertaking. From the early decades of Ottoman rule in northwest Anatolia, Ottoman imperial women made endowments, and their endeavors grew in size with the expansion of the empire itself. Ottoman sultans, like their predecessors, gave money or land grants to women who were favorite concubines (*haseki*) or to their own mothers (*valide*), daughters, and sisters. These grants, together with the monies women acquired from inheritance, dowry, stipends, investments, or gifts, provided the necessary capital for establishing endowments. The physical and functional prominence of their waqfs kept the names of imperial women on the lips of Ottoman subjects in cities around the empire. Women of the Safavid dynasty in Iran (1501–1723) provide an interesting comparison to the Ottomans. They had similar status and had sources of wealth that they used in generous and substantial patronage. However, Safavid wives and princesses seem to have been more openly involved in political affairs, more broadly educated (including in riding and the use of arms) and generally more independent in their lifestyles and use of their wealth.[56]

After the first two generations of Ottoman rule, the princes no longer participated in public building, perhaps since to do so would be to (pro)claim a status to which they were only entitled upon succession to the throne. Therefore, the largest public buildings established by the imperial household were the works of the sultan, his mother, daughters, and sisters, and this was their privilege. This assumes that women of the imperial household would not expect to accede to power, hence they could be permitted this symbolic prominence without threatening the sultan; on the contrary, their endeavors reinforced his stature along with their own.[57]

Nilüfer and Asporça, wives of Orhan, are the earliest of imperial Ottoman women about whose philanthropy there is evidence. Nilüfer was responsible for the building of a sufi tekke, a mosque and a bridge in Bursa. Her son, Sultan Murad I, also built an ʿimaret that bore her name in Iznik. Gülçiçek, concubine of Murad I and mother of Bayezid I, built a mosque and her own tomb in Bursa. Gülruh, concubine of Bayezid II (r. 1481–1512), built her tomb as well as a mosque and ʿimaret in Akhisar and two mosques in Aydın Güzelhisar and in Durakli Köyü.[58]

These women exemplify several aspects of waqf-making by imperial Ottoman women. First, they built the same kinds of institutions that men built. Second, they often constructed their own tombs, and established that the *Qurʿan* be read regularly in them. Third, endowments bearing their names were either established by themselves or in their honor. Finally, from the late fourteenth century until the time of Hurrem Sultan, the concubines made endowments chiefly in provincial towns of Anatolia and the Balkans, but, except for some tombs, not in the imperial capitals. This was a reflection of the fact that their sons were generally sent away from the capital to gain experience, with their mothers accompanying them to supervise their households and training.[59] Thus the patronage of these women was part of their contribution to the place that served as a temporary home. During those first two and a half centuries, the mothers of princes advertised the power and beneficence of the sultans to the provincial audience and not on the central stage of the capital.

A concubine generally established her individual importance within the household structure by bearing a healthy male child who survived into adulthood. Unlike the sultan's daughters, or the daughters of a wealthy family, imperial concubines might have little or none of their own property at the beginning of their affiliation to the imperial household. Moreover, they were slaves, and so, in theory, had to be manumitted or receive formal permission in order to establish endowments. A woman might accumulate wealth during her tenure as the sultan's favorite, but this was not comparable to the resources she could tap if she became the queen mother. The status of the *valide sulṭan* in the late sixteenth and seventeenth centuries was paramount.

Ḥafṣa Sultan, mother of Süleyman I, endowed a large complex of mosque, college, primary school, and sufi hospice in Manisa, one of the traditional towns of residence for Ottoman princes and their mothers. In 1513, at age nineteen, Süleyman had been appointed district governor to Manisa, and he lived there with Ḥafṣa until the death of his father Selim I in 1520.[60] While undertaking an endowment in the district seat of her prince-son was quite usual, Ḥafṣa's Manisa complex was the first by a concubine to include an imperial mosque. Ḥafṣa was also the first to be called by the title "Sultan." Together these events signalled the shifting status of the sultan's mother, her increased share in dynastic power.[61]

With the increasing prominence of imperial women, Hurrem Sultan was the first in a series of women whose actions gained publicity, and indeed notoriety, in the vortex of Ottoman imperial politics. Hurrem enjoyed unique status as the married wife of Süleyman, the mother of all but his eldest son, and due to her monopoly on the sultan's attentions. Unlike the women who preceded her, Hurrem apparently did not share the sultan's affections with any other women, nor did she leave him to accompany any one of her sons to his provincial appointment. Hurrem stands out then for her emphatic presence during Süleyman's lifetime, due to her own character, to his attachment to her, and to her exclusive claim to be future *valide* once Muṣṭafa, the rival son of the earlier favorite Mahidevran, had been put to death in 1553.[62]

Unlike the powerful women who followed her, Hurrem enjoyed her position as wife of the sultan and not as his mother.[63] This was always recalled by the appellation "Haṣṣeki Sulṭan," the favorite. Yet in the written texts connected to the waqf, her identity as mother of the future sultan took precedence over her connection to Süleyman. In the title deeds and waqfiyyas, she was known as *valide sulṭan,* perhaps to distract attention from the fact that she had vastly overstepped the traditional boundaries of a consort's building privileges.[64] Hurrem had translated her unique and preferential position into great power, a power reinforced by residence in Topkapı Palace and attested by the exceptional number, size, and location of her endowments. She was the first to have a mosque complex made in her name during the lifetime of her husband, and her double bath sits on the most prominent axis leaving Topkapı Palace, just beyond the Aya Sofya. By and large Hurrem continued the endowment activities practiced by the imperial women who preceded her, but her endowments were located not in provincial towns but in the imperial capitals and the holy cities. In addition to the Jerusalem and Istanbul complexes and the bath in Istanbul, Hurrem is credited or honored with ʿimarets in Mecca and Medina, water works in Edirne and a caravansaray, mosque, and ʿimaret in Cisr-i Muṣṭafa Paşa.[65]

After the time of Hurrem and her daughter Mihrimah, the most important women and women patrons were the *valide sulṭans.* Their prominence restored the locus of women's power to its more natural place in the body of the most senior and unchallengeable of all women affiliated with the sultan. The position of *valide sulṭan* became a much enhanced one, advanced by the transfer of the imperial harem permanently into the Topkapı Palace by Hurrem. With the increasingly rare sorties of the sultan at the head of his army and the end of the apprenticeship of princes as provincial governors, all members of the imperial family remained in more permanent residence in Istanbul during the late sixteenth century. This seems to have focused much of the building activity of imperial women in the capital. Hurrem's complex and bath, Mihrimah's mosques, Nurbanu's complex at Üsküdar and the Yeni Valide mosque complex at Eminönü all echo this development.[66]

Yeni Cami in Eminönü and the history of its construction provide one example of limitations on imperial women's beneficent activities. Safiye Sultan, mother of Sultan Meḥmed III, began work on the complex in 1597, but had to give it up when he died in 1603 and she moved to retirement in the Old Palace. As ex-*valide,* Safiye was cared for and enjoyed a regular pension, yet she no longer received the stipends, gifts, and grants which had enabled her to undertake the enormous project of establishing an imperial complex. In any event, the foundation hardly enjoyed the same rank among imperial complexes now that she was more distanced from the sultan, and so the propagandistic effect of completing it would have been diminished. Ultimately, the Yeni Cami was completed some fifty years later by Hatice Ṭurhan, the then-reigning *valide* of Sultan Meḥmed IV. Under her patronage, the project regained its significance as an imperial endeavor. When completed, its status and Ṭurhan's were marked by the ranking of positions in this mosque in the highest category of appointments for religious functionaries, a category which included the largest sultanic mosques in Istanbul.[67] Prior to completing the Yeni Cami, Ṭurhan had sponsored the construction of the Seddülbaḥir and Ḳumḳale fortresses at Çanakkale, on either side of the Dardanelles. As *valide* of the child sultan Meḥmed IV, she was the senior member of the Ottoman household (once the previous *valide* had been assassinated). Her patronage reflected her power, and the choice to build fortresses, her sense of responsibility and identity.[68]

Along with the *valide sulṭan,* the daughters and sisters of the sultan, related to him by blood from birth, had the most obvious family ties. They appeared in the harem stipend rolls and received additional income grants and other gifts. Waqfs were founded in their names and by them. The role of daughters seems to have become more prominent from the time of Mihrimah, daughter of Süleyman and Hurrem, although there were many daughter-philanthropists earlier and long after.[69] They too served as part of the "broadcast service" which made regular, concrete (or rather, stony) announcements of imperial beneficence throughout the realm. The increasing importance of the sultan's daughters in the late seventeenth century may have derived from their role in tying high-ranking officials to the sultan through marriage, as well as from the more circumscribed position of the *valide.* Marrying officials to princesses so that they became imperial sons-in-law (*damad*) served to strengthen bonds of loyalty and obligation to the sultan, as well as providing a mechanism for rechanneling the wealth collected by officials.[70]

Thus, the beneficence of Ottoman women is ultimately an activity configured not only by its heredity but by the immediate needs of the dynasty and imperial dynamics. Imperial women's physical location, political influence, and economic strength shifted over time. The people who changed places on the imperial stage were not necessarily the objects of direct public observation. Instead, beneficent acts were one sign which could be read as a notice of power shifts, and the shifts in modes of imperial beneficence could be read as signs of changing public idioms of power and prestige. While the visibility of their donations seems to share much with the beneficence of other imperial women, the choices of place, form, size, and timing were determined particularly from within the sultan's household; the stereotype of beneficent powerful women was reinforced and maintained with an obvious Ottoman stamp.

## The Gender of Beneficence

Beneficent undertakings were shaped by combined qualities of status, economic capacity, gender, or group solidarity. At the summit of Ottoman society, beneficent works, as embodied in imperial endowments, seem to have been configured by the identity of the founder as a member of the imperial family, and within that very circumscribed group, by the division of roles according to sex and status within the imperial household. These factors affected access to the revenues needed to make endowments, choice of city and site, timing, and subsequent management. An informal but extensive survey of imperial foundations from the fourteenth to sixteenth centuries reveals, on the whole, no dramatically gendered division of choices in the types of endowments created.[71] That is, imperial Ottoman women do not seem to have been systematically barred from establishing any particular type of institution. Religious and secular buildings, including mosques, caravansarays, libraries, water works, and fortresses all had women patrons.

The question remains: did the waqf-making of these women differ in significant ways from that of men in the imperial household? One kind of answer has already been given in showing how the princes were excluded from waqf-making while the princesses participated as a matter of course. Thus the function of an individual within the household could determine whether or not s/he had a role to play as a benefactor. Gender was only one factor determining waqf-making privileges, however, since here it was the blood tie to the sultan affording them access to the throne which kept out the princes. In contrast, men who were grand viziers, janissary commanders, and chief eunuchs all made waqfs notable for their size and importance.

In general, Islamic law stipulates where sex determines differential status, rights, and liabilities. No legal restrictions existed to curb the waqf-making of women, imperial or otherwise. Examples of women making endowments also show them following legal steps identical to those of men.[72] Islamic law recognizes the property rights of women, including their right to inherit and dispose of their property freely. If a woman possessed the necessary capital resources, she could make a waqf. Nor were there any social or cultural taboos against their making waqfs; they, like others, were encouraged to give. Ultimately, the chief constraint on the ability of women to make waqfs was financial, affecting the size of the waqf a woman could make. This limitation resulted from legal handicaps deriving from inheritance law, as well as from social and cultural norms that could affect women's ability to earn money or acquire capital.[73]

The bulk of their property, whether they used it for making endowments or not, came to women through dowry, inheritance, gifts, and stipends, from men. In this they resembled wealthy women in many other times and places in history. Women philanthropists, sincerely generous people, have by and large given away monies acquired from men. As if to emphasize how tied women have been to the money of men, even or especially the imperial or wealthy, a millennial article in *The Wall Street Journal* entitled "Fifty of the Wealthiest People of the Past 1,000 Years" listed only men as examples.[74] These super-wealthy men amassed their fortunes not only as businessmen, bankers, or industrialists, but also as rulers and conquerors and the legally preferred heirs to wealthy families, all of them positions by and large closed to women.

Women in different times and places in Islamic societies owned businesses, lent money, and traded. Where they were discriminated against in Islamic law was with regard to inheritance. Women received one-half the amount of men in the same family relationship. This could reduce their power to endow. It was not obliterated, however, as women *did* inherit. Moreover, they did not forfeit their property to their husbands when they married, as was the case in numerous other, notably Western Christian, societies.[75] Women in the Ottoman imperial household were given financial resources. They held land and revenue grants, received regular stipends and, depending on the individual, generous gifts. Yet when a sultan died there was no inheritance. The women, except for the new *valide sulṭan,* were retired on reduced stipends to the Old Palace. The new sultan's sisters and daughters retained a status affording them significant revenues, one to which his concubines, too, could now aspire.

Another financial restriction to women making waqfs resulted from their exclusion from the spoils of conquest and battle. In the Ottoman empire, the booty and loot amassed during its first 250 years created many fortunes for the sultans and their troops. Only as recipients of the sultan's largess and as heirs to the warriors did women have access to this wealth and only within the stipend-gift-inheritance-dowry circle of financial restrictions.

While not excluded from making endowments of any kind, some women did choose to bestow their beneficence especially on women. The first major endowment by Hurrem in Istanbul was situated near the area called Avret Pazarı (Women's Bazaar), perhaps a conscious choice in order to legitimize the first establishment of an imperial complex by a woman in Istanbul.[76] Kösem Sultan, *valide sultan* of Murad IV (r. 1622–40) and Ibrahim (r. 1640–48) made a waqf to fund dowries for poor girls.[77] In early Safavid Iran, Tajlu Khanum, wife of Shah Ismail, endowed the shrine of Fāṭima al-Maʿsūma in Qum, where women especially went to seek intercession. Numerous Safavid women followed Tajlu Khanum's example.[78]

Women may also have affected the shape of certain endowed buildings. Recently, it has been suggested that the layout of buildings in the Yeni Valide complex at Eminönü in Istanbul is the result of considerations based on the gender of its patrons: the *valides* Safiye and Ṭurhan. There, the imperial pavilion (*hünkâr ḳasrı*) was placed to allow the *valide* unrestricted visual access to the entire complex from within the pavilion, since both her status and gender prevented her from surveying the buildings openly in person. Moreover, the entrance to the pavilion itself is situated so as to enable everyone within the grounds of the complex to see the *valide's* ceremonial arrival and departure.[79] The magnificent entourage was intended to impress even if its central character could not be seen.

No legal restriction existed to prevent women from managing endowments. In her Haseki endowment in Istanbul, Hurrem retained the right to appoint the manager.[80] In Jerusalem, although she had a deputy, Hurrem kept administrative control over the waqf, as well as the right to change the terms of the endowment during her lifetime.[81] Baer observed for Istanbul in the sixteenth century that women founders were more likely to designate men than women as the managers and overseers of their endowments.[82] Yet his samples included no imperial waqfs. Meriwether found that the majority of managers were men in Aleppo as well during the later period that she studied, though her figures show more women than those of Baer.[83]

Why was there a seeming preference for men as managers? Imperial Ottoman foundations were often enormous, and their endowed properties spread over great distances. Effective managers were tapped from the ranks of the imperial corps of military-administrative officials or religious officials, all male. The careers of both managers and officials demanded mobility, experience in property and personnel management and revenue collection, and entailed some further on-the-job training, none of these easily available to women. However, examples from Mamluk Cairo demonstrate that in the context of succession by contest and not by dynastic order, other kinds of considerations could make women more attractive as managers and bring them the attendant wealth and status. Mamluk women served equally, if not more often, as the trustees of large endowments because of their greater longevity and relative insulation from the violence which struck Mamluk men; as a result, they provided some measure of protection for the greater foundations and the people they supported.[84] In the Jerusalem ʿimaret, members of prominent local families gradually took over the position of manager. Ironically, this allowed the office to be assigned on occasion to women from these families.[85]

Where women were clearly at a disadvantage was as beneficiaries in the large imperial waqfs. They did, it is true, enjoy access to the splendid mosques, the hospitals, the public kitchens, and the sufi residences and benefited from water works and bridges. Yet they were not among the ranks of stipendiary scholars and students in the colleges and only rarely in a position to enjoy the hospitality of the caravansarays. Nor do they appear as employees in the more menial positions in these institutions.

In sum, Ottoman imperial beneficence was clearly gendered. Women of the imperial household could make waqfs commensurate with their status, but their ability to do so depended on funds made available to them, in one way or another, by the sultan himself. Their choices of where and what to endow were also not limitless, but bound to some extent by the needs and conventions of the dynastic enterprise. The changes in these latter over time affected the choices available to women, so that there is nothing static in their waqf-making. In general, the beneficence of women is gendered, not because there are restrictions on women regarding beneficence. Rather, culture and law are gendered, and to the extent that they affect beneficence, it thus becomes gendered.

Was the beneficence of imperial Ottoman women more outstanding than that of their male counterparts? Yes and no. Within the imperial family, the sultan obviously made buildings and donations that were the most prominent or magnificent of his era. Yet he was the only man of the family to endow, whereas his numerous women relations and concubines could all be active patrons at any one time. Just as the sultan had no true female counterpart, the women of the family had no male counterparts. Thus their undertakings stand out in numerical terms.

If one considers the entire imperial household, the picture shifts so that the beneficence of women becomes part of a larger context. Within the extended imperial household the spectrum of high-ranking officials should also be identified as waqf makers. These included the viziers, the chief eunuch, and the imperial administrators and officers, some of whom were imperial sons-in-law. There were relatively few men of religion in this group, though they may have made smaller endowments. Again, all clearly were connected to the center of power but with no grounds for a claim to it. It was their access to property and revenue sources, chiefly through the sultan, which enabled members of the extended palace household and the high ranks of the military and administration to establish large endowments. They obtained revenues in the form of salaries or daily and annual allowances, gifts, and direct grants of property. The functions from which revenues derived influenced people's ability to make endowments. This condition was not necessarily prejudicial to women, who, like men of high rank, enjoyed generous material support from the sultan.

The beneficence of these women appears more outstanding, too, because it is one of their few public performances. While the men—even the infrequently seen sultan of the later sixteenth century—might appear in front of their armies, in council, on parade or in the mosques, the public persona of imperial women was always screened, behind the curtains of their litters, the fences of parks, the walls of buildings, or shuttered windows.

Changing structures and balances of power within the imperial household shifted the weight of women's waqf-making activities among mothers, daughters, wives, and concubines over the course of Ottoman history. A statistical study of these endowments might provide further material on which to base more substantial conclusions about gender as a factor in imperial endowment-making. However, it would be far more interesting to include the waqfs of viziers, commanders, imperial sons-in-law, eunuchs, and other high-ranking palace officials alongside those of different women.[86] A collective analysis such as this would offer a more complete picture of how differences of rank, function, proximity, and sex affected the endowment-making of the entire imperial household.

Powerful women are often donors, and they are often expected to be. The English designation "Lady Bountiful" became a sterotypical Western appellation for a kind and generous woman of means and status distributing assistance to those less fortunate than herself. The prototypical Lady Bountiful, wife of a deceased Sir Charles Bountiful, was a fictional character in an English play produced in 1707. She was reputed to spend half her 1000-pound-per-annum income "in charitable uses for the good of her neighbors . . . [having] cured more people in and about Lichfield within ten years than the doctors have killed in twenty."[87] Lady Bountiful was a paragon of generosity and effective charity, whose name became a standard English expression for the wealthy woman of good works. Another stereotype appears in Marianne, key symbol of the French Revolution and the Republic, who appears first as "Liberty leading the People," a figure in dynamic motion.[88] The expectations from powerful women were articulated in yet another way by Emma Lazarus in the poetic epigraph of the Statue of Liberty. Originally, the Statue was called "Liberty Enlightening the World," making her upraised arm the source of light leading people. Through Lazarus' pen she was reinvented as the "Mother of Exiles," beckoning protector of refugees seeking liberty and comfort.[89] For how could a woman of such stature not be a source of aid and relief? Yet in "The New Colossus," although Lazarus maintained the larger-than-life dimension of Liberty, she changed her from the strong leader into the steadfast figure who waits to succor and provide relief. Liberty stands motionless, fixed in space with open arms to gather in the weak and homeless. The anchoring of the Statue of Liberty echoes the transformation of women's roles and the idealization of them that took place with the sedentarization of the Turks. The charitable endeavors of imperial Ottoman women resembled those of their Selçuk, Mamluk, and Byzantine predecessors. Hurrem, exceptional in every way, was close to a full partner in Süleyman's beneficent enterprise. In Jerusalem, her ʿimaret stands as a monument to her own charity as well as to the idealized beneficence of powerful women. Hurrem becomes Helena; the two form a composite image of the lady bountiful.

Chapter Four

# Serving Soup in Jerusalem

*"Amma seʿadetlü sulṭanım bu diyarın fuḳarası çoḳtur."*
(But, my felicitous sultan, the poor of this region are numerous.)

## A report from the ʿimaret

Sometime during the months of January–February 1555, an imperial emissary named ʿAbdülkerim visited Jerusalem. He was on his way to Istanbul from Cairo, transporting a large sum in gold coins from the revenues of Egypt, when winter weather made the road north impassable at Ludd, near the town of Ramla. From there, he detoured to Jerusalem, and when he finally arrived in Istanbul, he submitted an extensive report describing the specific conditions he had found at the ʿimaret.[1] In the report, ʿAbdülkerim mentioned meeting two other imperial envoys when he subsequently resumed his journey northward from Ludd. Ḥamza and Ḥasan were on their way to Jerusalem from Istanbul to investigate the state of food and bread in the ʿimaret. They penned their own detailed account of food supplies, preparation, and distribution.[2]

ʿAbdülkerim's report, quoted below, illustrates the range of complications facing the nascent endowment.

> (Page a) At the time of the noon prayer, we arrived in Jerusalem unaccompanied; absolutely no one knowing [of our arrival], we came directly to the ʿimaret; upon finding the bread

and food cooked and ready, we placed a man [to watch] over it; we made him wait while we were performing the noon prayer, then we came back.

It is known to God, may He be exalted, that we found no particle lacking in the tastiness of the food and the weight of the bread, and that I had more than twenty portions of bread weighed. I found all of them [weighed] 90 *dirhems* each, after it was established that according to the noble waqfiyya each was to be cut [unbaked] at 100 *dirhems*.[3] When it was necessary to distribute [food], according to the regulations (*ḳanun*), after the bowls of those who came first for food were set down and completely finished, [food] was given to those who lived in the rooms of the residence (*ribaṭ*)[4], and afterwards to the servants of it, and [then] because the refectory was not large enough [to hold all the people at once], the food was given first to the poor of the scholars (*ehl-i ʿilm*), and then to the remaining *fuḳara* and *cumraya*[5] and then to the women.

But, my prosperous sultan, the poor of this region are many. Previously, food was distributed at one serving (*nöbet*); now food which was cooked for one serving begins to be cooked [for] two servings. I was amazed at the crowds and the cry for help from the sort of people who said "we are still hungry", not receiving [food] because the food and bread did not reach [them].

Let it thus be established to cook two servings of food; the cook must make an effort that there be somewhat more bread, or once again according to the first arrangement, it shall be necessary to cook one serving in the morning—one day rice, one day wheat—so that annually no person shall remain destitute (*maḥrum*).

With the perseverance and care and governance and protection of Meḥmed *ağa* of your servants, who is the director (*şeyh*) of the ʿimaret, the conditions of the food of the imperial ʿimaret were stated to be thus.

(Page b) And if an explanation is requested about the other conditions of the imperial ʿimaret, furthermore when I asked the nature of the manager [as to his] being capable, all the notables (*aʿyan*) of Jerusalem and the other *fuḳara* and strangers answered, and said: "Is it not known, that you ask: what is the condition of it? The manager of this ʿimaret is one who comes once a year, and then only for 15 days during which time he takes a stick in his hand; when food of the ʿimaret is distributed he does not approach, and when he comes to the bath building, he comes on horseback and looks on from in front of the building atop his horse, without dismounting, and once again returns to his room; and he does not procure all the supplies which are needed at the proper time, [but] he buys supplies out-of-season [hole in document]"[6]

In fact, my prosperous sultan, let the manager be that one who does not let his foot leave the ʿimaret and does not take his eye off the endowments. . . .

The true state of the case is thus: that the manager must [hole: make prosper?] the ʿimaret. In the present condition one silver coin (*akçe*) in ten is present from the yield of the endowments. They were ready and waiting for the yield of the market taxes (*iḥtisab*) and the tax of the village of Ludd, so that they could collect it and pay the daily allowance to the servants.

And affiliated to the ʿimaret, there was one of your servants called Bayram *çavuş* (emissary) from the imperial emissaries of Damascus; he himself has performed many good works (*hayrat*). And in that region, most of the time he is busy night and day serving the ʿimaret with goodness and devotion.

The noble orders of the Padişah, asylum of the universe, majestic personage, may God exalt and glorify his helpers, were given that [Bayram] take the place of the one who was present; he is well thought of now. Moreover a letter came to him from the manager; he showed it to your humble servant, and it said: "you should immediately examine the supplies required by the ʿimaret." Now for the oil and for some necessities which the ʿimaret required, he distributed 100–200 gold coins (*altun*) as loan to the *reʿaya;*[7] he was a capable person.

After it was permitted that the office of manager be given to a person like the person who is now the manager [Ferhad], may you [now] grant it to the aforementioned Bayram *çavuş*, your slave, who, besides being [watchful] over it day and night, making the imperial ʿimaret and its endowments prosperous, making the *fuḳara* comfortable and praying for God's benedictions, it is the hope that, with exertion and perseverance, by buying the supplies which are needed for the ʿimaret at the proper time, aside from all the expenditures, he will produce even more revenue from the accounting; let he himself obtain the account and deliver [it].

This kind of boldness [making this suggestion] is not merely from my mind. This is the wish of all the notables of Jerusalem and the other *fuḳarā* of the city, and her kadi and governor and ʿimaret servants, that by giving the office of manager as an act of grace to your servant Bayram *çavuş,* the food of the ʿimaret be well and the endowments flourish and be in a state of tranquility. For this reason they prayed and praised my sultan boundlessly in that noble place . . .[8]

And I went into the pantry of the imperial ʿimaret and saw all the things [there]. The honey was abundant, and the wheat was good, too. But there was only a sufficient quantity of fat (*yağ*) for twenty-five days. And the rice was in short quantity. But, if God wills, you will continue to give the order to your servant Bayram *çavuş,* to buy the supplies which are needed. Let [no one] suffer want. Thus let it be known to your noble person.

(Page c) And if an explanation is requested about the conditions of the bath which is being newly constructed in Jerusalem, a double bath was built, its domes were covered from the outside, the domes of the two dressing rooms were not; it was approximately half built. Thus let it be known to your noble person.

But it was established that great hardship is endured with respect to its water. Formerly, they obtained water; that water was needed for the bath, first in order that it be built. These words which we report are from the experts of that place. But from the beginning we were outside the building; we did not find anyone present from the persons who were procuring water. It is the hope that they may obtain it.

In short, in the present situation, there is no one besides [the director] Meḥmed *ağa* your servant who tended both the food and the bread of the imperial ʿimaret; if there were some words [spoken] against him, there is a hope that this too, my prosperous sultan, may not be registered; let it not be attributed to truth that the aforementioned [empty space] did not tend the food and bread nor care for the feelings of the *fuḳara;* he was capable in every way, he was among those who pray to God for you, who, being your sincere friend, is entitled to kindness and compassion; what more is needed to be said is that it be made known.

The present chapter examines more closely how the ʿimaret attempted to fulfill the purpose for which it was established. Certainly the managers attempted (more or less) to operate within the framework dictated by the waqfiyya; everyone had continual reference to the stipulations of the founder as discussed in Chapter 2. Routine activities as well as any necessary changes were supposed to be made within its parameters and all breaches were measured against it. Thus the waqfiyya continued to define the institution sustained by the endowment and to articulate its goals. It was to ensure them that the properties were meant to be managed to the best advantage of the endowment, a task which readily admitted change as necessary and beneficial. In addition, the law as defined by *sharīʿa, ḳanun* and *ʿörf*—Islamic law, imperial dictate, and local custom—determined the ways in which the manager could fulfill his basic task of running the ʿimaret within the context of laws regarding endowments generally.

Practical demands of everyday operations forced the managers continually to adjust the running of the kitchen to daily realities in Jerusalem and her surroundings. While the specific purpose of the foundation was to feed people deemed deserving and provide shelter for travelers and others, practical realities broadened its role. Due to the enormous supply needs of the kitchen, and the compass of the endowment properties, the ʿimaret and its manager became a substantial presence in the fabric of Jerusalem's urban and rural life, key figures in the local and regional economy and society.

From a close consideration of the early years of the Jerusalem ʿimaret, it emerges that the founding of such a charitable institution was not a single act, but rather a process. Its deed conveyed a sense of the intentions of the founder, the way in which the ʿimaret fit into the imperial vision of Ottoman sovereignty and beneficence. Although the date of the waqfiyya ostensibly marked a decisive moment for the endowment, Chapter 2 has shown that such was not entirely the case. Properties yielding revenues to the endowment were tapped before the deed was made or exchanged out of it when the ink was barely dry. And, the complicated transfer of properties in and out of the waqf emphasized how extended the process of setting up an endowment could be and how unfixed the endowed status of properties was in actuality. Clearly, the guiding rationale behind the property transfers was to stabilize income and facilitate revenue collection.[9] Yet even after achieving this, management of an endowment was a dynamic endeavor. Properties, personnel, and produce were all in continual motion.

ʿAbdülkerim's report covered several crucial areas of waqf administration, including the competence of managers, food preparation, and distribution, the steady flow of sufficient supplies to the kitchen, the supervision of revenue-producing properties, and the clientele of the soup kitchen. By exploring each of these subjects, this chapter elucidates how this large institution fulfilled its original mandate in Jerusalem. At the same time, aspects of the economy and society of Jerusalem (and of the empire as a whole) emerge more vividly.

## ON MANAGEMENT

The day-to-day workings of an endowment were in the hands of its manager. Those who ran the Jerusalem ʿimaret or institutions of comparable size managed a kind of corporation, in which they had to supervise the assets, collect revenues regularly, make all necessary disbursements for maintenance and operations, and make investment decisions when appropriate. Their most immediate daily task was to keep the kitchen functioning to prepare and distribute food. To do this, the managers had to see to personnel and supply, as well as acting as building subcontractors, landlords, tax farmers, and farm superintendents. Individual staff members saw to specific duties in the kitchen, refectory, storehouses, mills, and bookkeeping, but the manager ran the entire operation. In various ways, his duties also resembled those of a provincial governor, the leader of a military campaign, or the commander of the *ḥajj;* like them, he dealt with the logistics of supply, staff, and revenues.

Managers were obliged to draw up an annual accounting of the financial activity at the waqf—revenues received, expenditures on purchases of goods, salaries and repairs, loans and debts contracted—for the overseer in Istanbul. These accounts registers (*muḥasebe defterleri*) reflected the activities of the managers and showed the surplus revenues to be forwarded to the imperial treasury in any given year.[10] The supervisor and the sultan were also the address for reports or complaints from the manager himself or from others, such as villagers, officials, or townspeople, about any problems with the waqf. Alternatively, the local kadi was called upon to resolve questions, problems, or disputes connected to the functioning of the endowment or interpretations of its stipulations. The kadi was duty-bound to make decisions that served the best interests (*maṣlaḥa*) of the local Muslim community with respect to the endowment, meaning decisions that contributed to its sound functioning.

Five different managers held office during the first decade after the ʿimaret was established. At the time of his appointment, each one already possessed a large revenue grant (*ze'amet*) in the Syrian region, indicating that these men were well-established in their careers in the military-administrative ranks of the Ottoman empire.[11] As officers and as *ze'amet* holders, each man already had some experience managing revenues and people. Ḥaydar *bey kethüda* (agent or steward) held a *ze'amet* in Trablus province. 'Ali *kethüda* and Ferhad *çelebi* (gentleman) were among the *ze'amet* holders in Aleppo province. Ṭurgud *ağa subaşı* (police magistrate) and Bayram *bey çavuş* drew their incomes from *ze'amets* in Damascus province.[12]

Aside from being an indication of mid-career status, the possession of a *ze'amet* also meant that each man had a source of income independent of his salary as 'imaret manager. These personal financial resources were important since the managers might have to contribute to the expenses of the endowment should some pressing need arise for which the cash was lacking. 'Abdülkerim's report makes it clear that the job required a large investment of time and energy, along with competence and money. "Let the manager be that one who does not let his foot leave the 'imaret and does not take his eyes off the endowments,"[13] he says, commenting on the chorus of derision over Ferhad *çelebi*, the manager referred to in his report. Yet it was both expected and explicitly stated in the waqfiyya that the manager should be

> a person renowned for his deep attachment to religion and known for his appearance of integrity and honest. He should be . . . a man of serious endeavors in carrying out his duties, who would welcome guests and not turn them away. He should strive and show his aptitude and should guard himself as much as possible from negligence and carelessness, . . . pay the greatest attention to it, so that all vestiges of [her] illustrious [personage] should thus grow and increase day by day.[14]

## GETTING STARTED

According to this official job description, continual and careful attention were demanded of the manager. Records of operations also confirmed this as a reality of his work. Ḥaydar *kethüda* was the first manager of the 'imaret, although his three years in the job were mostly in the period prior to its initial endowment in 1552. At that time he was called "Ḥaydar *kethüda*, manager of the Sultan's endowments in Jerusalem," with responsibility for the tombs of Abraham, Isaac, and

Jacob and the mosque in Hebron, and the tomb of Moses, the Dome of the Rock, and the Church of the Holy Sepulcher in Jerusalem.[15] At this date, apparently, the Ottomans still had not sorted these sites and endowments into units to be managed separately. After Ḥaydar's term, the managers of the ʿimaret were appointed to that one institution alone. Ḥaydar was probably appointed to direct the new endowment because he was already a manager of proven competence. In addition, no official position as manager existed for the new endowment, since it had not yet been formally constituted.

Ḥaydar spent much of his time organizing workmen and materials for the repairs and renovations needed to convert the former house of Ṭunshūq into a public facility. Carpenters, stonecutters, builders, their apprentices, other unskilled laborers, and porters were drawn from among the local population with supplemental workers hired from elsewhere in the larger province of Damascus. The manager had imperial authorization to bring workmen to Jerusalem as needed. Stone, wood, nails, plaster, lime, iron, tools, food, and fodder had to be purchased locally or imported.[16]

A large establishment like the *ʿimaret* also required a steady supply of water. However, Jerusalem did not have abundant sources of water inside the city or very nearby. Some wells and, more commonly, cisterns for collecting rainwater existed inside the city walls, but the city depended on the water piped in from far south of the city and stored under the Ḥaram al-Sharīf. Under Süleyman, the entire system of aqueducts had been repaired and six fountains added as part of his extensive investments in Jerusalem during the 1530s and 1540s. This entire water system was maintained by a separate endowment.[17]

When the ʿimaret was built, water channels were constructed to connect it to the main water system of the city, which distributed water from the Ḥaram. Pipes were also laid to the new bath under construction nearby. Together, the needs of the kitchen and the bath meant a significant increase in demand on the general water supply of the city. Thus Hurrem's new waqf had to contribute to the waqf for water, to ensure sufficient inflow to Jerusalem from Wadi Abyar. Ḥaydar, however, was accused of interfering with the general water supply and causing harm in his efforts to establish a fixed flow of water to the ʿimaret.[18] Competition over water resources was an ongoing feature of life in Jerusalem, pitting the city's residents against each other and together against the bedouin and peasants outside the walls who persistently tried to claim a share of what was piped toward the city.[19]

Ḥaydar not only oversaw all the repairs needed on the ʿimaret buildings, but also managed the revenue-producing properties of the endowment. The first property deeded, the village of Amyūn, was formally transferred to Hurrem only in 1550–51, yet revenues were paid to the waqf from other sources beginning in late 1549.[20] Unfortunately for the waqf, the caravansaray, soap factory, mills, and village near Trablus in northern Syria yielded less than half of the revenues expected from them, and part of this had to be spent on repairs to the places themselves in order to keep them functioning.

The curious thing is that Ḥaydar and the properties were all in place before the initial deed of endowment was issued in the spring of 1552. Even the kitchen in Jerusalem seems to have begun serving food as early as Ramaḍān 958/Sept.–Oct. 1551. Thus, the waqfiyya did not initiate the functioning of this endowment. Rather, it served as a written record of what was already in existence, meant to concretize and regulate future activities more than to constitute a chronological point of departure. In this case, the waqfiyya had a defining legal function, but it was also an important political tool, the means of publicizing imperial beneficent actions performed in a specific location. As with the survey registers, there was a delay in issuing documents relating to provincial activities, since the information was reported back to Istanbul where official records were drawn up.

Hurrem's Jerusalem ʿimaret also belongs to a class of endowments which were not entirely original constructions or institutions. Like the shrine of Seyyid Baṭṭal Gazi in Anatolia,[21] it was created by occupying an existing place and assuming the responsibility for its upkeep, meanwhile adapting and expanding it to more distinctly Ottoman purposes. The same was true of the sufi residence at Dayr al-Asad in the district of Safed. There, Sultan Selim I handed over a Christian monastery to a certain Shaykh Asad after the Ottoman conquest of the region in 1516–17. The shaykh was an important local spiritual leader, and the newly converted monastery now enjoyed imperial support, part of the Ottoman program of colonization in the region.[22]

Complexes such as those of Fatiḥ Meḥmed and Süleyman in Istanbul illustrated another pattern, being constituted as wholly new endeavors. These and many of the other imperial endowments claimed empty space and infused it with activity, ritual, and construction. They were less bound by the constraints of existing structures and traditions, particularly in places like Istanbul, which had been Christian territories prior to the Ottoman conquest. Hence, these large complexes built from the ground up expressed more thoroughly Ottoman conceptualization of the use of space and materials, and of the shape of institutions. Projects like the Haṣṣeki Sulṭan ʿimaret, on the other hand, were common throughout the Ottoman provinces, restricted in one way or another by what had come before.

## TAX ARREARS AND FIREWOOD

ʿAli *kethüda,* Ḥaydar's successor, continued to supervise the early organization of the endowment. During his eighteen months as manager, construction work on the baths continued, the kitchen operated in high gear serving meals, and new properties joined the revenue rolls of the endowment. These properties included the two soap factories in Trablus, along with the taxes on tobacco and firewood there. Closer to Jerusalem were the villages of Ludd and Jīb, and the farm of Qayqaba.[23] As the list of endowment properties expanded, increased funds became available to operate the ʿimaret. However, payments due did not simply arrive in Jerusalem on fixed dates and in full as assessed; someone had to go and collect them. Expanding assets meant more and longer tours through the properties. This is reflected in the increased number of collection agents (five instead of one) in the later waqfiyya.

ʿAli shared many concerns of other revenue holders in the area. Whether they were waqf managers, revenue holders appointed to *tımar*s, or appointed collectors of the imperial domain, the greater part of their incomes usually derived from agricultural produce. Taxes or payments due were assessed as a proportion of annual yields, and were collected in kind. More importantly, yields fluctuated depending on rain, heat, pests, and rural stability. Deferred payments were not uncommon in this kind of economy, and ʿAli spent part of his time organizing the collection of arrears owed to the waqf from the time of his predecessor.[24] Later registers indicate that his successors did likewise. Unfortunately, no accounts registers or reports were found dating from ʿAli's tenure, though this is as likely an accident of preservation as any direct reflection of his own competence.

Ferhad *çelebi,* the man so criticized in ʿAbdülkerim's report, succeeded ʿAli *kethüda* as manager of the ʿimaret in the early summer of 1554. No new properties were added to the endowment during the year and a half of his tenure, though construction of the ʿimaret bath proceeded.[25] Ferhad, as noted, was insufficiently attentive to this latter project: he could not be bothered even to dismount and inspect the premises carefully when he came to visit. He was repeatedly criticized, chiefly for his absences and lack of diligence about the affairs of the endowment. This was especially problematic with regard to the kitchen functioning and the bath construction, since both required constant supervision and purchase of supplies. The costs of foodstuffs varied according to the seasons, and the manager had to be conscientious about stocking the larders in order to ensure that the ʿimaret had sufficient provisions to cover its needs.[26]

Despite his inattention to the bath, Ferhad's own reports give the impression of a very effective revenue collector, more so than his predecessors. In what looks like an attempt to salvage his reputation after the harsh criticisms of ʿAbdülkerim's report, Ferhad submitted a register of revenues and expenditures for the seventeen months of his tenure. He summarized his achievement thus:

> Of the aforementioned 10627 gold *sikke* coins [total collected], 4245 *sikke* and 34 silver *para* coins are from the arrears of the former managers, and 3230 gold *sikke* and 31 *para* are [collected] in the time of this humble one, and 3151 gold *sikke* and 25 *para* are from the revenue generated by the new waqf villages of Ludd and Jīb, and by incidentals.
>
> The former manager of the waqf, the deceased Ḥaydar *kethüda* collected 5495 gold *sikke* in two years, and the manager after him, the deceased ʿAli *kethüda* collected 5487 gold coins in one year and four months; and this humble one, I collected 7484 gold *sikke* and 25 *para* in one year and five months. According to this account, it was 1989 gold coins more than Ḥaydar *kethüda* and 2097 more than ʿAli *kethüda*.[27]

Not only did Ferhad collect more than either of his predecessors, he managed to collect monies owed to the waqf from their tenures as well.[28] Moreover, these figures were not simply entered in the accounts register, but Ferhad included this paragraph explicitly describing his industry on behalf of the waqf.

The revenues amassed were put to immediate use. Ferhad spent money required to develop the ʿimaret further. Under his supervision, two construction projects were carried out on the extensive kitchen buildings. The first was a granary built over the storeroom and oven. Since the original granary had been located in a structure with an open courtyard and water wells, the grain there spoiled rapidly, becoming rotten to the point where it was utterly useless for cooking. For the cost of the granary—20,236 *para*—Ferhad requested imperial assistance, as he could not raise the necessary funds locally.[29]

The second project for which Ferhad requested and received funds was the roofing of the woodshed. Uncovered, the wood got wet in the winter rain and made cooking very difficult. Moreover, one month after he took office, the ʿimaret began to serve meals twice a day instead of only once. As stipulated in the endowment deed, soup was now ladled out along with a portion of bread both morning and evening.[30] This change in the serving practices may have prompted Ferhad's search for funds to defray the cost of roofing. ʿAbdülkerim's report had emphasized that the increased food preparations strained the capacities of the endowment and made it more imperative to conserve and maximize all resources. Hence, a roof for the woodshed became both more necessary and more difficult to fund from available monies, though at 1677 para it cost a mere tenth of the new granary.

Firewood was one of the basic necessities of the ʿimaret. It was the only non-edible ingredient of the cooked dishes listed in the endowment deed and among the regular expenditures of this kitchen and most others, too. Firewood was even listed among the supplies purchased and transported by the army when on desert campaign.[31] Unlike many basic ingredients stocked in the ʿimaret larder, firewood was not delivered as a payment in kind from endowed villages but rather was purchased on command from the village of Jīb, northwest of the city.[32] Unfortunately, ʿimaret managers in the past had not always settled their accounts with the villagers. Ferhad was thus obliged to pay for firewood delivered under his predecessor ʿAli, as well as that purchased during his own tenure.[33]

Ferhad himself held a lease on the agricultural revenues from the village of Jīb, which were endowed for the waqf of the Mamluk Sultan Īnāl in Cairo.[34] This meant that he acted as a kind of revenue farmer for the waqf in Egypt while managing the Jerusalem ʿimaret. The combination of responsibilities to the two waqfs effectively made Ferhad the sole revenue collector for the village of Jīb, although there was no connection between the two endowments. In fact, each of the managers discussed here combined his position in the ʿimaret with other fiscal involvements in the immediate area, whether as a revenue holder in his own right or as lessee of revenues belonging to someone else. The possibility of controlling different kinds of revenues collection was one way for Ottoman officials to consolidate power locally, even in a short-term appointment. It allowed one person to broaden the scope of his authority beyond the circumscribed bounds of his formal appointment.

Moreover, the farming of waqf revenue collection described here is entirely comparable to the farming of other types of revenues throughout the empire. This situation indicates further how deeply integrated waqf properties were to the general Ottoman system of property management, not isolated or insulated from it merely because they were part of a waqf. The same mechanisms of registration, lease, collection, and payment were employed by all. Differences between them had more to do with local particularities than the category of the properties or the type of revenue holder.

The role of Ferhad points to another key aspect of many imperial endowments: extensive rural holdings generated most of their revenues. Problems in the villages that affected production or delivery of the revenue-producing crops or animals were thus the concern of the managers. In this they shared a long list of problems and concerns with holders of tımars or tax farmers in the region. Further, the Haṣṣeki Sultan waqf "institutionalized relations between the city and its rural hinterland."[35] It became a fixed point of reference for part of the rural population, and contact with Ottoman authorities was channeled through the waqf manager and revenue collectors. The manager also sent revenue collectors who provided relief in hard times and saw to problems of local security. Peasants might appeal to him for assistance or to report anything amiss. Thus, although the relationship appeared to rest on a one-way monetary obligation, the need to preserve and protect rural revenue sources created more dynamic interactions between the urban institution and its agrarian assets.

In contrast to the changing roster of tımar holders who could be assigned rural revenues, the ʿimaret was a local constant. While other villages watched their taxes due shift from the holdings of one *sipahi* to another, the waqf villages (except for those exchanged) remained part of the endowment for many generations. For these peasants, the waqf was part of their identity. When they made petitions, filed suits, or appeared in written records it was most often with an identification to the waqf. The registers of imperial decrees, the *mühimme defterleri,* contain a large number of orders issued in response to these petitions and other reports on ʿimaret affairs, far more than to any other single matter in southern Syria during the latter half of the sixteenth century. This may mean that these villages, because they were part of this waqf, had a more direct line of communication to Istanbul. The villagers, too, may have been conscious of their special status and, feeling protected by it, petitioned and complained more readily.[36] The question of how local identities were constructed is an enormous and largely unexplored terrain in the pre-modern Middle East. As the destination for payments due, this waqf (or any other) looks like one strong component of regional peasant identity.

Expenditures on food supplies for the ʿimaret usually comprised the largest single category of expenditures. In a period of sixteen months from 1554–55, they represented thirty-nine percent of the total. Together with other necessities (3 percent) and the servants' salaries (6 percent), direct operating expenses altogether consumed almost half the revenues. Construction of the storehouse, woodshed, and bath in that year took another 36 percent, with the bath alone accounting for 27 percent. Other expenses included repairs to the waqf properties in Trablus (2 percent), repayments of loans to the waqf (5 percent), debts for firewood (1 percent), repairs to the aqueduct from Wadi Abyar, and repairs to a mill in Jerusalem. In addition, it turned out that some revenues collected from the village of Jīb actually had belonged to a *tımar* holder, who had to be reimbursed.

Finally, the ʿimaret had to pay for the transport of its wheat and barley from the village of Ludd to Jerusalem, as well as for purchases of wheat, barley, and lentils that remained stored in the village.[37] This latter expense provides an interesting insight into the management of the waqf. On the one hand, this "purchase" might have been a bookkeeping technique to keep track of grains actually belonging to the waqf but simply stored in Ludd after having been collected from that village and others nearby.[38] On the other hand, if the ʿimaret was purchasing additional foodstuffs from the granaries of Ludd, then obviously the grains delivered in payment of revenues due did not fulfill the supply demands of the kitchen. Here, more grain was purchased from a village that was already one of the regular revenue sources of the waqf. For the villagers, the possibility of selling surpluses offered an additional source of income and, at the same time, linked the waqf and village economies that much more closely.

Ferhad would seem to have had his hands full to ensure that collections and expenditures were carried out with some expedition. As for his seeming successes at increasing revenues, these must be qualified with the recognition that Ferhad was the first to make significant collections from Ludd and Jīb, endowed to the waqf only shortly before his tenure began. He did show, however, that the waqf could be run at a profit. Revenues exceeded expenditures by 117 gold *sikke,* and these were forwarded to Istanbul.[39]

## FOOD FOR ALL

Ferhad was also the first to confront changes essential to accommodate the large numbers of people who arrived at the kitchen at mealtimes. The Haṣṣeki Sultan ʿimaret obviously attracted many people. Whatever the composition of the crowd that came to the door, it exceeded initial expectations and preparations. Ferhad, however, had to devise a solution to the overcrowding that did not include turning people away unfed. One suggestion was to reduce the quantity of soup and bread given to each person or else to provide only one meal per person per day. Two important differences from the normative dictates of the endowment deed appear here. First, the deed specified precisely how many people were to be fed: the staff; the residents of the fifty-five rooms; and 400 poor and pious people. Yet the terse and somewhat exasperated "but there are many poor people here," found in 'Abdülkerim's report, suggests that more people than provided for lined up expecting to eat and that the manager felt compelled to feed them. Certainly they could not be sent away hungry from the ʿimaret of Hurrem Sultan, for who, they seemed to ask, would believe that the beneficence of a *sulṭana* did not suffice for all? 'Abdülkerim and Ferhad appeared to concur in this attitude, seeking ways to stretch available resources. Ferhad, however, was additionally concerned to run the waqf successfully so as to enhance his reputation and gain some form of promotion or recognition.

Second, the deed said that two meals per day were to be served. Whereas both of his predecessors oversaw the serving of food only once per day, under Ferhad two servings of food began to be cooked.[40] In this way, there would be less pressure at each meal. In fact, the endowment deed stipulated two meals be served daily, and it is not clear why the change had not been implemented when that deed was issued, some two years before Ferhad took office. However, the original deed also seemed to indicate that the same people would be fed twice a day—certainly this was the case for the employees and the residents of the rooms. If the solution to overcrowding was to serve two meals, it implied that half the current crowd would be served each time. Feeding people twice a day represented a commitment to their sustenance, even if the fare was basic and limited in quantity. Feeding them once a day represented a different kind of commitment, to supplement and succor, but not to sustain fully. The ʿimaret could meet the basic needs of some of its clients, the more privileged ones, but it could not adequately feed all comers.

The apparent shortage of food at the kitchen was a real problem, since 'Abdülkerim's report described how the kitchen was preparing soup and bread according to the quantities stipulated, and yet the numbers of poor people who came to receive food overwhelmed the existing capacity. "But, my prosperous sultan," says the report, "the poor around here are very numerous; I have been amazed at the cries for help from the people who say 'we are still hungry!' "[41] This passage leaves little doubt that the quite literally poor were among the regular clients of this kitchen.

When the number of meals increased, larger quantities of all supplies were necessary and, as indicated in 'Abdülkerim's report, they would have to stretch farther than before. In fact, the only real increase in food served was in the amount of bread. By adding twenty *baṭmān* of wheat to the daily supply, 275 more loaves of bread were to be baked for distribution.[42] This crisis may have prompted some of the property exchanges and additions discussed in Chapter 2, since these actions aimed at improving productivity as well as increasing revenues absolutely. Interestingly, while Ferhad was reproached for his superficial management of certain aspects of the endowment, he was not blamed for the larger crowds and insufficient food available. No one questioned that these were problems of Jerusalem which merely manifested themselves at the ʿimaret.

The mention of a "former practice" of serving only one meal a day suggests yet again that some kind of public kitchen may have existed before Hurrem Sultan established hers, one which served as the basis in setting up the ʿimaret. Burgoyne, in his work on Mamluk Jerusalem, discusses how large and impressive Ṭunshūq's residence was but says nothing about any public or charitable functions it may have performed. As this woman was known for her piety and other works around Jerusalem, perhaps meals had been distributed to the poor from her kitchen and continued to be in some way after her death. The endowment of Hurrem Sultan may then have reinforced this existing institution, inadequate to the demands on it or weakened over time. The disparity in menus between the endowment deed and an expenditures register from mid-April 1555 is another indication that some previous institution was being replaced. The expenditures included lentils to be cooked with vinegar as one of the dishes at the ʿimaret. Yet no lentil dish was found in either version of the waqfiyya, nor is one commonly found in other ʿimarets; such a dish was distributed at the *simāṭ* in Hebron, however. A note in the register says that lentils were not available and so wheat was cooked instead of them.[43]

Despite shortages, the food served was of a certain quality. The report of ʿAbdülkerim gave high marks to the cooks and bakers, saying that the food was tasty and the bread, after weighing a broad sample of loaves, came up to required weight. Yogurt or pepper provided seasoning, with additional bulk and variety in flavor coming from seasonal vegetables. Perhaps the maintenance of standards in cooking was due to the mixed clientele of the kitchen. Perhaps, too, it was a reflection of the injunction that alms should be given from the best of what one has, not the meanest part.[44] Yet though it was supposed to achieve a certain standard, the quality of the food in Jerusalem remains an open question. Nothing indicates that it resembled the stinking, inedible filth described by Muṣṭafa ʿAli in Istanbul which the medrese students threw to the dogs.[45] But it is unclear whether it was as good as the tasty fare served to him at the ʿimarets of Gazi Evrenos bey in the Balkans, where:

> twice a day four or five kinds of food are distributed freely to the travellers. . . . These institutions are so efficient, the food offered to the travellers is so delicious and soul-nourishing as it has been mentioned and even more delicious and more pleasant than the food prepared by home-trained cooks. Their stewed meat is well-seasoned, their soup and hamburgers are plentiful, and their noodles and noodle soup are of equal quality. Moreover, during the nights of the fast there are always on every table a *baqlava* like the disk of the shining moon and sweeter than sugar, and countless tasty delicacies of the sausage (*būmbār*) and *herīse* (kind of meal pudding) type. As a matter of fact this humble [author] has repeatedly been a guest in these institutions and has found its boundless delicacies even more than what we have said here.[46]

Increased demand prompted a further suggestion for economizing at the ʿimaret during Ferhad's tenure. It was proposed to halve the portions served to each person from the richer dishes of *dane* and *zerde* that were prepared on Friday nights and during Ramadan. Instead of a full ladle, each person would receive one-half. At the same time, however, the portions for widowed women—one loaf of bread and one ladle of soup—were explicitly maintained. In this way, they had some privilege among the poor, perhaps to make up for the discrimination they suffered as the last to eat on most other days.[47]

The overflow of clients also added to the workload on the staff. Doorkeepers complained of the extra work created by large numbers of people coming in and out of the ʿimaret, particularly as their own salaries were low. These were raised. More burdensome was the increased kitchen work. While wheat for bread flour was ground at a mill, the wheat for soup was pounded in the kitchen by hand. When one meal per day was served, wheat and rice were alternated. With two meals a day, wheat had to be prepared every day, and wheat pounders quit in succession to protest the additional work required. Eventually, a recommendation to hire two wheat pounders instead of one and to increase their salaries was accepted.[48] The need for more staff was seen most clearly in changes between the earlier and later endowment deeds. The first included thirty-seven people while the second listed forty-nine, most of whom were subordinate kitchen staff such as bakers, dishwashers, and people to sift and clean wheat, along with revenue collectors and repairmen. Again, the endowment deed only served as a starting point for putting together a viable enterprise.

Ferhad's problems did not end once the challenge of how to feed more people was resolved. He faced problems of corruption among his staff as well. Very shortly after 'Abdükerim wrote his long report about the ʿimaret operations, an expenditures register was drawn up by 'Abdul-Raḥman, the kadi of Jerusalem, with the assistance of the two envoys sent from Istanbul. ('Abdülkerim had crossed paths with them near Damascus, as he made his own way north.) This register roundly criticized Meḥmed *ağa, şeyh* of the ʿimaret. According to the kadi, Meḥmed *ağa* was abusive of the staff and helped himself to food far beyond his daily allotment. Like the other employees, he was supposed to receive two ladles of soup and four loaves of bread each day. Greedy Meḥmed helped himself to six to eight ladles of food, with extra pieces of fat and some sixteen loaves of bread.[49] There is no clue as to whether he was feeding only himself from these portions or whether he was also trying to take out food for others.

In contrast to the kadi, 'Abdülkerim had nothing but praise for Meḥmed *ağa,* who, he said, faithfully looked after preparation of both food and bread. Curiously, 'Abdülkerim's report also cautioned against accepting any criticism of Meḥmed, simultaneously expending several lines of reproach against Ferhad. After Ferhad was replaced, the kadi submitted another report in which he was the one to point out Ferhad's failings. These now included, in addition to the inattention previously mentioned by 'Abdülkerim, suspected embezzlement of ʿimaret funds.[50]

The checkered career of Ferhad as manager of the ʿimaret offers some insight into the vulnerabilities of an endowment as well as the possibilities for venality tempting its managers. While he successfully collected overdue revenues, at the same time Ferhad was lax in supervisory duties and perhaps greedy as well. As for Meḥmed, the conflicting reports on his abilities as *şeyh* of the ʿimaret could point to a rivalry between the authors of the reports as well as recording his own questionable actions. Meḥmed or one of his friends may have persuaded the visiting 'Abdülkerim to support him. Ultimately, the incident demonstrates vividly the vulnerability of the Ottoman administration, dependent on the one hand on the local people who staffed a wide range of provincial Ottoman institutions, and on the other hand, reliant on Ottoman observers to report on local—and perhaps unfamiliar—situations.

An institution as large as the Jerusalem ʿimaret, with close to fifty employees, far-flung properties, and a huge kitchen operation was bound to run into problems with personnel. In Jerusalem, there were no separate menus for the staff and the poor who came to eat; the only difference between their meals was in quantity. How tempting, then, for those with easy access to help themselves to extra portions of food.

## BUILDING A BATH

Ultimately, Ferhad was replaced by Bayram *çavuş,* who had often been deputized by him to see to matters at the ʿimaret. ʿAbdülkerim's report was replete with praise for the man who had contributed money and time to the construction and management of the ʿimaret even before his appointment. As the agent of ʿAli *kethüda,* the former manager, he had given a loan of 556 *sikke* to the ʿimaret to help cover expenses.[51] Bayram was first appointed as waqf manager in the winter of 1555–56.[52] He served only a few months, was then replaced by a certain Ṭurgud *ağa* and subsequently reinstated during the summer, remaining manager for two more years, until the summer of 1558.[53] During his tenure, Bayram continued to prove his devotion to the welfare of the ʿimaret, as well as his competence in managing it. ʿAbdülkerim had specifically recommended Bayram for the position of manager, stating: "This is the wish of all the notables of Jerusalem and the other *fuḳara* of the city, her kadi, governor and ʿimaret servants, that by giving the office of manager as an act of grace to your servant Bayram *çavuş,* the food of the ʿimaret be well, the endowments flourish and be in a state of tranquility."[54] The available record of Bayram's tenure indicates that this confidence in him was not misplaced.

Bayram clearly enjoyed a widespread reputation in the Jerusalem district as a fair administrator. Testimony before one of the kadis of Jerusalem exemplifies his standing. In it, witnesses from the town and nearby village condemned the conduct of one ʿAli Bali, a *sipahi* who had so abused the peasants of the village in his *tımar* that they fled, leaving their lands untended and the nearby road unguarded. The peasants claimed, however, that if Bayram were appointed as representative (*mutakallim*) for the village, then the peasants would return and the village could recover.[55] Bayram's talents as an administrator were not exploited only in various official positions. He was a prominent merchant and property owner in Jerusalem, a wealthy man who could himself afford to endow sufi residences, and a primary school as well as construct an impressive house for himself. These were located in the same street as the ʿimaret, and in later centuries seem to have been incorporated into its precincts.

As manager of the ʿimaret, Bayram's most immediate project was the completion of the double bath that was part of the endowment properties. There were already at least five public baths in the city when it was built.[56] This new double bath was known as Ḥammām al-Sulṭān and it was intended for public use while generating revenues for the endowment. Somewhat removed from the ʿimaret, it was located down the hill and around the corner, at the intersection of al-Wād and the Via Dolorosa. By the mid-nineteenth century, the bath was in ruins, and the site was eventually sold to the Armenian Catholics, who put up a church and monastery there.[57]

Baths, where they existed, could be important assets for endowments. The ʿİmaret-i Hatuniye in Trabzon built by Gülbahar, mother of Selim I, had two baths in its endowment. Bathing was a necessity for religious ritual purity as well as for basic hygiene. Hence, in theory, baths provided a stable and healthy income.[58] However, Jerusalem, with a problematic water supply even in normal years, was a less than optimal site for a profitable bath. The heavier demands for ritual cleaning created by pilgrims, which might ordinarily have ensured a steady income, were offset by the realities of seasonal water shortages, so that the baths could not always be kept open.[59] The long rainless summer, along with years of real drought, contributed to its fluctuating revenues. Even when open, the interconnection of the water channels in Jerusalem could lead to contamination when pipes were broken.[60]

Construction of the bath began by imperial order, and the work lasted almost two years, from June 1554 to April 1556.[61] Initially, 3000 *sikke* were sent to Jerusalem for this purpose, though in the end the total cost came to twice that—6017 *sikke*. The shortfall for the bath (as well as for food costs at the ʿimaret) was largely made up through loans. Mevlana Yetimi, the manager of an endowment which included revenues from the Church of the Holy Sepulcher, contributed 120 *sikke* from the waqf as well as 24 *sikke* 2 *para* from his own money. Some villagers of Ludd contributed 63 *sikke* 2 *para* worth of cooking oil and honey to the ʿimaret stores. Finally, Bayram collected the huge sum of 2107 *sikke*. One-third came from Aḥmed Paşa, the *bey* of Damascus, apparently as a gift from the *cizye, resm-i ʿarus,* and *bad-i hava* that he collected. The remainder was a loan from Bayram's own coffer. "Since the building of the bath was important, and had difficulties about money, Bayram *çavuş* paid from his own [money]."[62]

Each of these contributions adds some insight into the relationship of the institution to its local situation. After the Ottoman conquest, one person managed all the major endowments in Jerusalem, including, initially, the Church of the Holy Sepulcher and the ʿimaret. Although they continued under separate management, by the mid-seventeenth century the endowments again became linked, as demonstrated by the appointment of two people sharing the two offices of deputy of the manager and guardian of the keys of the Church.[63] Contributions to the bath project, even as loans, were likely to find favor in the eyes of those keeping track of the ʿimaret's condition, and the favor gained might be used for personal protection or promotion in the future. Nor can purely pious motives be discounted as inspiring the donations.

Although Ferhad was manager during most of the construction period, Bayram was clearly more energetic and devoted to getting the bath built and running. This was no simple project. In addition to ensuring sufficient funds to pay for laborers and supplies, skilled workmen had to be hired and adequate building materials purchased. The professional builders came from Istanbul and Damascus, while the unskilled laborers were probably hired in the immediate region.[64] Local materials were used to the extent possible, and although some marble was imported through the port of Jaffa,[65] this was generally considered too costly. Stone being in short supply, the waqf acquired a decrepit house adjoining the bath and plundered it for materials.[66] Finally, construction was hampered in the winter by the wind and cold that descended on the city for several months.[67]

In this manner, the building of the bath proceeded in fits and starts over almost two years, interrupted by lack of funds, materials, and water. Under Bayram, the remaining third of the construction work was finished in the last three months before it opened. Upon completion, the first concessionary took over its operations on 15 Cemaziüevvel 963 (27 March 1556), leasing the bath for 60 *para* per day, on which basis it would, in theory, earn the waqf 21,600 *para* or 531 *sikke* per year.[68] This was the sum paid by two lease holders in its first year of operation, and in the years that followed, the bath continued to be leased for 60 *para* per day.[69] However, in the four-month period from mid-June to mid-October 1558, the bath was idle for twenty-two out of 120 days, presumably due to lack of water during these summer months. The twenty-two days were then recorded in the expenditures section of the register, presumably because the lease holders had to be compensated for their lost income.[70] The bath provides another telling example of what the running of a foundation entailed for its manager. He was expected to supervise construction and keep the accounts, as well as make up the shortfall when necessary. Bayram earned great personal capital by putting up the money needed for the bath even before he became manager. On this basis he was appointed manager in the first place. His efforts generally were also recognized, and shortly after his reappointment his annual salary was raised by 3,000 *akçe* per year.[71]

Alongside the huge project of finishing the bath, Bayram oversaw smaller but no less important matters. For the kitchen to function effectively, it had to have the necessary equipment. This included numerous kinds of cups and bowls, ladles and cauldrons for cooking and serving, as well as scales, weights, knives, and long-handled bakers' shovels. Equipment used daily by the cooks and the bakers remained in the kitchen and bakery, while the pantry-keeper stored implements needed less regularly.[72] One further piece of equipment provided by the ʿimaret manager was a cauldron for processing indigo. It was loaned seasonally to the villagers of Jericho (at least while the village was part of the waqf) who grew and processed indigo as one source of their revenues.[73]

Missing equipment or funds to buy it came from Istanbul, particularly in the early years, since later these items would be purchased from the annual revenues of the waqf. In the summer of 1556 the following items were requested: two cauldrons for cooking *dane* and *zerde* that would be smaller than the vast daily soup cauldrons, a large serving tray, three pairs of large baskets for carrying bread from oven to table, ten jars for storing oil and honey, iron for making bars for the kitchen windows, and buckets with which Shaykh Aḥmad al-Dajjānī and his followers could collect their daily food allowance.[74] Each item offers a small insight into the world of this ʿimaret. The cooks had a professional attitude to their task, wanting specialized equipment and not just making due with the available pots. The baskets conjure an image of large piles of fresh loaves, while one can imagine trays of *zerde* on Friday evenings. Were iron bars required on the kitchen windows to prevent after-hours pilfering of provisions stored in the great jars?

Removing food from the ʿimaret was not condoned. A special exception to this rule was made for the sufi master in Jerusalem, Shaykh al-Dajjānī and his sixteen disciples, who had been given the Franciscan Monastery on Mt. Zion in which to live and conduct their rituals.[75] They were not specifically mentioned in the ʿimaret waqfiyya, though they received food at the ʿimaret from its early days. Dajjānī and his followers obviously had special status to be allowed to take their food away from the ʿimaret. Their settlement on Mt. Zion was in some ways complementary to the establishment of the soup kitchen. Each building occupied a high point of the city; the ʿimaret was close to the

Christian quarter while Dajjānī took over a Christian site, overlooking the Jewish quarter of the city. In tandem, the two institutions marked both the Ottoman and Muslim presence in the city. A daily procession of sufis bearing food from the ʿimaret to Mt. Zion only emphasized this further.

In sum, Bayram was an effective manager, welcomed from the outset as an improvement over Ferhad *çelebi* and a conscientious collector of money owed to the waqf.[76] Not only did he increase revenues, but he also reduced costs: for milling wheat from thirty to sixteen *akçe* per day, and ten to six *para* for each *baṭmān* purchased of clarified butter. Both ground wheat and butter were staple ingredients of every meal prepared at the ʿimaret. These economies thus constituted important savings, 140,425 *akçe* per year, according to Bayram's own calculations. Despite his other achievements, Bayram too felt it necessary to boast of his successes in collecting revenues, measuring himself against his two predecessors.[77]

The ʿimaret was formally endowed during Bayram's tenure. This occasion might have entailed a celebration or marked the beginning of operations had it been in another place. Yet the deed was issued and signed in Istanbul, hundreds of miles from Jerusalem, while no significant practical change occurred at the ʿimaret.

## DEALING IN GRAIN

Under his successor it became evident that Bayram, too, had had his share of problems and made some decisions that did not turn out well for the waqf. While the mixed record of these managers may have been due to some personal failings, it also resulted from endless challenges. Success and failure had to be measured against the enormity of the task, as well as the chance of decisions turned bad.

Thus Ṭurgud *ağa*, who followed Bayram, had to close the accounts of his predecessor and rectify his mistakes as part of the ongoing management of the ʿimaret. Upon examining the accounts, Ṭurgud discovered that Bayram still owed the waqf money from the profits of the ʿimaret on the sale of wheat and olive oil, as well as from the sale of water buffalo. In addition, Bayram had leased the *hans* that belonged to the waqf in Trablus, without a guarantor, to a man named ʿAli who was now bankrupt while owing the waqf some 2500 gold coins.[78] Two years after Bayram left office, Ṭurgud was still pursuing this matter, encouraged from Istanbul to find Bayram and make him pay the outstanding money.[79]

In the meantime, Ṭurgud had already produced a register of revenue collections that demonstrated his own capacity as a manager. Whereas Bayram collected 861,473 *akçe* for the year 964, Ṭurgud recorded 1,311,591 *akçe* for the following year, an increase of over 50 percent. In order to highlight the scope of his achievement, Ṭurgud submitted a village-by-village list of revenues, comparing his yield with that of Bayram and also with the projected revenues recorded in the imperial survey registers (*tapu tahrir defterleri*). While Ṭurgud manifestly outdid his predecessor, he also made the survey seem practically irrelevant, since he collected almost ten times the revenues projected there.[80] True, the figures in the registers were at least ten years old, yet the disparity was still extraordinary.[81] Either Bayram and Ṭurgud managed the ʿimaret during increasingly fertile years, which surpassed the expectations reflected in the survey, or they both squeezed the peasants beyond their presumed capacity, or the survey registers were themselves not only inaccurate, but inadequate.[82] Each of these factors probably contributed something to the disparity.

Large crop yields did occur in these years. Orders from Istanbul addressed the matter of grain sales from the waqf surpluses since the ʿimaret villages produced large quantities of wheat and barley. In very good years, the yields from these villages exceeded the demands of the ʿimaret. While in theory the grain could be sold on the local market, in practice the whole area enjoyed high yields, which drove down the prices while reducing demand. As a result, the manager might judiciously choose to store the grain until needed or until prices rose.[83]

In the summer of 1559, orders arrived from Istanbul authorizing the sale of grain from the waqf stocks to Muslim grain dealers arriving from Rhodes. The stored waqf grain had become infested with bugs, and so it was thought best to sell off what was still good. All authorities involved in the deal—the bey of Rhodes, the bey of Gaza, and Ṭurgud—received direct orders on how to proceed, warning them that this authorization was unique and specific. Under no circumstances were they to sell any grain but that of the waqf and not to anyone but those who came with a certificate (*temessük*), especially not to unbelievers.[84]

It is not clear whether Ṭurgud was expected to make the trip from Jerusalem to Ramle, where the granaries were, and from there to Jaffa where the Rhodian merchants would land. However, he was obliged to have someone present to oversee the sale. This transaction adds to the list of tasks included in the waqf manager's job, and it also describes one aspect of the extensive Ottoman efforts to control grain sales and traffic around the empire. All exports of grain, even between regions of the empire, had to be authorized from Istanbul.

From its founding, the ʿimaret was bound into the Mediterranean grain trade. Not only did it sell surpluses, but it depended on imports of rice from Egypt to stock its pantry, since rice was not produced in significant quantities in the immediate region. A reciprocal trade in surplus waqf grain between Egypt and southern Syria also evolved. The ships that carried the rice from Damietta to Jaffa sometimes returned with wheat and barley from the ʿimaret.[85] Six months after the grain sales were ordered, the Istanbul authority again issued a permit, this time for relief assistance, in response to a report from Ṭurgud that the most recent crops had been attacked by grasshoppers. As a result, grain was now in short supply and prices had risen significantly. Likewise, the bey of Egypt was authorized to sell grain to Ṭurgud's agent, but to beware of imposters as well.[86]

Ironically, this last order was issued only days before a reply to another letter from Ṭurgud. In this order, Ṭurgud again received permission to sell off a large quantity of grain that was close to rotting from what remained in storage. Now, he was directed to sell the grain to the Ragusans (Dubrovnik), to whom he was to issue a certificate witnessing the sale.[87] Dubrovnik enjoyed a special status in the Ottoman empire, autonomous and left to see to its commercial fleet and the vigorous traffic of goods arriving and departing in all directions. The Ragusans were active merchants in both import and export, particularly as carriers of grain from the Ottoman empire to the Italian states.[88] It was perhaps for this reason that Ṭurgud's authorization carried a caution that no grain but that of the ʿimaret waqf was to be sold to the Ragusans. The temptation of the profit to be gained selling to the eager Italian merchants might easily induce others to sell surpluses, thus leaving the region with no grain stocks.

Either the previous sale to the Rhodian merchants had fallen through, or more stocks of grain belonging to the ʿimaret were being unloaded. Why they should be sold off when some form of shortage existed is curious. Apparently, the rotting grain was good enough to sell to the Ragusans, who had clients for it, but it was not fit to use in the ʿimaret. Thus the ʿimaret maintained a standard in the quality of the food it served, possibly because of its imperial identity, possibly because the clientele sometimes included important people. It is also possible that Ṭurgud contrived the story of the bugs in order to make a profit on sales that might otherwise not have been authorized.

The uncertainties of agrarian production were one of the chief concerns of the waqf managers as well as of almost all revenue holders. The managers were dependent on agricultural yields not only for the revenues of the endowment, but for the supply and stable functioning of the public kitchen. Any crisis of production—drought, pests, theft—thus created a dual threat: no cash for purchases and nothing to buy. Even local disturbances could upset cultivation, as happened in the village of Ranṭiyya during the first year of Ṭurgud's tenure. While he increased yields by an average of 50 percent everywhere else, a fight in Ranṭiyya with neighboring villagers caused a decrease in yield of almost 40 percent.[89]

Because grain supplies were so closely controlled, the solution to a crisis had to be negotiated via Istanbul. This made the managers somewhat less flexible in their ability to respond rapidly in an emergency. It also meant that the central authorities in Istanbul remained closely informed of such matters or believed that they were. In this specific case, imperial oversight may have been particularly close because the ʿimaret was an imperial project and was in Jerusalem. Obviously, however, illegal trafficking in grain went undocumented, at least when it was undiscovered. Smuggling, always a temptation, sometimes a possibility, was probably frequently a reality.

Concerns over agricultural production kept the managers of many waqfs closely involved in the affairs of their villages. Peasants might seek relief from the manager, being forgiven outstanding taxes or granted enough money for seed in a year when a poor harvest left them with nothing to plant the following season.[90] In such situations, endowment managers, and especially the managers of the large waqfs, had more resources than other revenue recipients, since the endowment depended on a mixture of revenue-producing properties that left it less dependent on any single one. *Tımar* holders, who held grants of revenues from one or two villages, would be hard put to provide extensive aid in an emergency or to absorb a large loss.

Ṭurgud had to contend with crises other than those imposed by nature. Like villagers all over, the peasants living in waqf villages suffered rival claims to their produce. These came sometimes from other Ottoman officials, sometimes from bedouin in the region. For example, Ṭurgud appealed to Istanbul for help protecting the village of Qāqūn, the only village in the endowment in the district of Nablus. Qāqūn was a district seat, a village with a regular market, and an important source of revenue to the waqf.[91] Local bedouin raided the town regularly, taking food and fodder and imposing levies illegally. Ṭurgud apparently saw the market as the magnet for the bedouin and requested that it be moved to another village.[92]

In another case, Ḥasan *çavuş*, who managed the ʿimaret twenty years after Ṭurgud, appealed for help during a trip to Istanbul. The military agents (*voyvodas*) who acted for governors in the districts of the ʿimaret villages had been entering these villages and disrupting them. They reportedly came twice a month with contingents of fifty to sixty men and helped themselves to food and fodder for their horses without compensating the villagers. As a result, peasants were abandoning their villages. It was this latter phenomenon that was most threatening to the waqf, as it would be to any revenue recipient, since unworked lands meant decreased revenues. As the imperial response to Ḥasan made clear, the agents could justly expect hospitality in villages they entered, but they were ordered to travel in smaller contingents and to compensate the villagers properly.[93]

The order replying to Ḥasan's complaint was sent to the kadis of Jerusalem, Gaza, Safed, and Nablus, since the endowment claimed revenues from villages in each of these districts. This demonstrates how the jurisdiction of the ʿimaret manager extended to all the districts, requiring him to be mobile and have a staff he could dispatch to survey the more remote properties. While he did not have the authority of a governor, he was responsible for the status of all the waqf properties. His authority intersected that of numerous governors, with whom he had to maintain good working relations in order to secure their cooperation in looking out for his properties. In essence, then, the manager of a large waqf was responsible for an economic unit which was superimposed on other economic-administrative units of the empire. It was an additional locus of authority, identity, and revenue, another dimension in the intersecting segments of Ottoman provincial administration.

## ADDING TO THE ENDOWMENT

Ṭurgud did not spend all his energies on improving revenue collections and dealing in grain. Under his supervision, with the approval of the kadi and the governor of Jerusalem, the kitchen of the ʿimaret was expanded, both to increase its capacity and to improve conditions for the cooks. Four years after ʿAbdülkerim's report was delivered, two new hearths and two chimneys adjoined the original kitchen, requiring an increased budget for firewood, which was also granted.[94]

Managers often left accounts for their successors to continue collecting and paying, as with any ongoing business. This also reflected the nature of the local agrarian economy, where villagers paid their taxes in installments and the effects of good and bad harvests were absorbed by the revenue holders. Ṭurgud, however, left his successor with an addition to the waqf revenues, as well as outstanding payments.

After his death, the properties which had comprised Ṭurgud's earlier revenue assignment (*ze'amet*) were endowed to the waqf. The villages of Shafa 'Amrū, Dhīb and Kuwaykāt in the district of 'Akkā (Acre) to the north, and 'Īsāwiyya and Jadīrā in the district of Jerusalem would yield 12,132 *akçe* annually for the waqf.[95] By Muḥarrem 972/August 1564 they had been brought into the endowment in exchange for properties in the province of Sidon worth 21,520 *akçe,* which were then transferred to the holdings of the imperial domain. Interestingly, the properties in Sidon were the ones added to the 'imaret endowment by Süleyman in 967/1560, two years after the death of Hurrem Sultan. All of these latter were located at some remove from Jerusalem, in the province of Damascus. They included the village of Ḥārā and two farms in the Sidon district, and a farm in the Iqlīm Tuffāḥ district.[96] Here again, the exchange demonstrates the tenuous connection between the revenue-producing properties of the endowment and the purpose they supported. Despite the fact that Süleyman's addition of the Sidon properties was clearly a gesture of homage in remembrance of Hurrem, it was the gesture and not its specific substance which was important, since the actual properties were exchanged only a few years later.

Apparently, Ṭurgud did not decide himself that his *ze'amet* properties should be incorporated into the waqf. The imperial order to effect the exchange only acknowledged him as the previous manager and a *ze'amet*-holder in the province of Damascus. It stated that since Ṭurgud had died, his *ze'amet* was to be added to the waqf in exchange for something not suitable for it.[97] Though the *ze'amet* properties were worth less on paper than the ones exchanged out of the waqf, their proximity to Jerusalem allowed for easier and more thorough collection of revenues, and so ultimately they were more valuable to the waqf.[98] The same was the case when Jericho was removed from the endowment just before the final waqfiyya was issued.

Perhaps the inclusion of Ṭurgud's *ze'amet* holdings was in some way a gesture to his loyal service. Or, his death simply made available a source of revenue whose purpose could be changed by imperial command because there was an immediate need. A further effect of the exchange was to reduce the revenue-yielding properties available for assignment to men like Ṭurgud. His former *ze'amet* properties were now endowed, and the exchange had removed properties from the waqf to the imperial domain. This was part of a larger trend at the time, one that reflected overall the declining centrality of revenue assignments (*tımars, ze'amets*) supporting the military-administrative staff of the empire. In their place, revenue sources were farmed out of the imperial domain to bidders from among the military-administrative ranks.

Ṭurgud was succeeded by ʿAbdülkerim, who was removed four years later under suspicion of having been lax in collecting revenues.[99] The same ʿAbdülkerim, or possibly another, was manager three years further down the line and was removed again: for embezzelment and for abusing the peasants.[100] The litany of complaints about Ottoman officials which appeared in the records of imperial orders during these early years is elucidated by the accounts records of the ʿimaret. These reflected a steadily increasing, if imperfect, inflow of revenues from the properties and the accompanying expenditures made on food, personnel, repairs, and incidentals. One could infer that when the waqf managers were effective beyond a certain degree, they made the peasants uncomfortable, taking too much of their produce or far more than the peasants had been forced to yield up in the past. Drawn from the same pool of military-administrators during these years, the complaints against the managers make them appear no better nor worse than their counterparts who served as provincial and district governors.[101]

Compared with their counterparts in Istanbul, Bursa, and Edirne, the Jerusalem managers appeared to be doing a fair job, perhaps in part due to inspections like the one carried out by ʿAbdülkerim. Of the efficacy of such inspections, Muṣṭafa ʿAli wrote in his familiar caustic style:

> it is obvious to all thinking men that it would be an easy thing for themselves [the sultans] or for their vezirs to show an interest and to inspect their food. That they [the ʿimarets] are in spite of this in such a disorder and that the inadequate funds concerning the allocations for food cause dearth and shortage in the three provinces [Istanbul, Bursa, Edirne] and throw the *medrese* students into throes of hunger is clearly the opposite of good policy and wisdom. But if they were now and again inspected and investigated, if their soup and bread were brought to the Imperial Palace and looked at, if the heads of the administrators whose misdemeanor has been established were chopped off for the sake of the public order, God knows, the improvement of the charitable foundations and the joy and relief of all deserving ones would be certain, and the August king would constantly gain bountiful merit and [eternal] reward.[102]

During the first years of the ʿimaret's operation, ʿAbdülkerim's report and others describing difficulties plaguing the ʿimaret reached

Topkapı Palace from Jerusalem. A negligent manager, a dishonest director of the ʿimaret, a half-built bath, missing equipment, insufficient revenues, and, perhaps the most problematic, more people seeking food than the ʿimaret was expected or designed to accommodate. From a more optimistic perspective, however, these same reports included accounts of revenues and expenditures that stated directly or by implication that repairs had been made to the buildings, the kitchen was functioning successfully to prepare food for hundreds of people each day, revenues were being collected and disbursed for needed supplies, the new bath was half completed, and the staff included some dedicated and competent individuals. The quarter of ʿAqabat al-Sitt had become more populous meantime (along with the rest of the city), and several employees of the waqf were listed among its residents, including the *şeyh* of the kitchen, one of the inspectors, the doorman, and the clerk.[103]

In Jerusalem, managers succeeded each other after one to three years in office, with Ṭurgud serving an exceptional four. The length of their tenures increased the stability of the ʿimaret in its early years. It is not surprising that there should be criticism of one manager by another. They wanted to emphasize their successes, to diminish their flaws. Management of the waqf was not at all a simple matter. The endowment was a large enterprise, and the ʿimaret was a huge ongoing operation. Moreover, it was funded chiefly by revenues from local agriculture. Not only did these have to be collected from approximately thirty different sources, but they fluctuated seasonally and annually based on yields susceptible to natural forces as well as human interventions. Built assets of the endowment, whether revenue-yielding or consuming, had to be maintained constantly, constituting another concern of the managers, as well as a logistical challenge for them. The abundant fixed tasks that constituted the manager's job were continually punctuated by unexpected developments. Daily operations were the constant; construction, repairs, disasters, and emergencies demanded periodic attention and divided the energies of the man in charge. Each manager was also a different personality with a distinct background and network, each with his own relationship to Ottoman officials and local Jerusalemites.

The complex realities that taxed the abilities and energies of the manager reflected the effects of the local environment on the implementation of the imperial plan of the endowment. Such influences were not unique to this ʿimaret or only to ʿimarets; they affected every aspect of Ottoman provincial rule. In this way, each administrative unit or institution—province, town, endowment—was a reinterpretation of a particular central schema. The flexibilities which were part of Ottoman imperial rule and also of the law pertaining to endowments all left a large margin for adjustment to local conditions based on custom and practice. It was this flexibility that enabled the adaptation and success of Ottoman administration and institutions in the very different regions of the empire. Because of the nature of Ottoman rule, the process of adjustments left a dense record of queries and authorizations.

At the same time, local acquiescence to work within, and sometimes around, the various imperial institutions and hierarchies reflected the success of the Ottomans in persuading local populations to support the imperial endeavor—not that they were necessarily co-opted, but they did not automatically resist. That this dynamic persisted for hundreds of years, in myriad forms, attests to the flexibility of the institutions and the elasticity built into imperial expectations. That local people continued to attach themselves to the endowment reflected its ongoing utility to a wide range of people in Jerusalem, many of whom had developed a dependency on the ʿimaret, whether for prestige, salaries, or subsistence. Altogether, the ʿimaret was an Ottoman institution, operating in a local setting, heavily dependent on imperial and local support and cooperation for its success.[104] This success, to the extent it existed, was an affirmation of imperial power and ideology. As Muṣṭafa ʿAli pointed out, the proper running of an ʿimaret favored those who came to eat there and redounded to the greater glory of the benefactor.

Yet the ʿimaret was obviously only one idiom of Ottoman power and only one articulation of imperial ideology. It belonged, however, to a particular aspect of power and ideology that was, it is argued here, emphatically Ottoman: food. In the next chapter, the micro-system of Jerusalem traced and analyzed here is de-magnified in order to examine the empire as a whole and to understand how Jerusalem and its ʿimaret fit into the larger, more complex organism.

Chapter Five

# Feeding Power

> They give food, for the love of Him, to the needy, the orphan, the captive; We feed you only for the sake of God; we desire no recompense from you, no thankfulness.
>
> (*Qurʿan*, LXXVI:8–9)

> But the ʿimarets of the previous sultans are those in which a loaf of bread and a cup of soup are continuously given generously to the poor and destitute, young and old, and to the traveler twice a day, each day, up until this one. I [Evliya], this wretch, have travelled for 51 years and in the territories of 18 rulers [but] there was nothing like our enviable institution. May the beneficence of the House of Osman endure until the end of days.[1]

Food was a key factor in the creation and preservation of Ottoman imperial power. The ability of the Ottomans to supply and distribute food to their subjects in turn fed their own power, constituting a source of legitimacy for the Ottoman dynasty and reinforcing its claims to sovereignty. This was the result of the singular amalgam of cultural practices, administrative forms, military demands, and economic policy that constituted the Ottoman empire by the mid-sixteenth century.[2] Food permeated ritual practices and acquired important symbolic meaning. Yet it was also the necessary basis of human life; everyone needed to eat. As a result, giving food was a consummate act of charity. Imperial beneficence, so central to the legitimization and representation of imperial power, thus made important contributions to the distribution of food. The Ottomans had the power to feed, and their power was nurtured by feeding.

The large food matrices touched the majority of urban dwellers in one way or another. However, food production was largely in the hands of the rural peasantry, who were restricted in their movements and obliged to maintain production of basic foodstuffs. The transport and processing of food engaged merchants, sailors, and nomads. Altogether, the organization of food supply and feeding systems stretched across the spaces and populations of the empire. These systems aimed to have an immediate and practical impact on the subject populations of the empire, ensuring sustenance. At the same time, the responsibility for and commitment to food supply bound people into relationships of patronage and benefit, of obligation and privilege, of vendor and client. Food was an agent in creating economic, social, and political hierarchies and defining power relations. Celebrations and feasts were the occasions for extraordinary public distributions as well as public displays of power and allegiance. Many ceremonies and rituals incorporated food.

A conglomeration of food-related activities commands our attention in this chapter, from the preoccupation with adequate acquisition, supply, preparation, and distribution, to the rituals and symbolic meanings of foods and feasts. It addresses the supply of food to the cities and palaces, to the army, and to the *ḥajj* caravans. Public kitchens throughout the empire were a distinct strand in these intertwined organizations of food supply and distribution. While they did not originate *ex nihilo* under the Ottomans, they did become particularly widespread during Ottoman rule and stood (as Evliya observed) as a signature Ottoman institution. After discussing the broader phenomenon of ʿimarets, the chapter closes with a discussion of how and why food became a predominant agent and symbol of power in the Ottoman context.

## PROVISIONING

Provisioning was not a preoccupation particular to the Ottomans, but rather a common concern for rulers of urban populations throughout the world. Many contemporary European monarchs ruled areas far smaller and more homogeneous than the Ottomans, yet depended on the delivery of foodstuffs from foreign sources. The Ottoman empire, in contrast, was largely autarchic. Supply concerns there focused more on moving basic goods within the empire, preventing unauthorized sales to foreigners, controlling quality, and not on insuring sufficient imports, as was the case with Venice and Genoa, for example.[3] Yet the logistics of provisioning the vast span of Ottoman territory resulted in regulated and intersecting systems; these further shaped Ottoman administrative practices, as regulation and supply required codification and responsible, experienced personnel. For all these routines, as is usual with the Ottomans, extensive written evidence survives.

None of these food systems worked perfectly or undisturbed. Supply networks were vulnerable to weather disruptions, piracy, state imperatives, or simply the temptation to sell or hoard for a larger profit. Natural disasters could create temporary hardship or long-term suffering. Famines came and went as a result of pests and drought, and relief was more difficult away from coasts and alternate sources of food. Thus the systems as discussed here are presented in a model form, with the understanding that they suffered countless interruptions and imperfections.

Provisioning channeled the attention and energies of officials in the capital city Istanbul and the provincial towns alike. Daily and emergency stocks of basic necessities were essential for all urban locations. For the larders of the Topkapı Palace, as well as for the residences of senior officials and notables, generous and various provisions had to be acquired. The army on campaign—for months, sometimes years—engendered another vast system of supply and delivery of basic foodstuffs along its projected routes. Moreover, the annual *ḥajj* caravans guiding pilgrims to Mecca and Medina organized similar provisioning networks overseen from Cairo and Damascus. Finally, food was the agent and object of institutional and informal patronage and poor relief.

## *Istanbul and Topkapı Palace*

Istanbul was at the hub of a great system that directed both essential and specialty items toward the capital generally and specifically to the imperial palace. The most important commodities were wheat and meat, along with barley, rice, and other staples like onions, cooking fats and oils, salt, seasonal vegetables, yogurt, and honey. Fuel wood and water were essential for cooking. In the sixteenth century, none of these commodities flowed to the Istanbul markets on the currents of free market trade. Each was collected, conveyed, stocked, and sold according to imperial prescription. Of course, demand was not an absent factor, nor profit and novelty absent possibilities, for the merchants and consumers. Yet a controlled regime of requisitioning aimed at regulating the overall quantity and quality of foodstuffs in Istanbul.[4]

Grain to feed Istanbul was produced mainly in Thrace and in the Black Sea and Danubian provinces of the empire, then shipped from Tekirdağ on the Marmara Sea from the ports ringing the northwest Black Sea coast between Istanbul and Caffa in the Crimea. After the conquest in 1517, Egypt contributed important quantities of wheat and rice to Istanbul, as well as to the Hijaz and the Syrian provinces. Some portion of what arrived in the capital represented the annual tax payments of peasants. Additional stores were purchased in or requisitioned from provincial markets at prices fixed by the Ottoman government. Delivery of grain, the bulkiest commodity, was facilitated by the location of the city at the juncture of important waterways. Grain arrived via the Danube, the Black Sea, and the Bosphorus, as well as from the Mediterranean and the Aegean through the Dardanelles to the Sea of Marmara. Without the possibility of shipping sufficient quantities of grain by water, Istanbul could not have sustained her huge civilian and military populations.[5] Even so, navigation on the Black Sea was not a simple matter technically for much of the year. Shipments coming across the Mediterranean and the Aegean were vulnerable to piracy or successful (and illegal) counterbidding by European merchants, along with the perils of sixteenth-century navigation.[6]

Camel caravans in Anatolia and the Balkans, as well as wagons in the Balkans, were alternate modes of transport. The Turcoman tribes developed a hybrid species from Bactrian camels and Arabian dromedaries that was particularly suited to the climate and terrain of Anatolia. Turcoman or Arab camel breeders and drivers maintained enormous herds which they hired out to the sultan, the army, merchants, pilgrims, or whomever for the transport of food, equipment, people, and merchandise. While camels could not replace shipping as a low-cost vehicle for transporting high-volume commodities like grains, other foodstuffs and essential items did come regularly to Istanbul overland.[7]

Arriving stocks were offloaded along the Golden Horn and delivered directly to warehouses or stores in the city or to the Topkapı Palace. Foodstuffs and raw materials for manufacturing were equally supervised and controlled, both to regulate their distribution and to ensure the proper collection of taxes due to the state. The most important markets along the Golden Horn each had a separate quay and scales, for example: Yağkapanı (oil, fat), Unkapanı (wheat), Balkapanı (honey) and Yemişkapanı (fruit).[8] Not only were the markets separate, but the preparation and sale of foodstuffs was divided amongst numerous specific cook shops and stores. Once again, it is Evliya Çelebi who provides an extensive catalogue of these from the mid-seventeenth century.[9]

Wheat was distributed from the city granaries near the quays to the millers and from there to the bakers. As with virtually all the city trades and manufactures, the bakers were organized as a guild, with a hierarchy of masters, journeymen, and apprentices preparing breads of different qualities and prices. The sultan was responsible for providing bread daily to his subjects in Istanbul and as a result was personally involved in ensuring grain supply to Istanbul. The grand vizier himself inspected the bazaar every week to check on supplies and manufacturing quality.[10] While some people purchased their daily supply of bread (sometimes more than once a day), others bought wheat for grinding, or flour, prepared their dough at home, and then took it for baking to neighborhood ovens. More well-to-do people maintained separate baking ovens at home.[11]

Meat arrived in Istanbul mostly on the hoof from the Balkans. People of means, merchants and artisans, were appointed to supply a fixed number of animals for purchase and delivery to the city butchers. Owners of large herds were required to send between five and ten percent of their own animals to the markets. These suppliers were called *celep-keşan*, and were usually named to the task because they possessed the financial resources necessary to convey large numbers of sheep and goats overland to the capital. For this obligation they earned relief from other levies, yet it was a costly and difficult charge.[12] Again, as with grains and bread, butchered meats of different qualities were sold to individuals and also to shops preparing cooked foods. While bread of some quality was daily fare for most everyone, meat consumption varied enormously and, as the ʿimaret menus demonstrate, was not a regular ingredient in the cooking pots of poorer people.[13]

Prices of basic foodstuffs and raw materials for manufacturing sold in the Istanbul markets and elsewhere were continually fixed and readjusted by the kadi in consultation with local merchants and manufacturers. The fixing of maximal prices (*narh*) and frequent market inspections all functioned as means to control production and distribution.[14] Market inspectors (*muḥtesib*) oversaw the setting of prices, the fair use of weights and measures, the quality of merchandise and the moral behavior of people in the markets.

Topkapı Palace maintained stocks of basic goods in its own storehouses separate from those of the city. Descriptions of meals and feasts, left by Ottoman chroniclers and foreign visitors alike, record the variety of foods prepared and eaten at the palace. Trained and practiced cooks and bakers transformed basic goods into an abundant array of dishes. This hierarchy of kitchen staff prepared daily meals for the palace, including the imperial household, servants, government officials present in one capacity or another, visitors to the palace of whatever status or rank, and artisans working in palace workshops. By 1526, some 277 cooks and bakers were preparing food for several thousand people per day, while by the mid-seventeenth century the number of cooks and servants working in the imperial kitchen had expanded to 1370.[15] Foodstuffs and cooked dishes were also distributed from the Topkapı Palace to other palaces around the city.[16]

More than one kitchen functioned on the palace grounds. Most evident and impressive was the row of ten hearths topped by high chimneys along the entire southeast side of the second court of the palace. Eight among them were separate kitchens serving different groups in the palace, while the remaining two were confectionaries (*ḥelvahane*).[17] Other, smaller kitchens throughout the palace served special groups; for example, the *kuşhane* (lit. birdhouse), prepared food only for the sultan and his immediate household, while the harem had a separate kitchen of its own.[18]

## *Provincial towns*

In every region, local networks similar to that centered on Istanbul existed to supply provincial and district towns. Emporia such as Aleppo and Cairo probably rivaled the markets of Istanbul, while the markets of major cities like Damascus, Edirne, Bursa, and Salonika offered residents an ample variety of special foodstuffs in addition to the essentials. Enforced supply networks, price controls, and market inspections were typical not only in the big cities like Istanbul and Bursa, but in smaller places like Ankara and Jerusalem as well.[19] In each town or city, the local governors and kadis oversaw and managed the markets with assistance from the market inspector and other authorities.

A corollary to regulating the movement and sale of foodstuffs was the control over food production. This was accomplished by restricting the movement of peasants, who incurred penalties or additional tax liabilities for changing their place of residence of their own accord. Nor could they deliberately change the type or the quantity of crops they cultivated without receiving official approval. This being said, the various revenue holders could forgive taxes and/or distribute seed in years of drought or infestation in order to ensure the short-term survival of peasants and the long-term stability of agricultural production and revenues.[20]

Jerusalem had a smaller and less wealthy population than the large towns mentioned above. With just under 3,000 tax-paying households at mid-century, it was comparable in size to cities like Çorum, Amasya, Niğde, and Aksaray in Anatolia.[21] It was a town of secondary, if not tertiary, administrative status with no important manufactures, except olive oil, olive oil soap, and souvenirs for the pilgrim visitors. No easy roads or convenient waterways led to its gates. Thus, the provisioning of Jerusalem operated on an even smaller scale and its markets offered a narrower range of basic and luxury foodstuffs than the larger towns of the empire. This was mirrored in the smaller number of professional, manufacturing, and service guilds in the town, approximately sixty, compared to c.260 in Cairo and 1100 in Istanbul.[22]

What set the town apart and gave it special status was its religious importance. As the principal destination for Jews and Christians making pilgrimages and a secondary stop for Muslims after Mecca and Medina, Jerusalem drew large numbers of visitors every year. The pilgrims swelled the population repeatedly, if temporarily, and created additional demands on the food supply matrices of the city. There is no means to infer how many Muslims or Jews passed through. As for the Christians, in the year 961/1553–54, anticipated revenues from taxes on the Church of the Holy Sepulcher were pegged at 120,000 *akçe*. These revenues derived from the tax of 45 *akçe* that Christians paid to enter the church. As the church was a destination for all of them, simple arithmetic would say that over 2500 Christians pilgrims came to Jerusalem every year, on average.[23] But the entry tax to the Church changed according to the remote or proximate origins of Christians, and the numbers of visitors may have fluctuated to extremes as a result of shifting political and military relations between the Ottoman empire and its enemies, so this number is only an estimate.[24]

The public kitchen set up by Hurrem Sultan, therefore, was a partial response to the city's need to feed all these people, as their presence was tied to the sanctity of Jerusalem and hence to the sultan's obligation to provide for the holy cities. It had a fixed clientele of local residents, including its own staff. Yet of those who came to the ʿimaret for meals, some portion likely came from the transient population, as ʿimarets were set up with them in mind as well.

*The army on campaign*

During Ottoman military campaigns, a provisioning system operated comparable to the one aimed at the cities, bending local, regional, and imperial lines of supply and drafting large merchants to ensure provisions to the army, whether in camp or on the move. Extended campaigns remained a constant feature of the Ottoman enterprise for several centuries.[25] Most often, major military operations lasted from early spring through late fall, creating a six-month season during which sufficient quantities of foodstuffs had to be made available for purchase along the route to and from the front. However, preparations began well in advance, and some of the imperial campaigns, notably those against the Mamluks and Safavids to the east, kept the troops away through the winter and into the following campaign season.[26]

The organization and supervision of these supply operations were crucial for the success of any campaign. Skills and experience similar to those required of the provincial governors in this period were necessary to ensure military provisioning. It is thus not surprising that, for the first few centuries, Ottoman commanders were also provincial governors, especially because provincial administration was in some ways inseparable from the preparation and organization of military campaigns. The work of Ottoman officers overlapped extensively the civilian and military spheres, and it was only in the later sixteenth century that the two began to separate into distinct corps.[27]

In order to gather and move grain supplies for military food and fodder, the Ottomans employed several devices. Peasants were required to deliver specific quantities of foodstuffs as a form of taxation (*nüzul*). This obligation might be converted into cash if people were too far from the campaign route to make delivery practicable. Individuals—peasants or others—could be assigned to deliver foodstuffs to particular locations to be sold at government-determined prices (*sürsat*). In addition, government agents purchased bulk supplies in local markets at government-fixed prices (*iştira*).[28]

For all that they appear to have imposed on the rural population, a basic goal of these provisioning mechanisms was not to disrupt unduly the people living along the campaign route. No plundering was permitted, and the penalty for commandeering supplies without authorization could be death. Because the steady inflow of revenues required a stable and working peasant population, the government rightly feared the potentially damaging effects of the army in transit. Even with the threat and implementation of severe sanctions against unruly troops, however, peasant flight from the villages along the way was not uncommon. On the eastern frontier, the scorched earth policy of the Safavid army when in retreat both drove away local peasants and destroyed the foodstuffs the Ottomans might have purchased en route. Under the circumstances, the Ottoman supply system encountered formidable problems, and the troops more often resorted to grabbing stores from local people.[29]

Muṣṭafa ʿAli sketched a picture of how this system ought to have worked in his critique of the Ottoman campaign in the east that began in 986/1578–79. Discussing its faulty logistics, he says:

> [A]s soon as the Sultan's intention of conquering the lands of Iran and his great haste and interest in the subjection of Georgia and Shirvān were expressed first of all an adequate amount of provisions and preservable grains like barley and millet should in the course of two years successively be stored in storehouses in the border regions of Erzurum, Van and Baghdad. . . . [This operation should proceed] in such a way that no one stretches out his hand to plunder the subjects of the Iranian provinces and to destroy their property, on the contrary, most of the burdens that are imposed upon them should be eased, and of some they should be kindly released. [Thus] the poor people should be treated kindly. In particular, that winter one victory-favored general should spend the winter in Tabriz using the provisions stored in Van, and the other army-leader should rest in the region of Revan (Yerevan) and Azerbaijan with the provisions from Erzurum, likewise some of the provisions stored in the area of Baghdad should be sent to Kazwin allowing the Khan of the Tatars to spend the winter in the town of Kazwin itself. . . .[30]

The careful planning expected by Muṣṭafa ʿAli was based on his knowledge of other campaigns. Nothing was to be left to chance, and the great distances and difficulties of supply in eastern Anatolia were carefully considered in this plan linking stored supplies and garrison towns. According to Muṣṭafa ʿAli adequate provisioning required years of accumulation to overcome the terrain and the distance of some 250 kilometers separating one base from the next. His prescriptions were aimed not only at stockpiling adequate stores for the army, but also at safeguarding peasants from the abuses of emergency military requisitioning.

## *Janissaries*

Food and everything associated to it also played a central role in the life of the janissary corps. As with other groups—the cities, the palaces, the army on campaign—the janissary corps had to be supplied with foodstuffs, either distributed as part of salaries or made available for purchase in sufficient quantities. The symbolic importance of food was, however, very emphatic for the janissaries. To begin with, the corps itself was called the *ocak* (hearth) or *ocak-i Bektaşıyan* (hearth of the Bektaşis). The names of the officer ranks came directly from the kitchen: the *çorbacı* (soup maker) was the battalion commander, while lower-ranking officers including the *aşçıs* (cook) and *kara kullukçus* (scullions).[31] The use of these titles reflected the close affiliation of the janissaries to the Bektaşi dervish order. Among the Bektaşis, the kitchen and hearth were sacred, thus prompting the use of kitchen terms and occupations to denote the hierarchy among the dervishes.

The cauldrons (*ḳazğan*) of the janissary hearths have long been understood to be the focal icon of their loyalty to the sultan. By accepting his food, they reaffirmed their allegiance and obligation to serve. Eating from the same pot also worked to create group solidarity. The cauldrons, like the officer ranks, found their antecedents among the Bektaşis, evoking the sacred cauldron (*ḳazan-i şerif*) of the eponymous leader, Hacı Bektaş. In the *aş evi* or kitchen of Bektaşi residence complexes, a huge cauldron often won great reverence for its role in the special ceremonies of certain festivals.[32] When the janissaries were discontent and rebellion was cooking amongst them, they spilled out the cauldrons to announce their rejection of the sultan's gift of food. Spiritual and political at one and the same time, the reversal of these pots was the classic sign of janissary revolt.[33] As was obvious from the numerous reports quoted from travelers to the city, the cauldrons were a central icon of the ʿimaret as well, at least in Jerusalem. They announced its capacity to feed, and, when empty, stood in mute accusation of diminished power.

## *Ḥajj Caravans*

Each year, two large caravans departed from Damascus and Cairo in the direction of Mecca and Medina. The preparations for the passage of these long convoys of pilgrims, merchants, animals, and goods bore a strong resemblance to those necessary for a military campaign. While the army organized supplies and transit across Anatolia or the Balkans and Hungary for some 150,000 men in the late sixteenth century,[34] *ḥajj* caravans annually included tens of thousands of camels carrying people, merchandise, foodstuffs, and water. Numerous pilgrims also made the trip on foot. A very rough estimate puts their total number at between 20,000 and 60,000 per year.[35] However, the *ḥajj* route was sparsely inhabited compared to the European and Anatolian campaign routes. Instead of ensuring that local peasants were undisturbed, as was the case with the passing army, the pilgrims and merchants in the desert caravans instead required protection from attack by local bedouin along the way. The Ottomans supplied the military forces necessary to ensure the security of the caravans, in addition to negotiating the cost of safe passage through the territories of different tribes.

Sufficient food and water for the caravans had to be carefully organized and supplied for the journey to and from the Hijaz. The long trip through the desert might occasionally pass sources of water, but little if any food was produced there. Bedouin contracted to transport large quantities of grain from the producing regions of Syria and Egypt to specific halting points for purchase along the way. Thus pilgrims stocked and carried their own food and water to the extent possible. Private endowments and state funds covered the basic costs of food for poor pilgrims, as well as providing an additional supply of water carried by camels in the caravan.[36]

Altogether, responsibility for the successful conclusion of the annual pilgrimage lay with its commanders (*amīr al-ḥajj*) in Cairo and Damascus, respectively. They collected the provincial revenues earmarked to fund the *ḥajj*, organized sufficient camels, food, and water, and saw to the security arrangements. The task required logistical abilities as well as the personal connections to local and Ottoman notables, whose support was needed to ensure supply and safety.[37] Ultimately, the *amīr al-ḥajj* carried out many of the same tasks associated with provisioning as the provincial governors and the military commanders. It is not at all surprising to encounter men who combined the duties of provincial administration and pilgrimage command, nor to meet those who moved from one to the other. Talented and successful *ḥajj* commanders were crucial to the Ottomans, and their success in this regard brought them near immunity from rebuke and punishment for other abuses. Despite his violent attacks against local peasants, Ibn Farrukh was *amīr al-ḥajj* in Syria for many years in the first half of the seventeenth century, retained because he was able successfully to outfit the caravan and guide it to Mecca and back again to Damascus.[38]

Ottoman supply concerns surrounding the *ḥajj* were not limited to the caravans. Following precedents established by their predecessors throughout the Muslim world, the Ottomans also contributed generously to ensure the regular supply of food and water in the holy cities themselves. Enormous endowments, established before the Ottomans, existed to support the inhabitants of Mecca and Medina, as well as to guarantee sufficient water in these desert cities. One of the largest was a collection of Mamluk endowments that the Ottomans called the Great Deşişe. It funded the annual delivery of grain from Egypt to Mecca and Medina for making bread and *deşişe,* a porridge of crushed wheat and fat. The Ottomans preserved this endowment when they conquered the Arab provinces. Süleyman I and Selim II both made large additions to the Great Deşişe, while Murad III created a separate endowment called the Small Deşişe which contributed money to the poor of Mecca and Medina.[39] Additional endowments in Anatolia, Rümelia, and the Arab provinces, including North Africa, also contributed to the maintenance of the communities and buildings in the holy cities.[40]

Altogether, supplying the caravans and Mecca and Medina constituted a critical preoccupation for the Ottoman sultan. His obligation and ability to protect and provide for the holiest sites in the Muslim world was simultaneously the source of enormous prestige and no small amount of worry. While visible only rarely to foreign non-Muslims, the success or failure of the sultans to fulfill these obligations would be evident and communicated throughout the Muslim world, since pilgrims were not limited to Ottoman subjects but came from Muslim communities everywhere. In Süleyman's time, the responsibility for the *ḥajj* was still relatively new to the Ottoman sultans. Guaranteeing the pilgrimage was part of the duties of the leader of the Muslim world, an image Süleyman was consciously cultivating during the latter half of his reign.[41] The building of the Süleymaniye was very much part of this program, and the establishment of the Jerusalem waqf was Hurrem's contribution in the same project. Their roles were complementary in these endeavors though they also coincided, as for example in the two ʿimarets in Mecca and Medina founded by Süleyman in Hurrem's name.

In sum, the challenge of supplying the pilgrimage caravan and the holy desert towns, combined with the demands of daily urban supply and military campaign provisioning, occupied no small amount of Ottoman time and resources. Food was not the *raison d'être* of any of these enterprises; it was their *sine qua non,* recognized as such in Ottoman policy. The power to feed fed power. All provisioning successes, unsung though they might be, were at the heart of Ottoman stability and legitimacy, an obligation assumed by the sultans and expected of them. In the practical realization of this obligation, the sultan depended on the military-administrative corps, soldier-governors who rotated through an array of appointments. Each post combined military and civilian duties and one common task was to solve the logistics of food supply for large numbers of people, whether sedentary in towns or on the move in caravans or on campaigns.

## ON THE WORD ʿIMARET

Many features were shared among all the provisioning systems, as is by now evident. The ʿimarets fit into this interconnected network, the only piece really unique to the Ottomans. The use of the Arabic word *ʿimāra* in the form *ʿimaret* seems to belong only to Ottoman Turkish, where it means specifically a large public kitchen. Contemporary Ottoman records also employed other, diverse terms to signify a public kitchen: *aşevi, aşhane, yemekhane, darüʾl-iṭʿam* or *darü'z-ziyafet.*[42] An architectural treatise from the early seventeenth century records kitchens (*maṭbah*) separately from ʿimarets, confirming that an ʿimaret denoted something more than just a cooking facility, perhaps of a certain minimal size or capacity and emphasizing the regular distribution of meals on the premises.[43] However, the original Arabic meaning of "habitation and cultivation," or "the act of building, making habitable, bringing into cultivation," is not entirely forgotten, as ʿimaret could also be used as a synonym for *külliye,* the large mosque-*medrese*-ʿimaret type of complex built to develop cities and new settlements.[44] Even in Ottoman Turkish, the use was ambiguous at times, as with the Jerusalem project of Hurrem. It was commonly referred to as *ʿimaret-i ʿamire* (the flourishing/imperial ʿimaret), sometimes to mean just the enormous kitchen and sometimes to include the entire complex.[45]

European dictionaries record the multiple meanings of the word *ʿimaret,* reflecting how elastic its use must have been.[46] An early seventeenth-century German source gives an example of this, describing the kitchens in a way that makes them sound more like the hans or caravansarays:

> There were also charity houses established in Turkey, which were built for travelers and foreigners, within which food and drink would be distributed and three-nights' lodging had; these were called *ʿimaret* in Turkish.[47]

Such a characterization explains the relationship between the rooms and the kitchen in the Jerusalem ʿimaret. It also explains the diverse list of diners in ʿimarets around the empire, where travelers and foreigners received food along with scholars, students, and impoverished people. As others have pointed out, the common condition of the travelers, foreigners, and indigents was their lack of an immediate community, either of family, confession, profession, or location, to take responsibility for their care.[48] Students and scholars, too, could be far from home, without a communal safety net to give them daily assistance. At the same time, these latter earned the right to support as a result of their dedication to the study and teaching of religious texts.

Another source of confusion about *ʿimaret* is the usage of modern scholars. Barkan, in the general sense, talks about the Ottoman ʿimarets to show how endowments promoted the socioeconomic development and expansion of Ottoman cities.[49] Inalcik makes the *waqf-ʿimāret system* (here in the sense of *külliye*) the linchpin in explaining the evolution of Ottoman Istanbul as a specific case. Yet he exemplifies the multiple uses of the word when he explains: "Each complex, as it answered the basic spiritual and material needs of a Muslim community in religion and education, as well as in water supply and even (through the hospice *ʿimāret* or hospice kitchen) in food, became the center of a settlement which grew over time into a full-fledged *nāḥiye* [district]."[50] Yet only one page later, in discussing the founders of the ʿimarets, he uses *ʿimaret* in the other sense: "It was only the Sulṭāns and the vizirs who built such *ʿimārets* or large complexes."[51]

Inalcik in fact clarifies the continuous polyvalent usage of the word in Ottoman Turkish and in discussions of Ottoman practice, for it would seem that it had no fixed meaning. Rather, its broader and more specific connotations were always possible, and context alone indicated the immediate sense. Tanman, from the perspective of an historian of architecture, finds the confusion of terminology arising in the fourteenth century, with the founding of mosque-*zaviyes* that combined ritual and socio-cultural functions. Notwithstanding, numerous scholars have tried to insist on the correctness of the more general meaning and the corruption represented by the more specific or, for them, popular usage. Ergin, in his early study of the "imaret sistemi" claims that the narrow usage derived from the concern of most people with their stomachs, so that they focused only on the kitchens of the large complexes; these then came to represent the whole group of buildings in their eyes.[52] Perhaps this was the case. In the present work, *ʿimaret* is used only in the narrower sense of "public kitchen"; "*külliye*" or "complex" refers to the larger collection of buildings.

## PRE-OTTOMAN PRECEDENTS

Some observations on the modes and meanings of large-scale food distribution in pre-Ottoman times broaden our perspective and understanding of what molded the specifically Ottoman practice. The precursors to Ottoman food distributions served practical functions: feeding retainers, soldiers, celebrating festivals, or handing our emergency assistance during hard times. At the same time, all these occasions were imbued with symbolic importance. As so often, a genealogy of the ʿimaret does not present itself and it is difficult to know how the symbolism ascribed to earlier ceremonies may have translated through time and space. Widespread public distributions of cooked food on a daily basis, however, were rare in the Middle East prior to the Ottomans. Where they did exist, it was not in a common type of purposely built facility but rather in diverse spaces and configurations.

Two texts articulate ideologies about the place of food, which the Ottomans appear to have incorporated as a basis for their practice. The oldest substantial work of Islamic Turkish literature, the *Ḳutadgu Bilig,* put food at the hub of relations between the ruler and subjects of every rank. This eleventh-century "Mirror for Princes," borrowing extensively from Perso-Islamic tradition, recommended that a ruler give food to nobles, scholars, and commoners alike. Regarding nobles and scholars, the advice was to "give them to eat of your bread and salt" (*tuz etmek yitür*).[53] The giving and taking of bread and salt implied the construction and consolidation of bonds of loyalty and obligation, while the physical sustaining and nourishing aspect of this food donation is not emphasized. The expression "bread and salt" was not only a medieval construction but persisted through Ottoman and into modern times. Evliya used it to mean "the obligation of service" between a patron and his clients.[54] Redhouse's *Lexicon,* the standard English-language dictionary for Ottoman Turkish, gives "favor, charity" along with "bonds of friendship" as definitions. The contemporary Redhouse *Çağdaş* dictionary records the proverb *"Tuz ekmek hakkını bilmeyen kör olur"* (lit. May the one who does not recognize the claim of bread and salt become blind, or, God punishes the ungrateful).[55]

Symbolic food gifts suited the ruling and learned classes. However, the *Ḳutadgu Bilig* reduced the group called "commoners" to a ravenous mass: "They only know how to fill their bellies, and have no other care but their throats. . . . Therefore, my brother, associate with them and give them food and drink (*içgü aş*) continually, speak softly to them and give them what they ask for. For he who gives is the true beneficiary."[56] This last line echoes the Qurʾanic attitude to beneficent giving, focused on the spiritual and eschatological gain to the giver. At the same time, the political implications of this passage for a ruler are evident. Ensuring sufficient food for the majority of the population was one key to its acquiescence in his sovereignty. No complex construction of loyalty in exchange for symbolic sustenance came into play here, but rather the most basic satisfaction of human hunger to forestall discontent. By implication, the ruler had no expectation, and the large mass of urban residents no need, of the symbolic bonds created by bread and salt.

In the contemporary *Siyasat-nama,* the vizier Niẓām al-Mulk (d. 485/1092) articulated for his Selçuk patron Malikshāh (r. 465–85/1072–92) the Perso-Islamic tradition he had learned in the court of the Ghaznavids. The chapter entitled "Concerning the arrangements for setting a good table" emphasized the obligation of the ruler to lay out a generous meal first thing in the morning, no matter where he might be. Niẓām al-Mulk recounted that "[almost] the whole system of government of the khans of Turkistan consists in having abundant food in the hands of servants and in their kitchens." The generosity of the sultan's table was the measure of his power and so had to be greater than that of all other rulers. Tradition held that "providing abundant bread and food for the creatures of God (to Him be power and glory) increases the duration of a king's life, his reign and good fortune." To illustrate the truth of this, Niẓām al-Mulk offered stories of Moses, Abraham, and ʿAli.[57] Yet, notably, he says nothing of the symbolic importance of this feeding; it appears as a purely practical act.

Among the early concrete examples from the central Muslim lands, the Caliph Al-Nāṣir li-Dīn Allāh (r. 1180–1225) apparently attempted to institute more regular assistance in the capital Baghdad during his tenure. His mother, a Turkish slave named Zumurrud Khatun, was remembered as the founder of numerous pious institutions. Al-Nāṣir himself ordered that bread, meat, and alms be given to the destitute every day. This was in addition to the distribution that he underwrote on special occasions, such as supplementary alms during the month of Rajab and soup kitchens established in Ramadan. Finally, he distributed food, clothing, and alms to pilgrims departing on the *ḥajj*.[58]

Another kind of precedent is found in the Mongol ruler Ghazan Khan (r. 694–713/1295–1304), who established numerous waqfs in Tabriz after converting to Islam. Among these were a royal complex in Tabriz that included a public kitchen and endowments to serve gruel or soup (*aş*) to Mongol and non-Mongol princes and all deserving people who came there on the anniversary of the founder's death.

He also provided for the distribution of sweet dishes on Thursday evenings and other feast days. Ghazan Khan prescribed food for birds as well, endowing grain to be spread for them in the winter.[59] His vizier, Rashīd al-Dīn (d. 1318) was an equal—if not more generous—patron, endowing another complex in Tabriz which contained a public kitchen in a poor house as part of a hospice for travelers.[60]

Among these few pre-Ottoman examples of public kitchens to be found is that of ʿAli Shīr Navā'ī, founded as part of the Ikhlāṣiyya complex in fifteenth-century Herat. The sufi residence (*khānqāh*) in the complex functioned primarily as a public kitchen, serving food to the poor. It was reported that over 1000 people came to eat there daily, receiving at least bread but also soup or some other cooked dish according to the festivals and holy days.[61] If this and the others mentioned are indeed the earliest ʿimaret-like institutions in the Islamic lands, then they point very strongly to a Central Asian, Mongol-Turkic origin for the practice of providing food on a daily basis to people deemed deserving of this kind of support.

Under the Ottomans, the daily meals served at the Topkapı Palace can be seen as an outgrowth of the *toys*, Central Asian ceremonial feasts where important matters were discussed and the seated order of the participants signified greatly.[62] These large public feasts, that were both the privilege and obligation of Selçuk and Mongol rulers, realized the recommendations found in both the *Ḳutadgu Bilig* and Niẓām al-Mulk's *Siyasat-nama,* though they may have had an entirely separate origin. Regular descriptions in *The Book of Dede Korkut* give a sense of how common feasts were in an earlier era, marking every event of consequence. They were organized to honor specific people or consult with noble and powerful followers, commemorating important aspirations or events. At the same time, the language of their ritual suggests that the feasts were part of a symbolic package that included other forms of generosity as well.

> Rise and bestir yourself; have the tents of many colours
> Set up on the earth's face. Have your men slaughter
> Of horses the stallions, of camels the males, of sheep the rams.
> Gather round you the nobles of the Inner Oghuz and the Outer Oghuz.
> When you see the hungry, fill him;
> When you see the naked, clothe him;
> Save the debtor from his debt.
> Heap up meat in hillocks; let lakes of kumis [fermented mare's milk] be drawn.

> Make an enormous feast, then ask what you want and let them pray.[63]

Unrestrained generosity to loyal followers and needy people alike was the price for satisfying personal wishes. However, those who benefited from the largess were then called upon to support the wishes of their host.

To this disparate but related collection of feasts in the pre-Ottoman era may be added the tables (*simāṭ*) spread by the Fatimids in Cairo and Fustat during the tenth through twelfth centuries. Gifts of food and large-scale distributions were standard practice during various festivals and celebrations. People could come to public tables to break their Ramadan fast after praying at the Mosque of ʿAmr, and additional feasts appeared at *ʿīd al-fiṭr* and *ʿīd al-aḍḥa*. These food distributions were not only substantive but comprised a measure of sanctity as well, as they were offered by the Caliph, the Commander of the Faithful. Food given by the Caliph with his own hands was believed to possess *baraka,* "the power to transmit blessing and grace."[64] The morsel received from this distribution was preserved and not eaten. In addition, the capacity to be generous was itself shared at the feasts, since people were supposed to leave with large quantities of food which they in turn might distribute.[65] It is interesting to reconsider in this light the restrictions on removing food from the ʿimarets. While the prohibitions had a practical aspect, controlling carefully the flow of food, they also kept the recipients focused on the principal donor as the source of their nourishment. A founder who sought *qurba* and political gain besides had no interest in sharing the loyalty or gratitude of those who received food from him/her with any intermediaries.

Perhaps the best-known "table" was that in Hebron called *simāṭ al-Khalīl,* the table of Abraham, said to have originated in his practice of hosting and feeding all travelers.[66] According to the eleventh-century Persian traveler Nasir-i Khusraw, anyone who came to Hebron received daily one round loaf of bread, a bowl of lentils cooked in olive oil, and raisins.[67] The Mamluk sultan Qāytbāy (r. 1468–96) restored the Hebron *simāṭ* during his reign and took it as a model when he stipulated that wheat be sent annually to his own *madrasa* in Medina, to be distributed to the poor and other visitors, no matter what their status, so that none should have to buy food.[68]

In the early sixteenth century, the local chronicler Mujīr al-Dīn al-Ḥanbalī (d. 927/1521) found that the daily fare at the *simāṭ* was still lentils, while on Thursday evening seasoned rice (*ruzz al-mufalfal*) and pomegranate seeds were served. More sumptuous dishes were prepared for holidays.[69] Mujīr al-Dīn also described the daily procedure at the *simāṭ*:

> And this is the table of the Noble Abraham, peace be unto him, which is called the Dashīsha; at the door of the kitchen a drum is struck each day after the afternoon prayer, at the time of the distribution from the generous table. The people of the town and pious sojourners eat from it; the bread is made daily and distributed at three times: early morning, after the midday prayer to the people of the town, and after the afternoon prayer a general distribution to the people of the town and the newcomers. And the quantity of bread baked each day is 14,000 flat loaves, but sometimes it reaches 15,000. And as for the capacity of its waqf, it can scarcely be determined; and no one is kept from his generous table, neither of the rich nor of the poor.

To emphasize further the scope of operations sustained by the *simāṭ*, Mujīr al-Dīn enumerates the three ovens and four millstones employed to prepare bread, above which loomed the granaries stocked with wheat, all populated by a crowd of men busy grinding grain, stoking fires and attending all other necessary tasks. This entire enterprise, he says, must rank in the wonders of the world, rare even among kings.[70]

Accounts from Ottoman times, such as those of the seventeenth-century travelers ʿAbd al-Ghanī al-Nābulsī (d. 1143/1731) and Evliya Çelebi, attest to the continuing vitality of this public kitchen. Al-Nābulsī was impressed with the *simāṭ* and quoted Mujīr al-Dīn on the subject at length.[71] Evliya recounts that, when the moment was announced to the people of the town,

> each person had his bowl filled with the soup of Abraham, enough for the subsistence of men with their families. I [Evliya] was also fortunately among the group of those *fuḳara*. I received a plate of wheat soup, a gift from God. I never witnessed such a tasty meal at the table of either viziers or men of learning . . ."[72]

This thriving "table" in Hebron may have been one inspiration for Hurrem's ʿimaret in Jerusalem. Hebron and Jerusalem were called "al-Ḥaramayn," the two sanctuaries, in echo of the two noble sanctuaries, al-Ḥaramayn al-Sharīfayn, Mecca and Medina. In adding a public kitchen to Jerusalem, Hurrem ensured that each of the four holy cities had an institution to feed the hungry.

In addition to the *simāṭs*, distributions and forced sales of grain stocks were a common feature in pre-Ottoman Cairo and perhaps in other places as well. In the late twelfth and early thirteenth centuries the rulers kept stores sufficient to feed the population of the city for an entire year in case of famine. At such times, grain and bread were distributed either for free or at very low prices, and the rulers policed the notables holding stocks to ensure they neither hoarded nor overpriced their grain.[73] Rulers felt a strong obligation to assist the poor of every definition in hard times and imposed this obligation on other people of means as well. However, there does not seem to have been a state mechanism for distributing assistance during times that for many people would have been called normal or even prosperous. Possibly, the informal distribution of aid from individuals to people in their neighborhoods and from the guilds or sufi orders was sufficient to support the chronic poor.

One might also find antecedents of or precedents for the Ottoman ʿimarets in the mosques, *madrasas*, *maktabs*, and shrines that had food for students and teachers under the Ayyubids and Mamluks.[74] In the large Mamluk *madrasas* and *maktabs*, stipends for scholars and students alike were intended to cover (at least) basic subsistence costs, through it is not clear that there were actual kitchen facilities in these institutions. Where food was distributed, it was not necessarily plentiful. A daily bread ration could suffice for one person, but not for any dependents.[75]

Historian Adam Sabra says explicitly that while Mamluk institutions were well-endowed, it was not until the mid-fifteenth century that they came to have an important role in the regular distribution of food to the poor. At that time, there was a shift from endowing *maktabs* to endowing tomb waqfs and institutions to feed the poor, whereas previously, food distributions to the poor were common chiefly in times of crisis and festivals. The exceptions were smaller endowments that supported specific distributions to students, prisoners, the poor who came to a certain mosque, or a sufi residence. The reasons for the change are not altogether clear, though Sabra suggests that the financial crisis in Egypt during the second half of the fifteenth century may have contributed to it. Tomb waqfs were cheaper to build and maintain than the *madrasas* or mosques preferred in more prosperous times, and they often included funds for the distribution of bread, perhaps itself a sign of increased hardship.[76] Yet some of these distributions took place only once a week, on Friday evening. It is worth noting, too, that by the fifteenth century, the Ottoman practice of building ʿimarets was firmly in place. Possibly, the Mamluk practice was influenced by that of the Ottomans.

Hundreds of sufi residences, called variously *zaviye, ribāṭ* or *khānqāh* were scattered across pre-Ottoman Anatolia, the early Ottoman Balkans, and throughout the Muslim world, another type of institution that included kitchens. In general, each *zaviye* comprised a residence and a kitchen. The kitchens cooked food for the dervishes and also fed travelers, needy people, and those who came to pray at the tombs of *shaykhs* or participated in sufi rituals. Some also functioned as residences for poor or elderly people, with an endowment to hire a cook and a doctor when needed. The residences, like other institutions, distributed food as part of the celebrations of Ramadan nights and other festivals associated with the Prophet, as well as at the Persian New Year (*nevruz*), which became a fixed festival in the Ottoman calendar.[77]

The practical and spiritual aspects of food and feeding were utterly entangled in the sufi milieu. For while the convents cooked and distributed food, the world of sufi expression and ritual was bound up in imagery and terminology from the kitchen. This was emphatically so for the Mevlevis and the Bektaşis. Food imagery and metaphor were ubiquitous in the texts of Mevlana Celaleddin Rumi, where a tension between eating and fasting kept food a prominent concern among his followers. In the Bektaşi order, as discussed above, the entire nomenclature of the hierarchy was that of cooks and kitchen personnel.[78]

Sufi residences played an important role in the consolidation of Turkish and then Ottoman rule in Anatolia and the Balkans. Their number increased with the successive ingressions of Turkic peoples. Local rulers striving for predominance in Anatolia in the wake of the Mongol conquest and Selçuk demise contributed to sufi institutions. *Zaviyes* and *ribāṭs* competed for attention with the mosques endowed by sultans, constituting affordable demonstrations of patronage and power for rival leaders of lesser means.[79] Anatolian cities like Amasya, Tokat, and Sivas contained many such structures, as did the conquered towns and spaces of the Balkans. Nor was food distributed perforce only to people: like Tabriz, Sivas had a waqf for bird food to be put out during the harsh winter months.[80] As the Ottoman state rapidly expanded its borders and sought ways to absorb people effectively into the imperial endeavor, the residences served as spiritual centers, guest houses, and the nuclei of future settlements. Once Ottoman rule was established, the individual sultans continued to patronize particular sufi orders, creating endowments for new and existing residences in addition to endowing mosques and larger complexes.[81]

Finally, in this tour of pre-Ottoman precedents for the 'imarets, it should be noted that the Turks migrating into Anatolia also encountered a range of local Byzantine practices and traditions which were not completely at odds with their own. The Byzantine web of charitable organizations (although the empire was impoverished by that time) included distributions of food to needy and deserving persons, echoing practices established in the Turkic principalities.

## AN OTTOMAN INSTITUTION

The confluence of Turco-Mongol, Muslim, and Byzantine practices, together with the demands placed on the new sultanate and the institutions it fostered, gave rise to the particular form of the ʿimaret. Evliya Çelebi remarked that in all his travels he saw "nothing like our enviable institution."[82] The particular Ottoman origin of the ʿimaret as a form is also attested by its presence throughout the Ottoman lands—Anatolia, the Balkans, the Arab provinces. Institutional features shared among all these regions were rarely if ever indigenous to all three, but rather the product of their common Ottoman past, the result of an ongoing Ottoman cultural synthesis. Moreover, at least one architectural historian claims that no earlier structures have been found that are analogous to the Ottoman ʿimarets, and none are described in numerous books on Islamic architecture.[83] As noted above, formal measures for emergency food assistance had existed prior to the Ottoman era in the Middle East. However, the daily distribution of cooked meals to large numbers of urban dwellers year-round from a special building designed for that purpose appears to have been an Ottoman innovation, at least outside the holy cities of Mecca, Medina and Hebron.[84]

By various names, the large kitchens became an integral component of the Ottoman project of settlement, colonization, legitimization, and urban development. The first Ottoman ʿimaret was reportedly built in Iznik by Sultan Orhan in 1336.[85] Over the centuries, the number of ʿimarets grew.[86] Their capacities expanded along with the size of the complexes in which they were located, reflecting the increasing wealth and power of the sultans and the Ottoman empire altogether. Consolidation of the form and functioning of the ʿimarets was another aspect of a process of canonization that has been described as culminating under Süleyman in the sixteenth century. Along with the emergence of identifiably Ottoman idioms of aesthetic creation and legal codifications emerged the shape of the ʿimaret.[87]

By the 1530s, there were no fewer than eighty-three ʿimarets established in the Ottoman realms.[88] However, this figure did not include Istanbul, Egypt, the Hijaz and the numerous building projects undertaken after that time. Other sixteenth-century ʿimarets established by Süleyman I, Selim II, Murat III, Meḥmet III and their mothers, consorts, daughters, and viziers are absent from this total. An early seventeenth-century treatise says that the renowned architect Sinan (d. 996/1588) built seventeen ʿimarets.[89] Thus even before 1600, one hundred ʿimarets can be counted, while many more were founded after that, including ʿimarets in the Sultan Aḥmet, Nuruosmaniyye, and Mihrişah Sultan complexes in Istanbul.[90]

Among the ʿimarets established in Istanbul during the time of Süleyman were his own at the Süleymaniye and that of Hurrem attached to her mosque-hospital complex in the Haseki neighborhood, about two miles west of the Topkapı Palace. This latter served the *medrese* students and staff of the mosque, ʿimaret, and hospital that formed part of her endowment, along with twenty-four needy individuals who held certificates attesting to their right to eat there.[91] Leftovers were distributed to other indigents. In contrast, the ʿimaret in Konya close by the tomb of the great sufi Celaleddin Rumi was one, like that in Hebron, where there were no restrictions on who could eat. Its doors were open to all the poor, needy people, travelers, strangers, and other guests, no matter where they came from. No permits or other conditions were imposed to obtain eligibility.[92]

It was not only the capacities of single ʿimarets that made them such impressive and significant institutions, but also the cumulative impact where there were many ʿimarets in one town. Twenty ʿimarets in Istanbul fed 4000–5000 people every day.[93] In sixteenth-century Edirne, three imperial ʿimarets in complexes and eight other ʿimaret endowments fed an estimated 2,600 people daily out of a population of about 22,000. Thus, if the residents of Edirne constituted the chief clientele of the ʿimarets, over 10 percent ate regularly in public kitchens.[94] However, it is worth considering that Edirne remained a popular temporary residence for sultans as well as a busy transit point on the road to and from the Balkans. The large number of ʿimarets may have existed to bear some of the burden of hosting the many travelers who came through the city.

Public kitchens continued to be constructed after the sixteenth century. Yet while the need for ʿimarets probably did not diminish, they were not all equally well maintained. Muṣṭafa ʿAli's late sixteenth-century tirade against the ʿimarets of the Ottoman capitals certainly testifies to some lack of regular upkeep.[95] Evliya Çelebi's mid-seventeenth century account gives a further perspective on their durability. In Diyarbekir he found that six of the seven kitchens that operated in the past were not functioning. Only that of the Great mosque was providing food. Diyarbakir, however, stood out for the rundown condition of its ʿimarets compared to other towns Evliya visited: Bursa had twenty, Trabzon two, Konya eleven, Amasya ten, Skoplje four, and Elbasan three.[96] According to him, Jerusalem had three as well.[97] Evliya says that in comparison with the ʿimarets, the sufi residences were more constant as sources of food for the poor. Yet perhaps it was everywhere the case that these residences played an important role in food distribution, and thus they worked, if not in tandem, at least in a common endeavor with the ʿimarets.[98] They have already been noted as one basic precedent for the development of the ʿimarets. This last observation, however, raises a further question. Just as the competition between Selçuk rulers and upstart *amirs* found expression in their respective endowing of mosques and sufi sites, it is possible that the ʿimarets and sufi residences played some role in the competition between sufi institutions and those of mosque-based Islam, between the dervishes and the *ʿülema,* for both popular support and imperial patronage.

Ultimately, the Ottoman sultan's preoccupation with food was in part an outgrowth of his political and military capacities, and his general responsibility to provide for his subjects. In the first two centuries of Ottoman rule, this responsibility was captured in symbolic acts like being the first to serve out food and lighting the first fire of a new ʿimaret attributed to Orhan.[99] This latter topos may have had its origins in an anecdote attributed to Zaid b. Aslam and repeated by Nizām al-Mulk in his *Siyasat-nama*. According to the story, the Caliph ʿUmar encountered a destitute woman and her two children as he walked in disguise one night. Not recognizing him, the woman cursed the Caliph for ignoring their hunger. He, much chastised, went away and returned to her as soon as possible carrying foodstuffs, then set about lighting a cooking fire and preparing bread and soup for the three hungry souls with his own hands.[100]

Little has been written about the symbolic function of the ʿimarets. This is partly because most accounts emphasize their role in feeding the poor, meaning the needy or destitute. Yet their most numerous clients seem to have been their own employees, those of the complexes and the various stipendiaries in them. Food distributions were not always a form of poor relief or significant only for their economic and subsistence consequences. All had symbolic and ritual aspects that created layers of meaning beyond temporary sustenance or the sensual enjoyment of eating. Giving and taking food symbolized and actualized the dense networks of patronage woven with implications of rights and obligations. Imperial distributions, in their many contexts, encapsulated most symbolic aspects of providing food, and the sultan stood as the epitome of those who gave. His efforts to prevent famine had a motive beyond the worry to stave off any threat to the productive and fighting forces of his domains. If he could not ensure the basic welfare of his subjects, then the sultan had no right to the fruits of their labors, their loyalty nor to his own title.

The daily meals at Topkapı Palace were an outgrowth of Turcoman practices from Osman's time and before, a ritual reconfirmation of leadership and loyalty. In the early Ottoman period, the sultan also appeared regularly during the communal meals he provided to his followers, and their participation was an affirmation of loyalty to him. This practice continued until the introduction of the formal seclusion of the sultan at the end of the reign of Meḥmed the Conqueror in the late fifteenth century.[101] Even after the sultan had disappeared from public view, however, food was distributed daily to all who came to the palace, a symbolic survival of the prior ritual. The symbolic impact of food present in these distributions grew as a result of the sultan's own absence, signalled to all by the huge palace kitchen chimneys on the skyline.[102]

Offering and accepting food as rituals of allegiance and status between the sultan and his subjects were transactions of fundamental importance. In discussing evolving notions of loyalty and leadership in his study of Buyid society in late ninth and tenth-century Iraq, Mottahedeh noted the significance of giving and accepting benefit (*niʿmah*) in creating bonds between individuals.[103] Forming such bonds was important for the consolidation of the Ottoman state. The sultan handed out benefits that included food, money, slaves, land, and other gifts and, like any other individual, profited to the extent that what he gave earned for him a measure of gratitude and devotion. Moreover, the line dividing the benefits distributed from compensation paid was not always a very clear one. "Eating the sultan's bread" was an expression for receiving a salary.[104] "I eat the sultan's bread" were the words of an Ottoman envoy in Europe at the end of the fifteenth century, describing his own status to his foreign listener.[105] The implications of this relationship are made explicit in the closing remarks of one ʿAzīz Efendi in his *Ḳānūnnāme-i Sulṭānī*, a seventeenth-century reform treatise submitted to the sultan:

> In consequence of my position therefore although it in actuality exceeds the prerogatives of my station, yet because I am an aged, distinguished, and loyal veteran in the Sultan's service, in accordance with the requirements of the claims governing

> those who have received noble benefactions from the sovereign (*niʿam-i celîle-i şehriyârî ḥuḳûḳu iḳtiżâsiyle*) I have made bold . . . to submit to the feet of the sovereign . . .[106]

This passage articulates how the bonds created by the giving and accepting of benefits conferred the right to speak critically of imperial matters. ʿAzīz Efendi echoes the earlier Buyid articulation of a "claim for this benefit" (*haqq hādhihī an-niʿmah*).[107] Both define the two-way bond set up by the benefit, a two-way claim (*ḥaqq*): the just claim of the giver to loyalty and service which imposed the same loyalty on the recipient along with an almost intimate or familiar privilege to speak. This *ḥaqq* was exemplified in the provision and acceptance of food—most specifically, bread and salt. The negative version of expressions with this phrase was employed to indicate a failure to fulfill the implied obligations. When Muṣṭafa ʿAli wrote in 1581 to criticize the commanders Lala Muṣṭafa Paşa and Sinan Paşa in the campaign against Iran, he said: "None of them was animated by the zeal of religion or by the wish to fulfill his obligations vis-à-vis the king whom they owed bread and salt."[108] And he repeated, in upbraiding Şemsi Paşa for his unwillingness to relate a "curious story" to the sultan out of fear for his own position: "Not only will you be a creature without benefit and without harm, but you will have betrayed the King's bread and salt [that you have eaten]."[109] The expression *tuz etmek hakkı bilmedi* (lit. "he failed to recognize the claims of salt and bread") implied the failure to fulfill these obligations.[110]

The implication of loyalty due in exchange for sustenance invites a comparison between the ʿimarets and the janissary *ocak,* both of which traced their origins partly to the sufi residences. The janissaries and the corps of religious scholar-judges were parallel institutions by the sixteenth century, and the continued loyal service of both groups was essential to the survival and functioning of the empire. Thus, comparable to the symbolic significance of the janissary hearth, the daily distributions in ʿimarets and *madrasa*s to the large corps of scholars and religious functionaries enacted a ritual of allegiance between them and the sultan.

Yet the ʿimarets were not simply janissary *ocak*s in a different setting. For one thing, they were never called *ocak,* but rather the cooking place in them was called *maṭbah* (kitchen), which if anything recalls the *maṭbah-i ʿamire,* the imperial kitchen. In addition, the janissaries purchased their own food, although it was the sultan's responsibility to ensure that there were enough foodstuffs available for purchase. Moreover, no account exists of ʿimaret cauldrons being spilled out, of food being refused in this setting. Ultimately, this suggests a smaller role for the symbolic aspects of feeding at the ʿimarets, a greater emphasis on the basic sustenance they afforded. Too, the power or potential power of those who ate in ʿimarets could not rival that of the janissaries (even if the janissaries and *ʿülema* did sometimes make common cause against the sultan). Those who ate in ʿimarets were more dependent on them, more beholden to the sultan. In this, his beneficence reinforced a less tenuous loyalty than the one which anchored the janissaries. The sultans' offer of food to these latter and their acceptance was not framed by beneficence as much as by political and military power.

Finally, compared with the janissary corps, the clientele of an ʿimaret was not an entirely fixed group. Each ʿimaret had a slightly different character, and the individuals served could range from the most important mosque functionaries and scholars to passing imperial delegations to indigent beggers. Indigents, the most obvious people (to modern eyes) to seek out such a facility, were only one group to receive meals and not necessarily the largest. Together with other aspects of Ottoman provisioning policies in the sixteenth century, the public kitchens operated in a society where the state and beneficent institutions had a continual and considerable role in contributing to the daily livelihood of all kinds of individuals.[111]

The origins of these policies are to be found in the long-standing practice of incorporating food into rituals of loyalty and celebration as well as that of remunerating retainers with payments in kind, as well as in cash. As the numbers of these retainers grew, sorted out into well-defined branches of government, Ottoman forms evolved, creating the ʿimaret as a special institution. Ultimately, it brought together practices arising from disparate motives. What united these motives was that all recipients were considered deserving of the sultan's beneficence.

The offer and acceptance of bread and salt were part of the social transaction in the public kitchen. Both were first and foremost basic ingredients in the distributions because they were the consummate subsistence foods. And real food distributions were of crucial importance. Despite what the *Ḳutadgu Bilig* seems to imply, the tie of obligations and just claims between patron and beneficiary was as important at the level of the urban lower classes as it was among the higher ranking Ottomans. These ties linked the sultan with subjects of all ranks throughout the empire. Imperial power in the Ottoman lands therefore, was ultimately tied to the supply and distribution of food, symbolized by and articulated through it. While nourishing people of all classes, this same food sustained the sultan's sovereignty and his domain.

# Conclusion: Practicing Beneficence

"How could the plates of the poor who came be sent back empty?"

*(Gelen fakir fukaranın tabakları nasıl boş geri çevirilirdi?)*[1]

In the preceding chapters, Hurrem Sultan's ʿimaret in Jerusalem provided a vehicle for understanding the nature of Ottoman beneficence as the product of intersecting practices, policies, and ideals. One group of buildings may seem a narrow base from which to explore a topic of this scope, and in fact, at one level, this book constitutes only an introduction to the issues surrounding beneficence. These are many and complex, and by no means all particular to beneficence in Ottoman contexts. Rather, they tie the Ottoman world into more universal discussions of the motivations and modes of philanthropic giving, of gender roles and of deservedness to receive assistance, specifically food.

There are, however, some good reasons for focusing on a single endowment, in particular on the Jerusalem ʿimaret. ʿİmarets have received limited attention before now, the only published research being the important studies cited above of Turkish scholars from a generation or two ago. Yet, but for a few exceptions, ʿimarets developed as separate and sizable institutions only under the Ottomans. Their presence in cities around the empire was thus a mark of Ottoman sovereignty as well as a means of imparting an Ottoman stamp to the city. In each place, an ʿimaret, like other large endowed structures, became part of the local urban fabric, both human and built. It altered expectations, not to mention sights, sounds, and smells, and rerouted the movement of people in space. The Jerusalem ʿimaret became a familiar landmark in the center of the city, one that has persisted for 450 years. From the outset, cooking for 500 people and serving them twice a day certainly altered the ambiance of the ʿAqabat al-Sitt quarter where it was located.

The genealogy of ʿimarets is a microcosm of the Ottoman heritage: Turkic, Mongol, Muslim, Persian, Arab, and Byzantine. The more short-term impetus that led to their development sprang from the Ottoman preoccupation with provisioning, a preoccupation highlighted by Ottoman efforts to control the supply of food throughout the empire. Channeling foodstuffs and meals to specific places and people reinforced the signs of privilege associated with class and rank (or lack thereof). In the public kitchens, provisioning crossed paths with the long-term practice of making waqfs. Waqfs supported a wide spectrum of institutions and services, most obviously those connected with prayer and study. Focusing on what had been a subsidiary function in mosques and *medrese*s, which chiefly sustained spiritual and intellectual aspects of Ottoman Muslim society, the ʿimarets emphasized support for basic physical existence as well. Food distributed in them reached a broad cross-section of Ottoman subjects, from imperial emissaries to established merchants, and including scholars, students, waqf functionaries, sufis, and the urban poor. All these people shared a temporary parity as recipients of endowed meals, identified as deserving because they lacked an immediate household or family to feed them, with no stigma attached to the event. Yet they were reminded, simultaneously, of the distance between them by the quality and quantity of the food they received, the order in which they were served and the place where they ate.

Investigating one ʿimaret has provided the unique opportunity to understand how such an institution fulfilled its charge, the myriad tasks required to serve meals to so many people. Clearly, the managers were the key to effective operations, yet even the best had a difficult job and, ultimately, mixed successes. Corrupt individuals at times headed the ʿimaret, were employed by it, or tried to use its resources selfishly for personal gains. The ʿimaret suffered because of natural disasters, regional conditions, or imperial policies. In the wake of the defeat at Lepanto in 1571, Ottoman enemies and pirates successfully interrupted shipping in the eastern Mediterranean. Thus in 1573, the manager reported to the kadi that he could not provide meals because the supply of rice from Egypt to Jerusalem had been cut.[2] In another instance, the ʿimaret was closed entirely in March 1585 when it ran out of supplies as a result of the too frequent (every six months) replacement of its managers in the preceding years.[3] Yet this situation was only temporary, as evidenced by the numerous accounts registers compiled for the years shortly thereafter.[4] Temporary closures continued to threaten the ʿimaret over time, however, reiterating its dependence on the presence of a capable manager. It was again closed in October 1626 until late the following spring, this time because the manager had gone away without leaving anyone to take over his responsibilities.[5]

In each instance cited, the problem was reported to the kadi so that he might correct the matter, accompanied by the complaint that the situation was harmful to the poor. Yet it does not seem that the ʿimaret was ever closed for very long or thoroughly derailed from its stated goals, though it suffered various deviations and checks. Evidently the kadis and the imperial administration in Istanbul, to which complaints were also forwarded, undertook seriously their roles in preserving the ʿimaret and maintaining its operations. How much of their commitment derived from pious dedication and humanitarian concern is not possible to calculate. Pressures from interested parties in Jerusalem and in the capital surely had some impact on the survival of the ʿimaret as well.

This close focus on the ʿimaret has clarified how normal were many of the processes connected to the establishment, management, and preservation of waqfs, processes some of which have been labelled in the past as corrupt. The idealized picture of waqf, born from the exquisitely constructed intention as penned in pristine and orderly texts of endowment deeds and normative law, must give way. Alongside it stands the imperfect execution as described in the view of waqfs based on reports, accounts registers *(muhasebe)* and judicial protocols. These depict a living endeavor, run by and serving human beings in the short run, though the institution was made for God, to last an eternity. The Haṣṣeki Sultan ʿimaret exemplifies the vulnerabilities of all waqfs yet demonstrates, too, how the ʿimaret fulfilled a crucial function in the city of Jerusalem despite its imperfections.

Hurrem Sultan established her presence in Jerusalem by founding the ʿimaret, which marked again the long reach of her power and beneficence. In the imperial Ottoman context, she was identified only with paradigmatic Muslim women who fulfilled the same role. On the ground in Jerusalem, however, Christians confounded her with other beneficent women tied to the place, melding her into the topos of a universal female figure providing for the weak. Hurrem's choice of what to do with her property and her ability or freedom to define the elements to be endowed was circumscribed, if not by direct order, then by the expectations of a subject population and the symbolic and practical needs of the dynasty or government. Her actions had to take familiar forms in order to be understood, forms that had come to represent imperial power and beneficence.

Hurrem's gender was a crucial factor in configuring her place in the imperial hierarchy, and it gave her defined rights and limitations within the framework of Islamic law. To some extent, beneficent action enabled her to transcend the social and cultural restrictions placed on her. The same was true for women elsewhere. With the Ottoman model firmly in mind, further comparative work to explore the undertakings of women will open a new avenue for cross-cultural studies. Beneficence was the purview of imperial or wealthy women in many cultures. Their undertakings often seem similar: material or medical aid to the poor, foundations specifically to aid women, spiritual institutions. A few cases will suffice to demonstrate how different legal and cultural conditions configured their beneficence in discrete ways, how varied were the motivations for and consequences of women's beneficence.

In Imperial Russia, pious women of means used their wealth for charitable purposes, founding religious communities, hospitals, schools, and housing. Like Muslim women, these Orthodox Christians kept their property even when married and so possessed the means for philanthropy in their own right. Several paragons who set up foundations and worked among the poor served as models for other wealthy women to emulate in their charitable endeavors. The historical study of Russian women as philanthropists provides a suggestive comparison as, in their case, it ultimately fostered the establishment of formal charitable associations among women in the modern era.[6] It would be interesting to learn whether Ottoman women in the upper ranks of society had any sense of shared undertaking in their philanthropy, and whether this ultimately led them to create beneficent associations at some later time.

Eighteenth-century Italy exemplifies a different climate of philanthropic giving by noblewomen. In Turin, the increasing number of donations by women to religious and secular charities is understood to have been part of a strategy for asserting their property rights against the claims of their husbands and sons to the property women brought with them to a marriage. The ability to make decisions about how to use their money, even if it was only to give it away, was important to these women, and the beneficiaries were various convents and refuges for women.[7] The antebellum United States demonstrates a similar aspect of women's beneficence. There, the transformation of charitable associations into formal corporate entities gave married women control over property and legal autonomy as officers of corporations that they lacked as individuals.[8]

Legal discrimination against women worldwide, along with limits imposed on them by social and cultural norms, have been fought with gradual success. In the past, one key aspect of beneficence shared among women was its use as a tool to achieve what might otherwise be inaccessible: public action, voice, and status. Now, more women are able to attain these goals directly. Moreover, the nature of women's beneficence is also shifting. In recent decades alone, women in significant numbers have moved into professional positions where they compete more equally with men to create and expend personal wealth. As this happens, women also noticeably reassess their giving strategies and preferences, making more independent decisions about where to give, less obliged by traditional practices or family to support the beneficiaries chosen and sustained by their fathers and husbands.[9]

Narrowing the focus to one waqf (while keeping an eye on others) has revealed many characteristics of imperial waqfs across the Ottoman empire. Without the detail presented, one would have little sense of the widespread micro-economic influence of waqfs, the nature of their operations or the immediate social meaning of their presence. Yet without the broader context of waqf-making, of the beneficent roles of imperial women, and of Ottoman provisioning policies, it would be hard to appreciate the aims and agendas being played out through the collectivity of individual institutions. Altogether, this study has demonstrated how an institution that seemingly served the weak or disadvantaged (however temporarily) was in fact an agent of power: for the imperial dynasty, for one imperial woman, for the person who managed the ʿimaret, for the peasants tied to it, and for those privileged enough to eat there.

Differences between individual endowments certainly existed in specific form and purpose, as well as with regard to their imperial and local standing, management of the properties, the clientele, the menus, etc. Each has its own specific history. Yet the study of the ʿimaret points out some important shared features of imperial endowments as agents of Ottomanization in provincial settings. Alongside the military and administrative institutions, they constituted another link to the imperial center in Istanbul, another Ottoman institution which was, in time, co-opted by local notables although never detached from its imperial connection. Local subjects of the Ottoman empire who were appointed to imperial waqf posts developed an interest in the continuation and stability of Ottoman rule. This identification with the Ottoman imperial project engendered loyalty alongside local self-interest; even when the administrative posts of the Haṣṣeki Sultan ʿimaret were taken over by local families, used in the competition for local status and power, they still remained Ottoman appointments and the ʿimaret an Ottoman endeavor.[10]

In Istanbul, the chief eunuch who supervised the ʿimaret from the Topkapı Palace used the waqf, along with the many others he controlled, to dispense patronage through appointments. At another level, the bond to the center was fiscal, whereby the waqfs delivered surplus revenues to Istanbul or received funds when in need of support. More importantly, this link established a permanent avenue of intervention from Istanbul, as well as a pipeline for complaints and petitions from Jerusalem. Political and financial bonds tied the province and the center through the waqf, since the sultan was obliged to continue his support of imperial provincial institutions once established. It would be a mark of dynastic and imperial weakness to let them founder, especially as decrepit buildings were sometimes more readily visible than ineffectual administrators.

No less important was the way the ʿimaret intruded and merged with the organization of property, patronage, and power at the local level. Because it was a waqf, dependent for its income on endowed properties, the ʿimaret also altered economic relationships. The ties of large waqfs to the countryside through their landholdings were not superficial; they refashioned the identities of villagers both proximate and remote, aligning them with the purposes of the waqf through their regular payments in kind or in cash, as well as the supply of other goods for purchase. Yet the villagers had little or no connection to the beneficence served up at the kitchen. That was intended for the pious poor, the travelers, the indigent, and whoever else managed to receive a bowl of soup and a loaf of bread.

Considered from almost any angle, the waqfs were constructions wholly embedded in the political, social, economic, and cultural fabric in which they existed. To see them as isolated entities empties them of meaning. Despite what the law codes seem to say about property endowed, the capital (in whatever form) made over to endowments was not imprisoned, as the comparison with European *mortmain* might imply. Using appropriate legal procedures, it remained part of the market in property. This dynamism was crucial for the maintenance and circulation of properties, keeping them in use and allowing for their reuse.[11] The same was true of the institutions benefited by endowed properties—mosques, colleges, fountains—since they might receive additional endowments and find new patrons to ensure or enhance their continuing operations.

Yet waqfs were something more than just single institutions, albeit of great influence in their settings. Collectively, waqfs constituted one of the fundamental organizational idioms for society as a whole, comparable in their importance and effect to the dynasty and the military corps. They were numerous and widespread enough to shape fundamentally economic activity, property ownership, urban-rural relations, and the physical shape of cities. Ritual and education were sustained and defined almost entirely through their agency.[12] All of this, moreover, was packaged in the language of beneficence, from the most personal and selfish of projects to the most public and grand.

The founding of waqfs by members of the imperial household was also part of a collective undertaking to enhance the Ottoman dynasty, reflecting the widespread use of waqfs by the imperial household for image-building and legitimation, social welfare, urban development, and food supply. These endowments aimed collectively to foster and uphold the ideal of the Ottoman sultan as a beneficent and just ruler, providing subsistence along with spiritual and intellectual support for his subjects. Both Süleyman and Hurrem were ambitious, conscious of the enormously powerful and successful empire which Süleyman led, and deliberate about enhancing its status and their own.

While imperial waqf-making can be seen as part of a collective endeavor, the initiative for establishing beneficent institutions as waqfs lay with individuals, and the recognition or acclaim gained from doing so, whether in this world or the next, redounded to the individual. Each waqf was an individual endeavor, the act of a single person who thereby sought to draw himself or herself closer to God. Sultans and others alike made waqfs as part of a spiritual calculus, no matter what their additional motivations might be.

Mottahedeh has observed that: "Some forms of *niʿmah* [benefit], like public works, resembled the vow in that they were transactions between a single man and an abstractly defined category of men; but those men were presumed to be grateful individually, and 'to invoke God's blessing' on the donor specifically rather than to be grateful in any corporate fashion."[13] This idea explains the way in which the sultan might appreciate his connection to his subjects. The right and real possibility for any subject to petition the sultan directly reinforced this perception. Yet did the Ottoman subjects perceive the sultan in his capacity of waqf maker as an entirely distinct individual and personality? When the single donor in question was the sultan, a member of his family, or even of the ruling elite, it was not so simple or straightforward to define his or her actions merely as those of an individual, seemingly undifferentiated other than in size from those of a wealthy merchant or modest artisan. The sultan's endowments, and those of people closely tied to or identified with him, had an impact that resonated far beyond the immediate neighborhood of their buildings. In this regard, imperial endowments possessed an ambiguous character, representing the efforts of an individual and at the same time the beneficence anticipated from the person-as-sultan. He fulfilled an obligation to promote the well-being of Ottoman subjects and personified the ideal of the ruler such that his actions were determined not only by personal volition but also by the expectations of his office.[14]

The dilemmas over the role of individuals and the role of government which have produced debates over the responsibilities of the modern welfare states did not exist in the Ottoman empire. Yet inevitably, and inextricably, the sultan's actions belonged to both individual and state realms, while the dilemma was absent because there was no clear division between the two. For the sultan, there was no truly private realm because his role as head of government was never set aside. The beneficent works of sultans, and their households by affiliation, were not only those of individuals identified by their personalities and achievements, but also the work of their offices. This idea goes counter to the insistent individualism in beneficent works that is generally emphasized when discussing *ṣadaqa* as a Muslim practice.[15] However, large-scale charitable undertakings seem to spring, too, from a popular expectation of office, one embedded in both the donors and the beneficiaries, an expectation born of long-term cultural practice and identity.

The formal vehicle of waqf certainly enjoyed enormous and long-lived popularity, easily retrievable by the historian. The other formal institution of charity was *zakāt*. Not much is known about the obligatory alms tax, but it does not appear to have played any significant role as a source of poor relief or beneficent aid in Ottoman times.[16] However, *informal* beneficence may well have rivalled waqf as a source of support and subsistence. Informal beneficence, for the purposes of this discussion, included all forms of donation and distribution that were not codified, recorded, or regulated. As a result, they did not create systematic documentary evidence. Yet while informal they were nonetheless institutionalized, in the sense that distributions often occurred at predictable times (holy days, personal celebrations, state occasions) and places (mosques, palaces, wealthy private homes, parade routes). Moreover, informal beneficence was expected from people of certain ranks and classes. The combination of expectation and predictability lent a more fixed and institutional quality to what otherwise appeared as a haphazard event.

A few examples highlight some key features of informal giving. One Caʿfer Efendi, in extolling the beneficence of his patron Mehmet Ağa, said:

> Many times his noble person experienced hardship. Yet at those times of want he did not act ungenerously in any way. At those times even more than at times of prosperity, his house became a public kitchen *[ʿimāret]* for travelers, free and slave, and equally for the great and the humble and for all neighbors and strangers, and various delectables and foods were set out day and night.[17]

Not only was Mehmet generous in the normal course of things, but he made a point of maintaining his open door even in more straitened circumstances.

This theme recurs. In the early twentieth century, a certain Enis Paşa was forcibly retired from imperial service on a meager pension. He nonetheless maintained his kitchen as before. Daily, it served the twenty-three people who formed his household and never fewer than ten other guests. In addition to these, "there were many poor of the mansion" *("Konağın fakir fukarası çoktur")* who expected to receive food and whom the paşa was accustomed to feed. He also kept a bath attached to the house, open for use to people in the neighboring quarters. Even when the paşa's household itself had none, its depot still fed the faucets where the poor could get water.[18]

Thus the ʿimarets were not the only locations where food was distributed. As pointed out, mosques, *medreses*, and sufi residences traditionally fed some people, though not necessarily every day. Others, too, took an active role in feeding the poor and travelers. Evliya Çelebi noted this in describing the city of Bitlis:

> Formerly the soup-kitchens of Sheref Khan and Khatuniyye and Khusrev Pasha were operative, dispensing nourishment to all travellers and visitors. But now their *evḳāf* [waqfs] have fallen to ruin, and they dispense soup only for Ashura and during the nights of Ramazan. But in fact there is no need for them since all the houses have open doors and host wayfarers like public banquet-halls.[19]

In Evliya's Bitlis, the ʿimarets were reduced to only part-time distributions, reminiscent of those afforded by non-specialized institutions. The slack was taken up by private individuals.

It was also the case that the palaces of the princesses and other members of the elite in Istanbul, which regularly received distributions of cooked food and food stuffs from the Topkapı Palace, in turn fed a wide range of people from their own kitchens. Some of what they received was immediately passed on, either to individuals or institutions like ʿimarets or sufi residences.[20] Ṭunshūq's house in Jerusalem could well have been the source of similar food distributions to the surrounding neighborhood. Though only a few examples are given here of informal food distribution, the picture is quite suggestive. At several levels of society, perhaps almost all, the stronger regularly shared their food with the weaker. This was not an occasional event but rather a basic mechanism of subsistence built into the fabric of society.

What made voluntary beneficence so central a component in Ottoman society? It is striking that canonical charity had such a meager presence (or left so little trace) while at the same time a thriving culture of giving existed. The legal institutions of *zakāt* and prescribed maintenance payments to needy family members *(nafaqa),* which were intended to ensure the subsistence of weaker people in society, became subsumed by waqfs and direct informal distributions.[21] Clearly, people felt a compulsion, if not an obligation, to be beneficent, to help the deserving targets of charity. They also, it seems, were more enthusiastic about doing so on their own terms and not through any imperial office or central authority. The wealthiest and most powerful people in the Ottoman empire did not pay taxes. This did not, however, mean that they were unwilling to invest part of their income in the welfare of the larger population. Using waqfs and informal beneficence, however, they maintained control over their distributions, whereas *zakāt* would have been collected and disbursed by state agents. By retaining discretionary control over the monies that they distributed—whether in kind or in cash—the donors also preserved their own power and even enhanced it, as they acquired loyal clients. At the same time, they emphasized and preserved existing social hierarchies, in a daily ritual that acknowledged strength and confirmed dependence.

Beneficence was thus central to Ottoman society. The examples of Mehmet Ağa and Enis Paşa suggest that it did not necessarily result from surplus wealth nor was it a practice which was lightly undertaken. Beneficence such as that practiced by these two men was a social obligation taken on sincerely, at huge personal cost, based on a commitment to certain religiously taught values. At the same time, their generosity served to acquire and maintain a particular social status. It was a marker of that status, not to be relinquished easily, even in difficult financial circumstances. On humanitarian grounds, too, once taken on, the responsibility for sustaining those who accepted beneficence could not be casually shed. In a similar way, the 'imaret created expectations and commitments. Public kitchens and private households alike worked hard to fulfill the expectations they established, perceiving that their ability to do so buttressed their status and power—indeed, defined it.[22]

The idea of the poor person, the *faḳir*, is a reflection of how beneficence was used to reinforce the status quo and not tied necessarily to material circumstances. *Faḳir* described the sufi, voluntarily impoverished in the pursuit of spiritual wealth. At the same time, *bu faḳir* is a regular term used by Ottoman writers to refer to themselves, often translated as "this humble one." In their address to their patrons, these *faḳirs* and other clients emphasized their condition of subservience and dependence, making them suitable recipients of beneficence. If we understand that charity was legitimately aimed at all dependents, this explains the enormous spectrum of beneficiaries at the 'imaret and at countless other waqfs.

And the results? Did 'imarets and waqfs create a class of parasitic dependents, as is sometimes maintained? Without a sense of what percentage of daily nourishment was in fact obtained from public kitchens and informal handouts, and for what percentage of those who ate from them, we cannot say. This study has focused on the donors and the institutions they set up. To investigate further the recipients and the broad impact of the 'imarets on them is an entirely separate, perhaps impossible, task.

Examining the practice of beneficence and the identity of its donors and clients has elucidated many of the aims of Ottoman imperial beneficence. In every instance, the aim of doing good and thereby finding favor in God's eyes, was one motive for founding a waqf, although we have seen that waqfs achieved far more than this. Like the specific example of the ʿimarets, beneficence was an agent of control, channeling resources to predetermined activities, admitting specific people as recipients. It did not aim to change the social order but rather to preserve it. Food distributions were not intended to help people free themselves from dependence on aid but only to succor and sustain them, a way of life for both donors and recipients. In this, the Ottomans shared much with other pre-modern societies. However, Ottoman beneficence was an entire way of life, an ideal and many practices that engaged individuals throughout society. The practices, more specifically the ʿimarets, were a particular solution to one of the most persistent concerns of individuals and governments: how to ensure the welfare of dependents and self alike.

# Notes

## Introduction

1. From the endowment deed *(waqfiyya)* found in the Khalidi Library (Jerusalem), Tur. 4, ff. 49–52. This deed was published in facsimile and translation by St. H. Stephan, "An Endowment Deed of Khâsseki Sultân, Dated 24th May 1552," *Quarterly of the Department of Antiquities in Palestine* 10 (1944): 170–94. Translations in the present work are those of the author unless otherwise noted. "Employees" in this translation is a summary of the list given in the deed. Friday evening is actually the evening before Friday, i.e. Thursday evening, as days in the Muslim calendar begin from the previous sundown.

2. For plans of the building and outlines of the constructions on the site from various periods, see the contributions of David Myres, "Al-ʿImara al-ʾAmira: the Charitable Foundation of Khassaki Sultan (959/1552)," and Yusuf Natsheh, "Al-ʿImara al-ʾAmira: the Charitable Foundation of Khassaki Sultan (959/1552)," in *Ottoman Jerusalem. The Living City: 1517–1917,* ed. S. Auld and R. Hillenbrand (London: Altajir World of Islam Trust 2000), 539–82, 747–90. These extensive surveys are the only coherent guide to the physical character of the endowment and provide detailed explanations of most parts of the complex. Some remain to be clarified.

3. See TSAD #1585, dated 15 Şaban 958/15 August 1551, which lists repair costs during the two years preceding, including materials and labor.

4. Antoine Morison, *Relation Historique d'un Voyage Nouvellement Fait au Mont de Sinaï et à Jérusalem* (Paris: Antoine Dezallier, 1705), 387. (My translation. A. S.)

5. Ermete Pierotti, *Jerusalem Explored, Being A Description of the Ancient and Modern City, with Numerous Illustrations Consisting of Views, Ground Plans, and Sections,* trans. Th. Geo. Bonney (London: Bell and Daldy, 1864), I:150–53. On the title page, Pierotti is described as "doctor of mathematics, architect-

engineer, civil and military, to his Excellency [the Governor] Suraya Pasha of Jerusalem."

6. Yusuf Sa'id Natshe, "My Memories of Khassaki Sultan or 'The Flourishing Edifice,' " *Jerusalem Quarterly File* 7 (2000). See Ra'if Yusuf Nijm et al. *Kunūz al-Quds* (Milan: Matabi Brughiriyu, 1983), 249–52, which described in detail the state of the buildings and the repairs needed.

7. The term *haṣṣeki* (favorite) describes the woman preferred by the sultan, hence Hurrem was known as Haṣṣeki Sulṭan. On this see Pakalın, I:752–53 and Leslie P. Peirce, *The Imperial Harem: Women and Sovereignty in the Ottoman Empire* (New York: Oxford University Press, 1993), 63, 89, 95–96, 127–28.

8. For an introduction to the topic, see Y. Linant de Bellefonds, *"hiba," EI²*, III:350–51 and Franz Rosenthal, et al., *"hiba," EI²*, III:342–50.

9. The classic work on gifts is that of Marcel Mauss, *The Gift: The Form and Reason for Exchange in Archaic Societies,* trans. W.D. Halls (London: Routledge, 1990). Most recently, Natalie Zemon Davis has explored the status, meanings, and uses of gifts in *The Gift in Sixteenth-Century France* (Madison: University of Wisconsin Press, 2000).

10. Amy Singer, *Palestinian peasants and Ottoman officials* (Cambridge, UK: Cambridge University Press, 1994).

11. See, for example, the work of Robert D. McChesney, which examines the shrine complex at Balkh (Afghanistan) over a period of several hundred years, *Waqf in Central Asia: Four Hundred Years in the History of a Muslim Shrine, 1480–1889* (Princeton: Princeton University Press, 1991).

12. The Topkapı Palace Archives, the Başbakanlık Arşivi (both in Istanbul) and the Vakıflar Umum Müdürlüğü in Ankara all contain endowment deeds, accounts registers, and other documents about waqfs all across the empire. Where local archives remain—as in Damascus, Jerusalem, and Cairo—there are often similar records extant. In addition, the registers of judicial proceedings (Tur. *kadı sicilleri,* Ar. *sijillāt*) everywhere in the empire preserve details, though not systematically recorded, of waqf management. On the archives and their contents, see *Başbakanlık Osmanlı Arşivi Katalogları Rehberi,* Osmanlı Arşivi Daire Başkanlığı, yayın nu. 5 (Ankara, 1992), yayın nu. 26 (Ankara, 1995); M.A. Bakhit, *Kashshāf iḥṣā'ī zamanī li-sijillāt al-maḥākim al-shar'iyya wa'l-awqāf al-islāmiyya fī bilād al-Shām,* (Amman: Markaz al-Wathā'iq wa'l-Makhṭūṭāt, 1984); and Suraiya Faroqhi, *Approaching Ottoman History: An Introduction to the Sources* (Cambridge UK: Cambridge University Press, 1999) 49–57, 59–61.

13. I saw both of these 'imarets in operation in 1995. Freely, in 1983, said that the Eyüp 'imaret was the only one still operating in Istanbul; see John Freely, *Blue Guide: Istanbul* (London: Ernest Benn, 1983), 296. By 1999, at least one other, the Ahmediye in Üsküdar, was again functioning (personal communication from John Freely).

14. For different sorts of waqf critique, see W. Heffening, *"wakf,"* in *SEI,* 627–28 and H. A. R. Gibb and Harold Bowen, *Islamic Society and the West. Vol. 1: Islamic Society in the Eighteenth Century* (London: Oxford University Press, 1950), Pt. 2:165–78. For discussions of the critique, see McChesney, *Waqf in Central Asia,* 5; John Robert Barnes, *An Introduction to Religious Foundations in*

*the Ottoman Empire* (Leiden: Brill, 1987), 51–65; and D.S. Powers, "Orientalism, Colonialism and Legal History: The Attack on Muslim Family Endowments in Algeria and India," *Comparative Studies in Society and History* 31 (1989): 535–71.

15. It does not, however, offer a detailed disquisition on the enormous topic of waqf law as it developed in Islam, nor specifically on the Ḥanafī school of law *(madhhab)* that predominated under the Ottomans. On this latter, see W. Heffening and J. Schacht, *"ḥanafiyya," EI²*, III:162–64. On waqf law, there are dozens of sources. A useful beginning point will be the new article by Rudolph Peters, *"wakf," EI²*, XI:59–63.

16. Peirce, *The Imperial Harem,* 205–12.

17. *Aş* means "cooked food" and is also used to describe a kind of soup; *hane* designates a house, or a building or room set aside for a specific purpose.

18. Suraiya Faroqhi, "Sayyid Gazi Revisited: The Foundation as Seen Through Sixteenth and Seventeenth Century Documents," *Turcica* 13 (1981): 90–122; eadem, "The Tekke of Haci Bektaş: Social Position and Economic Activities," *IJMES* 7 (1976): 183–208; eadem, "A Great Foundation in Difficulties: Or Some Evidence on Economic Contraction in the Ottoman Empire of the Mid-Seventeenth Century," in *Mélanges Professeur Robert Mantran,* ed. A. Temimi (Zaghouan: CEROMDE, 1988), 109–21; Miriam Hoexter, *Endowments, Rulers and Community: Waqf al-Ḥaramayn in Ottoman Algiers* (Leiden: Brill, 1998); and Ronald C. Jennings, "Pious Foundations in the Society and Economy of Ottoman Trabzon, 1565–1640. A Study Based on the Judicial Registers (*Şer'i Mahkeme Sicilleri*) of Trabzon," *JESHO* 33 (1990): 271–336.

19. G. Baer, "The Waqf as a Prop for the Social System, 16th–20th Centuries," *Islamic Law and Society* 4 (1997): 264–97; idem, "Women and Waqf: An Analysis of the Istanbul Tahrîr of 1546," *Asian and African Studies* 17 (1983): 9–27; idem, "The Dismemberment of *Awqâf* in Early Nineteenth-Century Jerusalem," in *Ottoman Palestine 1800–1914,* ed. Gad G. Gilbar, (Leiden: Brill, 1990), 299–319; Ö. L. Barkan, "Osmanlı İmparatorluğunda Bir İskân ve Kolonizasyon Metodu Olarak Vakıflar ve Temlikler," *Vakiflar Dergisi* 2 (1942): 279–386; H. Gerber, "The Waqf Institution in Early Ottoman Edirne," *Asian and African Studies* 17 (1983): 29–45; and Bahaeddin Yediyıldız, *Institution du Vaqf au XVIIIe siècle en Turquie—Étude socio-historique* (Ankara: Imprimerie de la Société d'Histoire Turque, 1985).

20. Hoexter, *Endowments, Rulers and Community.*

21. McChesney, *Waqf in Central Asia,* 5.

## CHAPTER 1

1. All citations from the *Qur'an* are from A. J. Arberry, *The Koran Interpreted* (Oxford: Oxford University Press, 1983). Subsequent citations will give *sura* and verse in the text in parenthesis with no further reference.

2. Muslim b. al-Hajjāj al-Qushayri, *Ṣaḥīḥ Muslim* (Cairo: Dar al-Ghad al-'Arabi, 1987–1990), Kitāb al-waṣiyya 4.

3. Gabriel Baer, "The Muslim Waqf and Similar Institutions in Other Civilizations" (unpublished paper presented at the Workshop on Economic and Social Aspects of the Muslim Waqf, Jerusalem, 1981), 1. For a recent work which investigates philanthropy around the globe, see W. Ilchman, S. N. Katz, and E. L. Queen, eds, *Philanthropy in the World's Traditions* (Bloomington: Indiana University Press, 1998).

4. Most of the sources on waqf cited in this work have something to say on the subject. See Heffening, *"wakf,"* 625–26. McChesney's discussion serves as a complement to Heffening's; see Robert D. McChesney, *Charity and Philanthropy in Islam: Institutionalizing the Call to Do Good* (Indianapolis: Indiana University Center on Philanthropy, 1995), 2–5. See also Peter Charles Hennigan, "The Birth of a Legal Institution: The Formation of the Waqf in the Third Century A. H. Ḥanafī Legal Discourse" (Ph.d. diss. Cornell University, 1999), 209–31.

5. As told in Heffening, *"wakf,"* 625.

6. Bahaeddin Yediyıldız, *"vakıf," İA*, XIII:153–54.

7. J. Schacht, "Early Doctrines on Waqf," in *Fuad Köprülü Armağanı* (Istanbul: Osman Yalçın Matbaası, 1953), 443–52; Claude Cahen, "Réflexions sur le *Waqf* Ancien," *Studia Islamica* 14 (1961): 37–56; McChesney, *Waqf in Central Asia*, 7; Hennigan, "The Birth of a Legal Institution," 5; Peters, *"wakf."*

8. G. Baer, "Waqf Reform in Egypt," *Middle Eastern Affairs* 1 (1958): 61–76; J. N. D. Anderson, "The Sharia and Civil Law: The Debt Owed by the New Civil Codes of Egypt and Syria to the Sharia," *Islamic Quarterly* 1 (1954): 29–46; idem, "Recent Developments in Sharīʿa Law IX: The Waqf System" *Muslim World* 42 (1952): 257–76; idem, *Law Reform in the Muslim World* (London: Athlone, 1976), passim; Gregory C. Kozlowski, *Muslim Endowments and Society in British India* (Cambridge, UK: Cambridge University Press, 1985); Yitzhak Reiter, *Waqf in Jerusalem 1948–1990* (Hebrew) (Jerusalem: Jerusalem Institute for Israel Studies 1991); Aharon Layish, "The Muslim Waqf in Israel," *Asian and African Studies* 2 (1966): 41–76; and see the studies in Faruk Bilici, ed., *Le Waqf dans le monde musulman contemporain (XIXe-XXe siècles): Fonctions sociales, économiques et politiques* (Istanbul: Institut Français d'Etudes Anatoliennes, 1994), especially those by Bilici, Arda, Bolak, and Arslan on Turkey, Deguilhem on Syria, and Layish and Reiter on Jerusalem.

9. S. D. Goitein, *Muslim Law in the State of Israel* (Hebrew) (Jerusalem, 1957), 156–57; Norman A. Stillman, "Waqf and the Ideology of Charity in Medieval Islam," in *Hunter of the East: Studies in Honor of Clifford Edmund Bosworth. Vol. 1: Arabic and Semitic Studies*, ed. I. R. Netton (Leiden: Brill, 2000), 357–58; Marshall G. S. Hodgson, *The Venture of Islam* (Chicago: University of Chicago Press, 1974), I:292–94; and Michael Dols, *Majnūn: The Madman in Medieval Islamic Society* (Oxford: Oxford University Press, 1992), 469–70.

10. Norman A. Stillman, "Charity and Social Service in Medieval Islam," *Societas* 5 (1975): 105–15.

11. U. Haarmann, "Islamic Duties in History," *Muslim World* 68 (1978): 14; Semih Tezcan, *Bir Ziyafet Defteri* (Istanbul: Simurg, 1998), 9; and Peirce, *The Imperial Harem*, 198.

12. The same word is spelled differently in Latin characters depending on the language from which it is transliterated. Thus one may find *vakıf/evkaf* (Turkish) and *vaqf/vaqouf* (Persian), as well as other variants. *Ḥubs* (pl. *aḥbās*) is an Arabic synonym for *waqf* and the word more commonly used for this institution in North Africa, where the Mālikī school of law is prevalent. On the basic legal aspects of waqf, see Peters, *"wakf,"* who includes the classical Arabic bibliography on the subject. See also Yediyıldız, *"vakıf,"* which includes references to the extensive writing in Turkish not found in Peters. A nineteenth-century text of Ḥanafī law pertaining to waqf is Muḥammad Qadrī Pāshā (d. 1888), *Qānūn al-ʿadl wa'l-inṣāf li'l-qaḍā ʿalā mushkilat al-awqāf,* 3d ed. (Bulaq, 1902/1320 A.H.) General discussion in English about waqf law may be found in A. A. A. Fyzee, *Outline of Muhammadan Law,* 3d ed. (London: Oxford University Press, 1964), 223–81; the section entitled "The Law of Waqf" in George Makdisi, *The Rise of Colleges* (Edinburgh: Edinburgh University Press, 1981), 35–74; and Henry Cattan, "The Law of Waqf," in *Law in the Middle East,* ed. M. Khadduri and Herbert J. Liebseny (Washington, D.C., 1955), 203–22.

13. Peters, *"wakf,"*; Yediyıldız, *Institution du Vaqf,* 178–82, discusses the particular status of the *kapıkulları* (slaves of the sultan) as waqf founders. Men and women alike serving in the Ottoman upper echelons made endowments even though they were technically unfree; for this they required, and apparently obtained, imperial permission. The case of ʿOsman Ağa, chief eunuch of Topkapı Palace, illustrates the tenuousness of this situation. He was ordered to build a mosque by Sultan Meḥmed III (r. 1595–1603), and given permission to found a waqf for it. However, a few years later, Safiye Sultan, mother of Meḥmed III, had his waqf invalidated, claiming that ʿOsman was a slave and had never been given permission to build the mosque. D. Behrens-Abouseif, *Egypt's Adjustment to Ottoman Rule: Institutions, Waqf and Architecture in Cairo (16th & 17th Centuries)* (Leiden: Brill 1994), 173, 176.

14. See J. Mandaville, "Usurious Piety: The Cash Waqf Controversy in the Ottoman Empire," *IJMES* 10 (1979): 298. On cash waqfs, see also Colin Imber, *Ebus's-suʿud. The Islamic Legal Tradition* (Stanford: Stanford University Press, 1997), 142–46 and Murat Çızakça, "Cash Waqfs in Bursa, 1555–1823," *JESHO* 38 (1995): 313–54.

15. On different aspects of salaries as paid by waqfs, see Makdisi, *The Rise of Colleges,* 163–65 and Jonathan P. Berkey, *The Transmission of Knowledge in Medieval Cairo: A Social History of Islamic Education* (Princeton: Princeton University Press, 1992), 774-78, 82.

16. Schacht, "Early Doctrines on Waqf," 444–45.

17. Eugenia Kermeli shows how, under the guidance of the pragmatic *şeyhülislam* Ebu's-Suʿud Efendi, the Ottomans recognized some traditional monastic trusts in the Balkans and Thrace as comparable to family waqfs, with the monks constituting a family. See her "Ebū Suʿūd's Definitions of Church *Vaḳfs*: Theory and Practice in Ottoman Law," in *Islamic Law: Theory and Practice,* ed. Robert Gleave and Eugenia Kermeli (London: I. B. Tauris, 1997), 147, 152–53. See also Richard van Leeuwen, *Notables and Clergy in Mount*

*Lebanon: The Khāzin Sheiks and the Maronite Church (1735–1840)* (Amsterdam: Institute for Near Eastern and Islamic Studies, 1992), 34–36, 168–70; *idem*, "The Maronite Waqf of Dayr Sayyidat Bkirkī in Mount Lebanon During the 18th Century," in *Le Waqf dans l'espace islamique: Outil de pouvoir socio-politique*, ed. Randi Deguilhem (Damas: Institut Français de Damas, 1995), 259–75; and Moshe Gil on the "waqf of dhimmis" in *Documents of the Jewish Pious Foundations from the Cairo Geniza* (Leiden: Brill, 1976), 8–10.

18. Schacht, "Early Doctrines on Waqf," 446–49 and Peters, *"wakf."* See the Arabic endowment deed of the Haşşeki Sultan ʿimaret in the Türk ve İslam Eserleri Müzesi (TİEM) #2192, fol. 46v ff. or K.J. Al-ʿAsalī, *Wathā'iq Maqdisiyya Ta'rīkhiyya* (Amman: al-Jāmiʿa al-Urdunniyya, 1983), 141.

19. See Peters, *"wakf"*. One example of such a stipulation is from the *waqfiyya* of Aḥmed Paşa and reads: "if the vicissitudes of time prevent and their [the mosques and the soup kitchen supported by the endowment] restoration be rendered impossible, the income of the above-mentioned trusts shall be distributed among the righteous Muslims and poor monotheists" *(ṣuleḥa-i muslimine ve fuqara-i muveḥḥidine)*. M. A. Simsar, *The Waqfiyah of 'Aḥmed Pāšā* (Philadelphia: University of Pennsylvania Press, 1940), 140.

20. See Simsar, *The Waqfiyah of 'Aḥmed Pāšā*, 190–92, on the authority of the kadi and manager according to Ḥanafī law. On the nature of the kadi's relationship to waqfs and his role in overseeing their well-being, as part of his responsibility to the general welfare of the Muslim community, see Miriam Hoexter, "*Ḥuqūq Allāh* and *Ḥuqūq al-ʿIbād* as Reflected in the Waqf Institution," *Jerusalem Studies in Arabic and Islam* 19 (1995): 141–46.

21. Abu Yūsuf maintained that the verbal commitment was sufficient; see Goitein, *Muslim Law*, p. 160, on *qaul*. One example of a *waqfiyya* inscribed on the building itself is the Mirjaniya *medrese* in Baghdad, for which see Robert Hillenbrand, *Islamic Architecture: Form, Function, and Meaning* (New York: Columbia University Press, 1994), 28–29; another example is the Burujiyya medrese in Sivas, on which see Albert Gabriel, *Les monuments turcs d'anatolie* (Paris: E. de Boccard, 1934), 2:154–55.

22. The waqfiyya of the Haşşeki Sultan ʿimaret was copied into the Jerusalem *sijill* in 1203/1788–89. This text is reproduced in Shaykh Asʿad al-Imām Al-Ḥusaynī, *Al-Manhal al-Ṣāfī fī'l-Waqf wa-Aḥkāmihi* (Jerusalem, 1982), 78–93 and in Al-ʿAsalī, *Wathā'iq*, 127–42.

23. See Heffening, *"wakf,"* 627, who uses *mortmain* and the translation "dead hand" to emphasize this view. Heffening's article, written for the first edition of the *Encyclopedia of Islam* (1931), has been until very recently the basic general reference on waqf for scholars who need a succinct statement about the subject. He has thus made no small contribution to the generally negative views about waqf within and outside the field of Middle Eastern and Islamic history. The work of Fyzee is another much-cited modern work on waqf which has contributed its negative views to the general one, on which see Fyzee, *Outline*, 232–34. On corruption and waqfs, see also H. A. B. Rivlin, *The Agricultural Policy of Muḥammad ʿAlī in Egypt* (Cambridge, MA: Harvard University Press, 1961), 35 and Gibb and Bowen, *Islamic Society and the West*, Vol. I, Pt. 2,

pp. 177–78. For a cogent analysis of how negative attitudes to waqf evolved as part of colonial rule by the French in Algeria and the British in India, see Powers, "Orientalism, Colonialism and Legal History."

24. See Majid Khadduri, *"maṣlaḥa," EI*², VI:738–40 and McChesney, *Waqf in Central Asia,* 11–13.

25. *Qur'an* II:82, 83, 110, 215, 273, 277; IX:60, 103. See also M. Berger, *"khayr," EI*², IV:1151–53; T. H. Weir and A. Zysow, *"ṣadaḳa," EI*², VIII:708–16; and J. Schacht, *"zakāt," SEI,* 654–56.

26. On this see McChesney, *Charity and Philanthropy in Islam,* 8, and Schacht, "Early Doctrines on *Waqf,*" 447.

27. A. R. Hands, *Charities and Social Aid in Greece and Rome* (Ithaca: Cornell University Press, 1968).

28. Franz Rosenthal, "Ṣedaḳa, Charity," *Hebrew Union College Annual* 23 (1950–51): 429. Rosenthal's article deals specifically with the evolution of the term from its general meaning of righteousness to the specific one of obligatory alms-giving.

29. Mark R. Cohen, "Poverty as Reflected in the Genizah Documents," typescript, p. 2, to be published in the Proceedings of the Seventh International Conference of the Society for Judaeo-Arabic Studies, ed. Paul Fenton (forthcoming). My thanks to the author for sharing with me the typescript of his paper.

30. Weir and Zysow, *"ṣadaḳa,"* 708–09. For a much later period, extensive evidence on Jewish charitable organization and practice exists from the Cairo Geniza. Jewish practices in Fatimid Cairo and Fustat are discussed extensively by S. D. Goitein in *A Mediterranean Society,* Vol. 2 (Berkeley: University of California Press, 1971), 91–143. Gil, *Documents of the Jewish Pious Foundations,* 1–36, 102–17, also discusses the Jewish *heqdēsh* (endowment) with reference to its origins and evolution and, more extensively, the relationship between *heqdēsh* and waqf, as elucidated by the documents of the Geniza. Other influences on the initial evolution of waqf included ancient Sheban tradition from Yemen and Arabian tradition from the time of idol worship. See Goitein, *Muslim Law,* 155. Dedications of property to the Kaʿaba in pre-Islamic Mecca may also have served as a partial model for the early waqf, on which see Barnes, *An Introduction to Religious Foundations,* 7 (though Barnes gives this possibility little credence).

31. On Byzantine charitable institutions and their development generally, see Demetrios J. Constantelos, *Byzantine Philanthropy and Social Welfare* (New Brunswick: Rutgers University Press, 1968); idem, *Poverty, Society and Philanthropy in the Late Medieval Greek World* (New Rochelle, NY: Aristide D. Caratzas, 1992); P. W. Duff, "The Charitable Foundations of Byzantium," in *Cambridge Legal Essays* (Cambridge, MA: Harvard University Press, 1926), 83–99; and Evelyne Patlagean, *Pauvreté économique et pauvreté sociale à Byzance 4e-7e siècles* (Paris: Mouton 1977).

32. Judith Herrin, "From Bread and Circuses to Soup and Salvation: The Origins of Byzantine Charity," Davis Center Paper (Princeton, 1985), 16, 20, 26 and *eadem,* "Ideals of Charity, Realities of Welfare: The Philanthropic Activity

of the Byzantine Church," in *Church and People in Byzantium,* ed. Rosemary Morris (Birmingham: University of Birmingham, 1990), 153–58.

33. A. G. Perikhanian, "Iranian Society and Law," in *Cambridge History of Iran, Vol. 3(2),* ed. Ehsan Yarshatar (Cambridge, UK: Cambridge University Press, 1983), 661–63 and McChesney, *Charity and Philanthropy,* 5–6.

34. See the discussion in Barnes, *An Introduction to Religious Foundations,* 8–16, especially as it pertains to Roman and Byzantine influences, which he favors. Hennigan also stresses that the origins of waqf are not easily discernible. He contrasts this evolution of the institution with the clear genesis of the laws of inheritance *(ʿilm al-farāʾiḍ)* from explicit Qur'anic statements. Hennigan, "The Birth of a Legal Institution," 230–31.

35. In Cahen's opinion, waqf seems, in fact, to be an institution developed almost entirely within Islam, "*sui generis* . . . [an institution] which has less to do with separate religious institutions and more to do with the organization of society generally, whose explanation should thus be sought in the specific traits of Muslim society, its Arab past and the conditions of life during its first generations." Cahen, "Réflexions sur le *Waqf* Ancien," 55 (My translation. A. S.)

36. Haarmann, "Islamic Duties in History," 8–15.

37. Hodgson, *The Venture of Islam,* II:124.

38. An historical record of alms-giving, too, remains to be traced. Other than the *Qur'an,* writing about *zakāt* is found more extensively in legal texts than other kinds of evidence for historical practice. See Schacht, "*zakāt*" and McChesney, *Charity and Philanthropy,* 7. Normative legal texts might be used to investigate changing attitudes to *zakāt* as a reflection of changing practices, but such a study does not yet exist; see Stillman, "Charity and Social Service," 107–09. "Poor" *(faqīr)* and "rich" *(ghanī)* are used here as legal categories, defining who was eligible to receive alms and who was obliged to pay them. On this see Hennigan, "The Birth of a Legal Institution," 234, 237.

39. McChesney, *Charity and Philanthropy,* 11–12.

40. For more on *qurba,* see J. N. D. Anderson, "The Religious Element in Waqf Endowments, *Journal of the Royal Central Asian Society* 38 (1951): 292.

41. Stephan, "An Endowment Deed," 180. The Qur'anic citation is XXVIII:77.

42. *Qur'an* II:82, LVII:18 and see also Weir, "*ṣadaḳa,*" VIII:709–10, 712.

43. Halil Inalcik, "Istanbul: An Islamic City," *Journal of Islamic Studies* 1 (1990): 1–23 and Heffening, "*waḳf,*" 627.

44. Hodgson, *The Venture of Islam,* II:214.

45. Michael Chamberlain, *Knowledge and Social Practice in Medieval Damascus, 1190–1350* (Cambridge, UK: Cambridge University Press, 1994), 50–52 and R. Stephen Humphreys, "Politics and Architectural Patronage in Ayyubid Damascus," in *The Islamic World: From Classical to Modern Times,* ed. C.E. Bosworth and Charles Issawi (Princeton: The Darwin Press, Inc., 1989), 166–67.

46. Berkey, *The Transmission of Knowledge,* 95–107; Carl F. Petry, "A Paradox of Patronage During the Later Mamluk Period," *Muslim World* 73 (1983): 202; Gary Leiser, "The Endowment of the al-Zahariyya in Damascus,"

*JESHO* 27 (1984): 33–55; Michael H. Burgoyne, *Mamluk Jerusalem: An Architectural Study* (London: World of Islam Festival Trust, 1987), *passim;* Leonor Fernandes, "Mamluk Architecture and the Question of Patronage," *Mamluk Studies Review* 1 (1997): 107–20.

47. Ira M. Lapidus, *A History of Islamic Societies* (Cambridge, UK: Cambridge University Press, 1988), 164–67, 236, 279.

48. See Speros Vryonis Jr., *The Decline of Medieval Hellenism in Asia Minor and the Process of Islamization from the Eleventh Through the Fifteenth Century* (Berkeley: University of California Press, 1971), 221 ff. and Howard Crane, "Notes on Saldjūq Architectural Patronage in Thirteenth Century Anatolia," *JESHO* 36 (1993): 7.

49. Berkey, *The Transmission of Knowledge,* s.v. "salaries," "student stipends."

50. Barnes, *An Introduction to Religious Foundations,* Chapter 8 "The Decline of Religious Foundations," 118–53.

51. Hillenbrand, *Islamic Architecture,* 215–17.

52. On this see Ö. L. Barkan, "Osmanlı İmparatorluğunda Bir İskân ve Kolonizasyon Metodu"; Semavi Eyice, "İlk Osmanlı Devrinin Dini-İctimai Bir Müessesesi: Zâviyeler ve Zâviyeli-Camiler," *İstanbul Üniversitesi İktisat Fakültesi Mecmuası* 23 (1962–63): 1–80; Halil Inalcik, *The Ottoman Empire: The Classical Age 1300–1600* (London: Weidenfeld and Nicolson, 1973), 149–50; Ronald C. Jennings, *Christians and Muslims in Ottoman Cyprus and the Mediterranean World, 1571–1640* (New York: New York University Press, 1993), 40–68; Aharon Layish, "Waqfs and Sûfî Monasteries in the Ottoman Policy of Colonization: Sultân Selîm I's Waqf of 1516 in Favor of Dayr al-Asad," *Bulletin of the School of Oriental and African Studies* 50 (1987): 61–89; and Machiel Kiel, "The Vakifnâme of Raḳḳas Sinân Beg in Karnobat (Ḳarîn-âbâd) and the Ottoman Colonization of Bulgarian Thrace (14th–15th Century)," *Osmanlı Araştırmaları/Journal of Ottoman Studies* 1 (1980): 15–32.

53. Inalcik, "Istanbul: An Islamic City." On the different complexes, see Godfrey Goodwin, *A History of Ottoman Architecture* (Baltimore: Johns Hopkins University Press, 1971); Çiğdem Kafescioğlu, "The Ottoman Capital in the Making: The Reconstruction of Constantinople in the Fifteenth Century," (Ph.D. diss. Harvard University, 1996), 283–372; and also Freely, *Blue Guide: Istanbul.*

54. Muṣṭafā b. Ahmet ʿAlī *Muṣṭafā ʿAlī's Counsel for Sultans of 1581,* ed. and trans. Andreas Tietze (Vienna: Österreichische Akademie der Wissenschaften, 1979), I:54, 146.

55. A. K. S. Lambton, *Continuity and Change in Medieval Persia: Aspects of Administrative, Economic and Social History, 11th–14th Century* (New York: Bibliotheca Persica, 1988) 156–57.

56. Hennigan, *The Birth of a Legal Institution,* 81.

57. Koçi Bey, *Koçi Bey Risalesi,* ed. Ali Kemal Aksüt (Istanbul: Vakit Kütüphane, 1939), 56. Koçi Bey presented this memorandum to Murad IV in 1040/1630.

58. Halil Inalcik and Donald Quataert, eds., *An Economic and Social History of the Ottoman Empire, 1300–1914* (Cambridge, UK: Cambridge University

Press, 1994) 106, 126–27. See also Oded Peri, "Political Trends and Their Consequences as Factors Affecting the Founding of Waqfs in Jerusalem at the end of the Eighteenth Century," (Hebrew) *Cathedra* 21 (1981): 73–88.

59. Hennigan, "The Birth of a Legal Institution," 232.

60. Numerous scholars have pointed out that this value-laden *khayrī-ahlī* distinction is a modern one. See Cahen, "Réflexions sur le *Waqf* Ancien," 39–40, 47. Gabriel Baer also concluded that the *ahlī-khayrī* distinction belonged to legislation of the twentieth century, and not to Muslim laws pertaining to waqf, on which see "The Muslim Waqf and Similar Institutions," 21. See also Rabie's discussion of Maqrizī's three groups of waqfs in Egypt, including *"awqāf ahliyya,"* which were extensive estates in Syria and Egypt for "Sufi houses, schools, mosques and tombs," Hassanein Rabie, "Some Financial Aspects of the Waqf System in Medieval Egypt," *Al-Majalla al-Ta'rīkhiyya al-Miṣriyya* 18 (1971): 23. Here *"ahliyya"* appears to mean more "local, indigenous" rather than "family." Lambton, in *Continuity and Change,* says there is no "substantive distinction between private and charitable trusts" and that "both public and private ultimately serve the same purpose and both are bound by the same legal principles" (156). See also McChesney, *Charity and Philanthropy in Islam,* 12, and Hennigan, "The Birth of a Legal Institution," 1.

61. As related in Roy P. Mottahedeh, *Loyalty and Leadership in an Early Islamic Society* (Princeton: Princeton University Press, 1980), 78.

62. On the area near Trabzon, see Anthony Bryer, "Rural Society in Matzouka," in *Continuity and Change in Late Byzantine and Early Ottoman Society,* ed. Anthony Bryer and Heath Lowry (Birmingham, UK: Center for Byzantine Studies, 1986), 62. Goodwin lists a number of sites, in *A History of Ottoman Architecture,* 162 ff., 182. From a somewhat later period, the conquest of Cyprus (1571) produced similar takeovers of property by the Ottomans from the Venetians who had maintained the Byzantine institutions on the island. On this see Jennings, *Christians and Muslims in Ottoman Cyprus,* 404-41, 53.

63. Herrin, "Ideals of Charity," 159.

64. Lambton, *Continuity and Change,* 149–51.

65. Vryonis, *The Decline of Medieval Hellenism,* 348–55.

66. The matter of Byzantine influence has been a sensitive and controversial subject in Ottoman historiography. See Cemal Kafadar's remarks on the subject, reviewing the debate, in *Between Two Worlds: The Construction of the Ottoman State* (Berkeley: University of California Press, 1995), 24, 384-41.

67. Ethel Sara Wolper, "The Politics of Patronage: Political Change and the Construction of Dervish Lodges in Sivas," *Muqarnas* 12 (1995): 39–47.

68. Cornell Fleischer, "The Lawgiver as Messiah: The Making of the Imperial Image in the Reign of Süleyman," in *Soliman le Magnifique et Son Temps,* ed. Gilles Veinstein (Paris: Documentation Française, 1992), 159–77; Colin Imber, "Süleymân as Caliph of the Mulims: Ebû's-Suʿûd's Formulation of Ottoman Dynastic Ideology," in *ibid,* 179–84; and Peirce, *The Imperial Harem,* 166.

69. See the example of Hersekzade Aḥmed Paşa (d. 1517, holder of various high offices, including the grand vizierate) who retained the offices of

inspector and administrator for himself in his lifetime, then stipulated that they should pass to his sons and the fittest of his freed slaves, respectively, until they disappeared, at which time the Governor of Rümeli would be responsible for appointing capable persons to the two tasks. Simsar, *The Waqfiyah of 'Aḥmed Pāšā*, 126–29, 187–88.

70. İ. H. Uzunçarşılı, *Osmanlı Devletinin Saray Teşkilatı* (Ankara: Turk Tarih Kurumu, 1945), 177–80; Barnes, *An Introduction to Religious Foundations*, 65–66; and Yediyıldız, *Institution du Vaqf*, 197–99.

71. On this see especially Gülru Necipoğlu, "A *Kânûn* for the State, a Canon for the Arts: Conceptualizing the Classical Synthesis of Ottoman Arts and Architecture," in *Soliman le Magnifique*, ed. Gilles Veinstein, 195–216.

72. See Goodwin, *A History of Ottoman Architecture*, 215–39 and Gülru Necipoğlu, "The Süleymaniye Complex in Istanbul: An Interpretation," *Muqarnas* 3 (1985): 92–117.

73. On Jerusalem, see Amnon Cohen, *Economic life in Ottoman Jerusalem* (Cambridge, UK: Cambridge University Press, 1989) and Ammon Cohen and Bernard Lewis, *Population and Revenue in the Towns of Palestine in the Sixteenth Century* (Princeton: Princeton University Press, 1978), 84–104. On the development of cities in the Arab provinces under the Ottomans, see A. Raymond, "The Ottoman Conquest and the Development of the Great Arab Towns," *International Journal of Turkish Studies*, 1 (1979–80): 84–101.

## CHAPTER 2

1. Al-Ḥasan al-Baṣrī (d. 728), quoted in Weir and Zysow, "*ṣadaḳa*," VIII:710.

2. Natshe, "My Memories," 2.

3. On the ways in which different groups bargained and negotiated with the Ottoman government, implicitly or explicitly, see Karen Barkey, *Bandits and Bureaucrats: The Ottoman Route to State Centralization* (Ithaca: Cornell University Press, 1994) and Singer, *Palestinian peasants*, 2, 24–30.

4. One partial exception is the work of Ömer Lutfi Barkan in publishing the expenditures registers from the construction of the Süleymaniye complex. These registers give detailed accounts of labor and materials costs for this huge project and focus on the economic aspect of waqf-making. See *Süleymaniye Camii ve İmareti İnşaatı (1550–1557)* 2 vols. (Ankara: Türk Tarih Kurumu, 1972–79). Crecelius also provides some insights in his article on the waqf of Abū Dhahab in Cairo, where he follows the trail of documents that collected numerous properties in preparation for the founding of this waqf. See Daniel N. Crecelius, "The Waqf of Muḥammad Bey Abū al-Dhahab in Historical Perspective" (paper delivered at the conference on the Social and Economic Aspects of the Muslim Waqf, Jerusalem, 1979).

5. These are found in TSAE-7816/1–9 and TSAE-7702. For a more lengthy examination of the aesthetic qualities and the significance of their rich ornamentation, see Amy Singer, "The Mülknāmes of Hürrem Sultan's Waqf in Jerusalem," *Muqarnas* 14 (1997): 96–102.

6. Tülay Artan describes thus the vessels used to distribute food to the princesses' households in the eighteenth century, on which see Tülay Artan, "Aspects of the Ottoman Elite's Food Consumption," in *Consumption Studies and the History of the Ottoman Empire, 1550–1922*, ed. Donald Quataert (Albany: State University of New York Press, 2000), 163.

7. Stephan had access to the final Arabic version of the deed when he prepared his translation of the Turkish version (Tur.4). He does not say, however, where he saw the document. It is possible that he worked from the Arabic text which was copied "from the fine copy" into the protocols of the Jerusalem kadi (JS-280/pp. 18–27) in 1203/1788–89. This text is reproduced in al-ʿAsalī, *Wathāʾiq*, 127–42. Alternatively, there may be another "fine copy" of the Arabic deed which is not publicly available.

8. This was Stephan's contention in "An Endowment Deed," 171.

9. For a description and discussion of the *mühimme*, see Uriel Heyd, *Ottoman Documents on Palestine 1552–1615* (Oxford: Oxford University Press, 1960), xv-xvii, 3–6.

10. See İ. H. Uzunçarşılı, "Çandarlı Zade Ali Paşa Vakfiyesi," *Belleten 5* (1941): 550, for a transliteration of the text of this order *(ferman)*.

11. Yasser Tabbaa has found a bilingual waqfiyya in Damascus for the Manisa complex of Hafsa Sultan, Süleyman's mother, which may derive from the same kind of deference. See the discussion on H-Turk, from December 2000, accessible via <http://h-net.msu.edu/>.

12. All page references are to the Ottoman Turkish version of the deed, unless otherwise indicated. This document comprises 54 leaves bound into a single volume. See the description in Lawrence I. Conrad and Barbara Kellner-Heinkele, "Ottoman Resources in the Khalidi Library in Jerusalem," in *Aspects of Ottoman History. Papers from CIEPO IX, Jerusalem*, ed. A. Singer and A. Cohen (Jerusalem: Magnes Press, 1994), 289.

13. Literally, *al-mawqūf ʿalayhi* means the thing for which something is endowed, or the beneficiary.

14. All these buildings appear in both the Turkish and Arabic deeds with little or no differences except for the absence of the stable in the Arabic deed. It may be that it was assumed to be part of the *han* and therefore not mentioned separately. Natsheh locates it in the existing stable of Dar al-Sitt Ṭunshūq, on which see Natsheh, "Al-ʿImara al-ʿAmira," 764–65.

15. This according to Burgoyne's description of the Mamluk building, based on an architectural survey, for which see Burgoyne, *Mamluk Jerusalem*, 487–99.

16. Repairs are mentioned in JS 32/341 and JS 58/600 (1). On Ṭunshūq's house see Burgoyne, *Mamluk Jerusalem*, 42. See also D.H. Kallner-Amiran, "A Revised Earthquake Catalogue of Palestine," *Israel Exploration Journal* 1, 2 (1950–51): 223–46; 48–65.

17. See the descriptions of Myres and Natsheh which compare the extant buildings to the descriptions in the waqfiyya, in "ʿAl-ʿImara al-ʿAmira," 539–82, 747–90.

18. Literally, *al-mawqūf* means "the thing that was stopped, designated."

19. Ottoman administrative divisions, from the largest to the smallest, included the province *(beylerbeylik)*, district *(sancak)*, and subdistrict *(naḥiye)*. Lands belonged to villages *(ḳarye)*, seasonally inhabited farms *(mezraʿa)* and plots of land *(ḳitʿa)*. On each of these, see Pakalın and/or *İA*, s.v., for further discussion.

20. *Qaysariyya* is sometimes used as a synonym for caravansaray. On this see M. Streck, "*ḳaysāriyya*," *EI*[2], IV:840–41.

21. TSAE-7816/4; TSAE-7816/3 and TSAE-7816/5; TSAE-7816/6; TSAE-7816/7.

22. TTD 427/p.277; TTD 1015/p.223; TTD 289/p.107; TSAE-7816/7; and JS-70/p. 140. See also Singer, *Palestinian peasants*, 83 and 51–53, for an explication of these taxes and their calculation.

23. See the *ḳanunname* of Jerusalem in the opening of TTD 516 and TTD 515, as well as Singer, *Palestinian peasants*, 49.

24. TSAE-7816/8, /9 and TSAE-7702.

25. On security in the region, see the examples of Heyd, *Ottoman Documents*, 100, and the section there on the Bedouin. Even close to Jerusalem, a military escort was required to collect revenues from the villages, on which see Heyd, 144.

26. This exchange is recorded in one of the title deeds and is reflected in the Ottoman survey registers *(taḥrir)* of the area, TSAE-7816/8, TTD 516 (967/1560) and TTD 304 (964/1557). It was also referred to directly in an account submitted in early 964/1557: TSAD-4576 referring to 964/1557 and 965/1558 listed twenty villages, six *mezraʿas*, a community of water buffalo keepers and four tribes. These items (listed in a title deed from 964/1557) were endowed in place of the soap factories (their title was from 960/1553). A register of endowment income and expenditure lists arrears in their accounts (TSAD-3643/10 from 963/1555–6).

27. TSAE-7816/8. This document says it is reiterating what was transferred on 14 Ramazan 963, i.e. two to three weeks prior to the document's actual date.

28. TSAD-4576 from 965/1558.

29. TSAE-7816/9; TTD 1015/pp. 197, 199. On *ḥass-i şahi*, see Cohen and Lewis, *Population and Revenue*, 42.

30. Title deed TSAE-7702, as compared with survey registers from Gaza province, TTD 265 from 955/1548–9 and Jerusalem province, TTD 289 from 952/1545. Any survey register was somewhat out of date by the time its fair copy was drawn up in Istanbul. Thus, the register dated the same year as the endowment deed (TTD 304, 964/1557) understandably did not include the three additional villages, though they were by then indeed part of the endowment. The last survey of the sixteenth century lists them together with the others belonging to the endowment (TTD 546, 1005/1596–7).

31. TTD 289/p. 70; title deed TSAE-7816/8. For the dating of the survey registers and methodological comments on them, see Amy Singer, "*Tapu Taḥrir Defterleri* and *Kadı Sicilleri*: A Happy Marriage of Sources," *Tārīḫ* 1 (1990): 95–125.

32. On this question, see Singer, "*Tapu Taḥrir Defterleri* and *Kadı Sicilleri*," 119.

33. TTD 516/p. 66 and JS-70/p. 135.

34. The same note is found in the subsequent survey from around 1595–97, TTD 515, also found in Ankara. JS-70 is a copy of TTD 516. JS-70 and TTD 516 have the following note appended: *vaḳfa sancaḳ haṣṣlarindan ahar bedel verilüb işbu ḳarye-i Rīḥā vaḳıftan ihrac olunub sancağa verilmek ferman olunub defter-i icmalda/humayunda haṣṣ-i mir-i liva üzerine tarihi işaret olunmuştur*. Mazraʿat Ra's al-Diq, listed with the village of Buqayʿat al-Ḍān in JS-70, was listed in the title deed with Jericho. In JS-70 a note says it was exchanged *(mezbur mezraʿa vaḳıftan ihrac olunup sancaḳ haṣṣlarından bedel verilmiştir)*, but the note is absent in TTD 516, the original survey from which JS-70 was copied.

35. TTD 516/p. 68 and JS-70/p. 137; TTD 342/p. 4.

36. Dror Ze'evi, *An Ottoman Century: The District of Jerusalem in the 1600s* (Albany: State University of New York Press, 1996), 103.

37. This has also been demonstrated with respect to the Awqāf al-Ḥaramayn in Algiers, by Hoexter, *Endowments, Rulers and Community*.

38. Al-ʿAsalī, *Wathā'iq*, 132; Stephan says: "One of these [two baths] is now no more to be identified. The other, having become disused, was sold in the latter half of the 19th century to the Armenian Catholics, who built a church on the site and reused part of the building of the former *Ḥammâm as-Sulṭân* bought from the Khâlidi family" ("An Endowment Deed," 184). See also Stephan, "Three Firmans Granted to the Armenian Catholic Community," *Journal of the Palestine Oriental Society* 13 (1933): 238 ff. Stephan, it seems, misunderstood the term *çift hamamı* to mean two baths instead of one double bath, the one he described.

39. For the details of this, see Chapter 4.

40. The waqfiyya for this addition was copied into the Jerusalem *sijill* at the same time as the original deed, towards the end of the eighteenth century. I have worked from the text as published by al-ʿAsalī, *Wathā'iq*, 147–50. The two additional title deeds are TSAE-7816/10–11, dated beginning of Şevval 967/July 1560; the waqfiyya is from the end of the same month.

41. MD-3 28/p. 9; 15 Ramazan 966/21 June 1559.

42. In this regard, the map of southern Syria made by Hütteroth and Abdulfattah offers a striking demonstration of the links between properties endowed and institutions supported in the sixteenth century, and makes clear how extensive the property network could be; see Wolf D. Hütteroth and Kamal Abdulfattah, *Historical Geography of Palestine, Transjordan and Southern Syria* (Erlangen: Frankische Geographische Gesellschaft, 1977), Map 4.

43. Except where otherwise noted, all information on the personnel, salaries, etc., comes from the Turkish and Arabic texts of the endowment deeds.

44. These *muḥasebe defterleri* are discussed in Chapter 4.

45. Called Jaʿfar *agha* in the Arabic waqfiyya (Al-ʿAsali, *Wathā'iq*, 135) which makes it fairly certain he is the Caʿfer Ağa listed as the *babüsseʿadet ağası* in Süleyman's time; see Mehmed Süreyya, *Sicill-i ʿOsmanî* (Istanbul: Matbaa-i Âmire, 1308–11/1891–93. The *babüsseʿadet ağası* was probably the

*naẓır* until around 1590, when the *darüsseʿadet ağası* or *kızlar ağası*, who was the chief eunuch of the harem, took over as chief eunuch of the palace. On this see Uzunçarşılı, *Osmanlı Devletinin Saray Teşkilatı*, 173 and Pakalın, I:401.

46. Anyone who has ever purchased grains in bulk in an open market can appreciate why so many people were necessary to wash and pick over the large quantities of rice and wheat used daily in this kitchen.

47. *Çanaḳcı* means a potter; perhaps they were also expected to manufacture and/or repair all the crockery needed by the place. It seems from this number of dishwashers that the ʿimaret supplied cups as soup bowls for all those who ate there. Stephan has a slightly different configuration of people and positions in this section, which he got from the Arabic deed he saw. This suggests that it was not the published eighteenth-century *sijill* copy, which conforms in detail to the Arabic waqfiyya in Istanbul.

48. There are some other, more slight differences in the personnel listed in the two deeds; this is the only place where there is a significant difference.

49. Kemal Kürkçüoğlu, *Süleymaniye Vakfiyesi* (Ankara: Resimli Posta Matbaası, 1962), 38–40; A. Süheyl Ünver, *Fâtih Aşhânesi Tevzî'nâmesi* (Ankara: Istanbul Fethi Derneği, 1953), 5–6; and Ratip Kazancıgil, *Edirne İmaretleri* (Istanbul: Türk Kütüphaneciler Derneği Edirne Şübesi Yayınevi, 1991), 96–97.

50. Kazancıgil, *Edirne İmaretleri*, 40–41 and Yusuf Küçükdağ, *Karapınar Sultan Selim Külliyesi* (Konya: Karapınar Belediyesi Kültür Yayını, 1997), 125–31.

51. Gülru Necipoğlu, *Architecture, Ceremonial and Power, The Topkapı Palace* (Cambridge, MA: M.I.T. Press, 1992), 70 and Uzunçarşılı, *Osmanlı Devletinin Saray Teşkilati*, 380.

52. These nineteenth-century defters, listing stipendiaries and recipients of food, are from the Nezaret Sonrası Evkaf Defterleri (EV) classification of the Başbakanlık Arşivi in Istanbul. They are numbered: EV-13370, 13391, 13407, 13432, 13446, 13460, 13485, 13495, 13504, 13645, 13646; 16873, 16926, 16935; 18277; 17146, 17753. One defter is found in the Kamil Kepeci classification of the Başbakanlık Arşivi KK-3397, mükerrer 43.

53. See <http://planning.pna.net/jerusalem/JERUSALE.htm>, December 2000.

54. JS 33-2800/p. 525 17 Shawwāl 964/13 August 1557; JS-40 379/p. 76 3 Rabīʿ II 968/22 December 1560. For a more extensive discussion of the role of *subaşıs* in the villages, see Singer, *Palestinian peasants*, 24, 26–28.

55. MD 36 375/p. 34, 23 Muḥarrem 987/22 March 1579; and JS 31/435, translated in Amnon Cohen and Elisheva Simon-Pikali, eds. and trans., *Jews in the Moslem Religious Court: Society, Economy and Communal Organization in the XVIth Century, Documents from Ottoman Jerusalem* (Hebrew) (Jerusalem: Yad Izhak Ben-Zvi, 1993), 250–51. On the butchers, see Amnon Cohen, *Economic Life*, 21–23.

56. Küçükdağ, *Karapınar*, 130; on meat supply, see Robert Mantran, *Istanbul dans la Seconde Moitié du XVIIe Siècle* (Paris: Maisonneuve, 1962), 194–97.

57. These latter will be discussed in Chapter 4.

58. TSAD-1511 (pp. 12b-13a) lists specific tools in the ʿimaret. See Kazancıgil, *Edirne,* 99, on tinning.

59. Two separate smaller pots were specially requested in mid-1556; see TSAD-3528/20.

60. 1 dirhem = approximately 3 grams, thus each loaf weighed about 270 grams wet. See H. Inalcik, "Weights and Measures," in Inalcik and Quataert, *An Economic and Social History,* 988.

61. For a discussion of the composition and caloric value of food distributed in welfare and poor relief institutions in early modern Europe, see Robert Jütte, "Diets in Welfare Institutions and in Outdoor Poor Relief in Early Modern Western Europe," *Ethnologia Europaea* 16, no. 2 (1986): 117–36. For an evaluation of the nutrition content of the various ingredients at the ʿimaret, see Kenneth F. Kiple and Kriemhild Coneè Ornelas, eds., *The Cambridge World History of Food* (Cambridge, UK: Cambridge University Press, 2000), s.v.

62. On Konya, see İbrahim Hakki Konyalı, *Âbideleri ve Kitabeleri ile Konya Tarihi* (Konya: Yeni Kitap Basımevi, 1964), 977; on Damascus, see Yvette Sauvan, "Une Liste de Foundations Pieuses (Waqfiyya) au Temps de Selim II," *BEO* 28 (1975): 239; and on Ergene and Bolayır, see Ö. L. Barkan, "Osmanlı İmparatorluğunda İmâret Sitelerinin Kuruluş ve İşleyiş Tarzına âit Araştırmalar," *İstanbul Üniversitesi İktisat Fakültesi Mecmuası* 23, no. 1–2 (1962–63): 256 ff.

63. Kürkçuoğlu, *Süleymaniye,* 43 and Ünver, *Fâtih Aşhânesi Tevzîʿnamesi,* 4.

64. Peirce. *The Imperial Harem,* 124.

65. Ünver, *Fâtih Aşhânesi Tevzîʿnamesi,* 4.

66. Kürkçuoğlu, *Süleymaniye,* 43 and 45: *"sâyir amâyirde ne-vech-ile ziyafet ve ikram olunursa dahi ziyade edeler, noksân üzere etmeyeler."*

67. See Artan, "Aspects of the Ottoman Elite's Food Consumption," 141, where sheep's trotters were ordered especially from the Süleymaniye quarter to one of the princesses' private palaces.

68. Küçükdağ, *Karapınar,* 107; and see also Kazancıgil, *Edirne,* 99.

69. Kürkcüoğlu, *Süleymaniye,* 43 and Ünver, *Fâtih Aşhânesi Tevzîʿnamesi,* 4. (The transcription is incomplete; check the facsimile, 13.)

70. On the festivals see either *EI*[2] or *İA,* s.v.

71. See references in Tezcan, *Bir Ziyafet Defteri,* at 42–43, 58.

72. Al-ʿAsalī, *Wathāʾiq,* 139; Ömer Lutfi Barkan, "Süleymaniye Camii ve İmareti Tesislerine ait Yıllık Bir Muhasebe Bilânçosu 993–994 (1585–1586)," *Vakıflar Dergisi* 9 (1971): 155–60. See also Raphaela Lewis, *Everyday Life in Ottoman Turkey* (New York: Dorset Press, 1971), 121, who says it always contains nuts, raisins, and other dried fruits boiled with cereals.

73. Muṣṭafā b. Ahmet ʿAlī, *Muṣṭafā ʿAlī's Counsels for Sultans,* II:27, 144.

74. Tur. 4, f. 49–52.

75. Artan, "Aspects of the Ottoman Elite's Food Consumption", 155, 159–60.

76. Ünver, *Fâtih Aşhânesi Tevzîʿnamesi,* 5–6.

77. Sauvan, "Une Liste de Fondations," 243.

78. Konyalı, *Âbideleri ve Kitabeleri,* 977.

79. TSAE-7301/2, page a.

80. Tur. 4, 49–52.

81. Called in both deeds: *fuḳarā ve masākīn ve ḍuʿafā ve muḥtājīn.*

82. Tur. 4, p. 51.

83. Kürkçuoğlu, *Süleymaniye,* 31.

84. On this see Ze'evi, *An Ottoman Century,* 27, and Yusuf Natsheh, "Catalogue of Buildings," in *Ottoman Jerusalem,* ed. S. Auld and R. Hillenbrand (London: Altajir World of Islam Trust, 2000), 573. This is a topic that needs to be extensively investigated in the Jerusalem *sijills.*

85. Konyalı, *Âbideleri ve Kitabeleri,* 978; A. Süheyl Ünver, "Anadolu ve İstanbulda imaretlerin aşhane, tabhane ve misafirhanelerine ve müessislerinin ruhi kemâllerine dair," *Tıb Fakültesi Mecmuası* 4 (1941): 2397.

86. This was Inalcik's suggestion in a conversation we had on the subject in the early 1990s. However, he had no precise reference to corroborate this speculation, nor have I ever found one.

87. See Kallner-Amiran, "A Revised Earthquake Catalogue of Palestine," 229, for a sketch catalogue of the destructiveness of this earthquake, together with references to source information.

88. For these numbers, based on the Ottoman surveys, see Cohen and Lewis, *Population and Revenue,* 1978, 94–95. Some increase in population was due to improved record-making. The population total was calculated by assuming that each household comprised five persons, on average. On such calculations, see the discussion in Singer, *Palestinian peasants,* 166–67, n. 29.

89. Amy Singer, "Ottoman Jerusalem: Conquering the Urban Frontier" (paper presented at the Middle East Center of the University of Utah, October 2000).

90. See Auld and Hillenbrand, *Ottoman Jerusalem,* 7; J. P. Pascual, *Damas à la fin du XVIe siècle d'après trois actes de waqf Ottoman* (Damas: IFAED, 1983), and Muhammad Adnan Bakhit, *The Ottoman Province of Damascus in the Sixteenth Century* (Beirut: Librairie du Liban, 1982), 116.

91. Amnon Cohen, "The Walls of Jerusalem," in *The Islamic World: From Classical to Modern Times,* ed. C. E. Bosworth and Charles Issawi (Princeton: Darwin Press, 1989), 467–77; Myriam Rosen-Ayalon, "On Suleiman's *Sabīls* in Jerusalem," in *ibid,* 589–607; and O. Salama and Y. Zilberman, "The Supply of Water to Jerusalem in the 16th and 17th Centuries," (Hebrew) *Cathedra* 41 (1986): 91–106.

92. Peirce, *The Imperial Harem,* 63.

93. Tur. 4, pp. 9–10.

94. Peirce, *The Imperial Harem,* 188.

95. Tur. 4, p. 9.

96. On Muṣṭafa, see Peirce, *The Imperial Harem,* 55–56, 79–83. There was even an English play written about him entitled *The Tragedy of Mustapha, the Son of Solyman the Magnificent* by Roger Boyle, first produced in 1665. See *Five Heroic Plays,* Bonamy Dobrée, ed. (London: Oxford University Press, 1960).

97. Peirce, *The Imperial Harem,* 61.

98. Goodwin, *A History of Ottoman Architecture,* 206–11.

99. TSAE-7816/1–11 and TSAE-7702.

100. Islambol is a play on the word Istanbul: *"bol"* means full in Turkish, so the city is "filled with Islam." This name was also used by the Ottomans. Al-Quds al-Sharīf literally means "the noble sanctuary.' See also Kafescioğlu, "The Ottoman Capital in the Making."

## CHAPTER 3

1. "The New Colossus" was written in 1883 for the Statue of Liberty, which was unveiled in 1886. The poem was only affixed to the statue in the form of a bronze tablet in 1903. Bette Roth Young, *Emma Lazarus in Her World: Life and Letters* (Philadelphia: The Jewish Publication Society, 1995), 3–4.

2. TSAD-8466.

3. Ḥafṣa Sulṭan, mother of Süleyman, is also credited with the founding of the Jerusalem ʿimaret, a confusion perhaps due to the common connection to Süleyman. See J. B. Barron, *Mohammedan Wakfs in Palestine* (Jerusalem: Printed at the Greek convent press, 1922), 58. Barron, who was the Director of Revenue and Customs for His Majesty's Government in Palestine, does not give his source for this information, and he is the only one to mention Ḥafṣa. Yet Ḥafṣa could not have been responsible for the ʿimaret; by the time it was founded she had been dead for thirteen years. See Peirce, *The Imperial Harem,* 62, 199–200.

4. Dede Korkut, *The Book of Dede Korkut,* trans. Geoffrey Lewis (Harmondsworth: Penguin Books 1974), 117–32; Peirce, *The Imperial Harem,* 274–75; Gavin R. G. Hambly, "Becoming Visible: Medieval Islamic Women in Historiography and History," in *Women in the Medieval Islamic World: Power, Patronage and Piety,* ed. Gavin R. G. Hambly (New York: St. Martin's Press, 1998), 11.

5. Kathleen McCarthy, "Parallel Power Structures: Women and the Voluntary Space," in *Lady Bountiful Revisited: Women, Philanthropy, and Power,* ed. Kathleen McCarthy (New Brunswick: Rutgers University Press, 1990), 1.

6. Marina Warner, *Alone of All Her Sex. The Myth and the Cult of the Virgin Mary* (London: Weidenfeld & Nicolson, 1976), 221–23, 273–98.

7. Mujīr al-Dīn al-Ḥanbalī, *Al-Uns al-jalīl bi-ta'rīkh al-Quds wa'l-Khalīl* (Amman: Maktabat al-Muḥtasib, 1973), II:54, 64–65; Burgoyne, *Mamluk Jerusalem,* 485–86, 505; and M. van Berchem, *Matériaux Pour un Corpus Inscriptionum Arabicarum Deuxième Partie: Syrie du Sud II. Jérusalem 'Ville'* (Cairo: Institut Français d'Archaeologie Orientale, 1922–23), 310–12, who discusses at length her probable connection to the Muẓaffarid dynasty. On the Qalandariyya order, see Tahsin Yazıcı, "Ḳalandariyya," *EI*[2], IV:473–74.

8. On this incident, see Amnon Cohen, "The Expulsion of the Franciscans from Mt. Zion," *Turcica* 18 (1986): 147–57.

9. Jews, however, do not seem to have been among those who ever ate at the ʿimaret, because of dietary restrictions, but also due to the extent of relief available within their community.

10. N. Crouch, *A Journey to Jerusalem: Or, A Relation of the Travels of Fourteen Englishmen in the Year 1669* (London: printed by T. M. for N. Crouch in Exchang-Alley, 1672), 50.

11. Morison, *Relation historique,* 378–79. (My translation. A. S.)

12. W.H. Bartlett, *Jerusalem Revisited* (London: A. Hall, Virtue and Co., 1855), 88. On Bartlett see the *Dictionary of National Biography,* s.v.

13. Bartlett, *Jerusalem Revisited,* 89.

14. P. Gérardy Saintine (Xavier Boniface), *Trois Ans en Judée* (Paris: Hachette, 1860), 178–79. (My translation. A. S.)

15. Pierotti, *Jerusalem Explored,* I:150–53.

16. Natsheh, "Catalogue of Buildings," 710.

17. ʿĀshiqpashazādeh, *ʿĀshiqpashazādeh Ta'rīkhī. A History of the Ottoman Empire to* A.H. *883 (*A.D. *1478),* ed. ʿAlī Bey (Istanbul: Matbaa-i Amire, 1332/1914), 42.

18. Morison, *Relation historique,* 387–89.

19. Peirce, *The Imperial Harem,* 58. In the Ukraine today, Hurrem (Roxelana) remains very much alive in popular story and song, revered both for her kindness to compatriots who arrived in Istanbul as slaves and as the protectress of the Ukraine from Ottoman incursions. My thanks to Dr. Olexander Halenko for sharing with me his extensive knowledge of this material.

20. Carter Vaughn Findley, "Social Dimensions of Dervish Life as Seen in the Memoirs of Aşçı Dede İbrahim Halil," in *The Dervish Lodge: Architecture, Art, and Sufism in Ottoman Turkey,* ed. Raymond Lifchez (Berkeley: University of California Press, 1992), 182, 184; and Ayla Algar, "Food in the Life of the Tekke," in *ibid.,* 291–303.

21. Maurice Halbwachs, *La Topographie Légendaire des Évangiles en Terre Sainte: Étude de mémoire collective* (Paris: Presses Universitaires de France, 1941), 185. (My translation. A. S.)

22. See the discussion about competition for Christian-held sites in Jerusalem and Bethehem in the late seventeenth century in Oded Peri, *"The Ottoman State and the Question of the Christian Holy Places in Jerusalem and Its Vicinity During the Latter Half of the Seventeenth Century"* (Hebrew, Ph.D. diss., Hebrew University of Jerusalem, 1995), Chapter 3: "The Ottoman State and the Competition between the Christian Communities for the Holy Places," 142–224.

23. See Singer, "Ottoman Jerusalem."

24. F. de Saulcy, *Jérusalem* (Paris: n.p., 1882), 321–22, cites Josephus. On this Helena, see the article "Adiabene" in *Encyclopaedia Britannica Micropedia,* 15th ed. (1974).

25. Al-ʿAsalī, *Wathāʾiq,* 129–30.

26. See Margaret Smith and C. Pellat, "Rābiʿa al-ʿAdawiyya," *EI*$^2$, VIII:354–56 and Ruth Roded, *Women in Islamic Biographical Collections* (Boulder: Lynne Rienner Publishers, 1994), *passim.*

27. Tur. 4, p. 9 and Al-ʿAsalī, *Wathāʾiq,* 129–30. See also Tülay Duran, ed., *Tarihimizde Vakıf Kuran Kadınlar. Hanım Sultan Vakfiyyeleri* (Istanbul: Tarihi

Araştırmalar ve Dokümentasyon Merkezleri Kurma ve Geliştirme Vakfı, 1990), 246, 547, and Peirce, *The Imperial Harem,* 204.

28. In general, see Weir and Zysow, "*ṣadaḳa,*" VIII:711; on Zaynab, see V. Vacca, "Zainab bint Djaḥsh," *EI,* IV:1200 and Barbara F. Stowasser, *Women in the Qur'an, Traditions, and Interpretation* (New York: Oxford University Press, 1994), 115, 117; and D. A. Spellberg, *Politics, Gender and the Islamic Past: The Legacy of 'A'isha Bint Abi Bakr* (New York: Columbia University Press, 1994), and specifically, private communication from Spellberg (24 April 1995).

29. Linda Darwish, "Images of Muslim Women: 'A'isha, Fatima, and Zaynab bint 'Ali in Contemporary Gender Discourse," *McGill Journal of Middle East Studies* 4 (1996): 95, 108–11.

30. See, for examples, Ibn Khallikān, *Wafayāt al-A'yān* (Beirut: Dar al-Thaqāfa, 1968–72), 3:245–46 and Ibn 'Imād, *Shadharāt al-Dhahab* (Beirut: Dar Ibn Kathir, 1986–93), 2:178, 272, 3: Part V. And see also Roded, *Women in Islamic Biographical Collections,* 4–6; and for Mamluk examples, Carl F. Petry, "Class Solidarity vs. Gender Gain: Women as Custodians of Property in Later Medieval Egypt," in *Women in Middle Eastern History,* ed. Nikki R. Keddie and Beth Baron (New Haven: Yale University Press, 1991), 122–42.

31. Ibrahim Peçevi, *Tarīḫ-i Peçevi* (Constantinople: Matbaa-i Amire, 1281–83), I:425–27.

32. Nabia Abbott, *Two Queens of Baghdad* (Chicago: University of Chicago Press, 1946), 239–41; Wiebke Walther, *Women in Islam,* updated text (Princeton: Markus Wiener Publishers, 1993), 117–19; and Hodgson, *The Venture of Islam,* I:294.

33. Esin Atıl, "Islamic Women as Rulers and Patrons," *Asian Art* 6 (1993): 7–8.

34. Judith Herrin, "Public and Private Forms of Religious Commitment among Byzantine Women," in *Women in Ancient Societies,* ed. J. Leonie Archer, et al., (London: Macmillan, 1994), 186.

35. Timothy S. Miller, *The Birth of the Hospital in the Byzantine Empire* (Baltimore: Johns Hopkins University Press, 1985), 194; Judith Herrin, "From Bread and Circuses," 16–17.

36. Herrin, "From Bread and Circuses," 15–16.

37. Kenneth G. Holum, *Theodosian Empresses: Women and Imperial Dominion in Late Antiquity* (Berkeley: University of California Press, 1982), 23, 26–27.

38. Kafadar, *Between Two Worlds,* 15, 89–90.

39. Anthony Bryer, "Greek historians on the Turks: the case of the first Byzantine-Ottoman marriage," in *The Writing of History in the Middle Ages,* ed. R. H. C. Davis and J. M. Wallace-Hadrill (Oxford: Clarendon Press, 1981), 480–81 and Peirce, *The Imperial Harem,* 34, 36; and M. Çağatay Uluçay, *Padişahların Kadınları ve Kızları* (Ankara: Türk Tarih Kurumu, 1980), 3–5.

40. Peirce, *The Imperial Harem,* 40–41.

41. Ibid., 29–30.

42. Hambly, "Becoming Visible," 11, and Morris Rossabi, "Khubilai Khan and the Women in His Family," *Studia Sino-Mongolica: Festschrift Für Herbert Franke* (Wiesbaden: Steiner, 1979): 153–80.

43. Geoffrey Lewis, "Heroines and Others in the Heroic Age of the Turks," in *Women in the Medieval Islamic World,* ed. Gavin R. G. Hambly (New York: St. Martin's Press, 1998), 150. For Dede Korkut, see the introductory material in *The Book of Dede Korkut,* 9–23.

44. Ibid., 117. It is worth noting that Kan Turalı, having found a woman who fit this description, almost kills her in a fit of pique when she saves his life.

45. Lambton, *Continuity and Change,* 150–51, 271. On the notion of the shamefaced poor and their status in early modern Italy, see Sandra Cavallo, *Charity and Power in Early Modern Italy: Benefactors and Their Motives in Turin, 1541–1789* (Cambridge, UK: Cambridge University Press, 1995), 12, 111–12, 187–88.

46. R. Stephen Humphreys, "Women as Patrons of Religious Architecture in Ayyubid Damascus," *Muqarnas* 11 (1994): 36, 49.

47. Yasser Tabbaa, *Constructions of Power and Piety in Medieval Aleppo* (University Park, PA: Penn State Press, 1997), 48. The terms *ribāṭ, khanqah* and *zāwiya* are all used to described sufi residences. While in some places, the distinctions between them may be clear, in others it appears that the terms were used interchangeably, or that one was simply preferred over the others. On this see J. Chabbi, *"khānḳāh,"* $EI^2$, IV:1025–26, who defines the term as "a building usually reserved for Muslim mystics belonging to a dervish order." Chabbi says that all the terms—*ribāṭ, tekke, zāwiya*—are similar.

48. Ülkü Ü. Bates, "Women as Patrons of Architecture in Turkey," in *Women in the Muslim World,* ed. Lois Beck and Nikki Keddie (Cambridge, MA: Harvard University Press, 1978), 245–46, 250, and Crane, "Notes on Saldjūq Architectural Patronage," 11.

49. Atıl, "Islamic Women," 8.

50. Bates, "Women as Patrons," 246.

51. Petry, "Class Solidarity," 123–24.

52. Doris Behrens-Abouseif, "The *Maḥmal* Legend and the Pilgrimage of the Ladies of the Mamluk Court," *Mamluk Studies Review* 1 (1997): 92–95.

53. Ibid., 88.

54. Berkey, *The Transmission of Knowledge,* 162–65; Leonor Fernandes, "Mamluk Architecture" 115; and Petry, "Class Solidarity," 133, 136.

55. Adam Sabra, *Poverty and Charity in Medieval Islam: Mamluk Egypt 1250–1517* (Cambridge, UK: Cambridge University Press, 2000), 84–85, 87, 92–93.

56. Maria Szuppe, "La Participation des femmes de la famille royale à l'exercise du pouvoir en Iran safavide au XVI siècle," *Studia Iranica* 23, 24 (1994): 258.

57. Peirce, *The Imperial Harem,* 199.

58. Uluçay, *Padişahların Kadınları ve Kızları,* 3–5, 6, 23.

59. Peirce, *The Imperial Harem,* 47. For examples of tombs, see Pars Tuğlacı, *Osmanlı Şehirleri* (Istanbul: Milliyet Yayınları, 1985): on Bursa, 73–74, on Edirne, 106, 108.

60. M. Çağatay Uluçay, "Kanuni Sultan Süleyman ve Ailesi ile İlgili Bazı Notlar ve Vesikalar," *Kanuni Armağanı* (Ankara: Türk Tarih Kurumu, 1970), 229.

61. Peirce, *The Imperial Harem*, 279; Uluçay, *Padişahların Kadınları ve Kızları*, 29–30; and İbrahim Hakki Konyalı, "Kanunî Sultan Süleyman'ın Annesi Hafsa Sultanın Vakfiyesi ve Manisa'daki Hayır Eserleri," *Vakıflar Dergisi* 8 (1969): 47–56.

62. Peirce, *The Imperial Harem*, 55–56.

63. Ibid., 41.

64. Bates remarks on the practice of naming women in relation to men, in "Women as Patrons," 248. Peirce discusses these boundaries extensively in her article "Gender and Sexual Propriety in Ottoman Royal Women's Patronage," in *Women, Patronage, and Self-Representation in Islamic Societies*, ed. D. Fairchild Ruggles (Albany: State University of New York Press, 2000) 53–68.

65. M. Tolmacheva, "Female Piety and Patronage in the Medieval 'Ḥajj', in *Women in the Medieval Islamic World*, ed. Gavin R. G. Hambly (New York: St. Martin's Press, 1998) 165, n.25 and M. Tayyib Gökbilgin, "Hurrem Sultan," *İA*, V:595.

66. See on the various structures, s.v., in the *İstA*.

67. Peirce, *The Imperial Harem*, 206–07 and Lucienne Thys-Şenocak, "The Yeni Valide Mosque Complex at Eminönü," *Muqarnas* 15 (1998): 58–70.

68. Ibid., 66. See also M.C. Şihabeddin Tekindağ, "Çanakkale," *İA*, III:345.

69. See the lists of charitable endeavors recorded for each woman in Uluçay, *Padişahların Kadınları ve Kızları*.

70. Peirce, *The Imperial Harem*, 65–77.

71. This is based on Uluçay, *Padişahların Kadınları ve Kızları* and notes on endowments from around the empire, but not on an exhaustive survey of endowment deeds or other materials. To my knowledge, there does not exist a complete listing of endowments made by members of the imperial household during the entire Ottoman period.

72. Bates, "Women as Patrons," 257; Margaret L. Meriwether, "Women and *Waqf* Revisited: The Case of Aleppo, 1770–1840," in *Women in the Ottoman Empire*, ed. Madeline C. Zilfi (Leiden: Brill, 1997), 128–52.

73. On inheritance in Islamic law, see J. Schacht and A. Layish, *"mīrāth,"* in *EI*[2], VII:106–13.

74. Rachel Emma Silverman, "Rich & Richer," *The Wall Street Journal*, 11 January 1999, B6.

75. On the antebellum United States, see Lori D. Ginzberg, *Women and the Work of Benevolence: Morality, Politics, and Class in the Nineteenth-Century United States* (New Haven: Yale University Press, 1990), 50–51; on Tsarist Russia, see Adele Lindenmeyr, *Poverty is Not a Vice: Charity, Society, and the State in Imperial Russia* (Princeton: Princeton University Press, 1996), 111. From Muscovite times, Orthodox women had complete control over their property regardless of marital status. In comparison, English and American women in the nineteenth century lost extensive property rights when they married.

76. Peirce, "Gender and Sexual Propriety," 60.

77. Peirce, *The Imperial Harem*, 202.

78. Kishwar Rizvi, "Gendered Patronage: Women and Benevolence During the Early Safavid Empire," in *Women, Patronage, and Self-Representation*, ed. D. Fairchild Ruggles (Albany: State University of New York Press, 2000), 134, 139–40.

79. Lucienne Thys-Şenocak, "The Yeni Valide Complex of Eminönü, Istanbul (1597–1665). Gender and Vision in Ottoman Architecture," in ibid., 81–82.

80. Nimet Taşkıran, *Hasekinin Kitabı* (Istanbul: Yenilik Basımevi, 1972), 62.

81. Tur. 4, fol. 28–29.

82. Baer, "Women and waqf," 13 ff.

83. Meriwether, "Women and *Waqf* Revisited," 140–50 and Mary Ann Fay, "Women and *Waqf*: Property, Power, and the Domain of Gender in Eighteenth-Century Egypt," in *Women in the Ottoman Empire*, ed. Madeline L. Zilfi (Leiden: Brill, 1997), 31.

84. Carl F. Petry, *Protectors or Praetorians? The Last Mamlūk Sultans and Egypt's Waning as a Great Power* (Albany: State University of New York Press, 1994), 200–01.

85. See Al-'Asali, *Wathā'iq*, 311–12 for the *berat* (appointment document) of one such appointment from 1043/1633.

86. This research has begun in part with the work of Tülay Artan, who has studied the role of Ottoman princesses from the late seventeenth through the eighteenth century. See "From Charismatic Leadership to Collective Rule: Introducing Materials on the Wealth and Power of Ottoman Princesses in the Eighteenth Century," *Dünkü ve Bugünüyle Toplum ve Ekonomi* 4 (1993): 53–94 and eadem, "Noble Women Who Changed the Face of the Bosphorus and the Palaces of the Sultanas," *Istanbul (Biannual)* 1 (1993): 87–97.

87. George Farquhar, "The Beaux' Stratagem," in *Three Restoration Comedies*, ed. Norman Marshall (London: Pan Books Ltd., 1953), 187.

88. See M. Agulhon and Pierre Bonte, *Marianne. Les Visages de la République* (Paris: Gallimard, 1992), 23–25.

89. Young, *Emma Lazarus*, 3–4.

## CHAPTER 4

1. TSAE-7301/2, written on 10 Cumaziülevvel 962/2 April 1555.

2. TSAD-3643/8, dated to mid-Cemziülevvel 962/3–13 April 1555. Two versions of this report exist: 3643/8 uses Arabic terms *(ṭabbāḫīn, ḫubbāzīn)* while 3643/9 uses Turkish *(aşçıyan, etmekciyan)*. Otherwise, 3643/8 has more extensive marginal notes. It is also exquisitely penned, with each letter beautifully formed and each page carefully laid out. As Hurrem was still alive at this point, it is possible that an especially clean copy was made to submit directly to her.

3. This is the weight of dough, wet and heavier than baked bread.

4. *ribaṭ hücrelerinde.* This is the only instance where *ribaṭ* is used to describe the Haṣṣeki Sultan ʿimaret in any way. Apparently, it looked to this outsider like other sufi residences, perhaps due to the form, perhaps because people lodged there. It is an indication of how much overlap existed both in form and function between buildings of different names, as well as how much variety there was in buildings of the same name. Hillenbrand calls Islamic architectural terminology "notoriously vague", on which see Hillenbrand, *Islamic Architecture,* 219.

5. Persian *jamrī* (Tur. pl. *cumrāya*) means "poor" or "mean." See F. Steingass, *Persian-English Dictionary* (New Delhi: Cosmo Publications, 1977).

6. Such holes are an unfortunate yet not unfamiliar hazard of archival research.

7. The *reʿaya* were the tax payers in the Ottoman empire, largely peasants but not exclusively. They are distinguished from the *askeri,* the military, although the *askeri* referred to a much broader group of people who were exempt from taxes. It seems here that Bayram loaned the waqf money to buy supplies from the peasants.

8. The original document has a fold here, and the letters are obscured and broken up.

9. For a detailed study of property exchanges and purchases, and for a specifically similar situation, see Hoexter, *Endowments, Rulers and Community,* 116–18.

10. On *muḥasebe,* see Ö. L. Barkan, "İstanbul Saraylarına ait Muhasebe Defterleri," *Belgeler* 9 (1979): 1–380.

11. Revenue grants in the Ottoman empire took the form of rights assigned to officers to collect portions of the yields in kind or cash from various crops and taxes throughout the provinces. The smaller grants were called *tımar* and larger ones *zeʿamet.* For more on these, see Inalcik and Quataert, *An Economic and Social History,* 141. *Tımar* holders were the lowest on the scale of military-administrative functionaries who were assigned local sources of revenue. The scale included officer holders ranging from the tımar-holding cavalry officers *(sipahis)* to include the senior ranks of officers and governors whose larger holdings were called *zeʿamet* and *haṣṣ.*

12. *Kethüda* and *çavuş* are functions, *çelebi* and *ağa* are titles, and *bey* is a rank. See James Redhouse, *A Turkish-English Lexicon* (Constantinople: A. H. Boyajian, 1890), s.v. and Pakalın, s.v. for discussions of each.

13. TSAE-7301/2, page b.

14. Stephan, "An Endowment Deed," 187. See similar charges to the manager for the ʿimaret of Edirne in Kazancıgil, *Edirne İmaretleri,* 96–97.

15. TSK-Koğuşlar 888/pp. 162 bot., 230(a) and 283(a). The fees paid by foreign Christian pilgrims to enter the Church of the Holy Sepulcher were part of the waqf of the Dome of the Rock, on which see Cohen and Lewis, *Population and Revenue,* 96.

16. TSK-Koğuşlar 888/pp. 309a and 309a bot.; TSAD-1585 and TSAD-9414 are detailed accounts of the cost of materials and labor for this project.

17. Rosen-Ayalon, "On Suleiman's *Sabīls*," and Salama and Zilberman, "Supply of Water to Jerusalem" (Hebrew).

18. TSK-Koğuşlar 888/pp. 283a.

19. TSAD-7301/2 from 962/1555; and the section on water in Singer, *Palestinian peasants*, 101–04.

20. See the title deeds: TSAE-7816/2 (21 Rebiülahir 957/9 May 1550) and TSAE-7816/1 (22 Zilḳa'de 957/1 Jan. 1551); the Turkish waqfiyya, Tur. 4; and TSAD-2149 recording revenues from 11 Şevval 956 to the end of Zilḳa'de 959/2 Nov. 1549–17 Dec. 1552.

21. Faroqhi, "Sayyid Gazi Revisited."

22. On Dayr al-Asad, see Layish, "Waqfs and Sûfî Monasteries."

23. On all these properties, see the title deeds TSAE-7816/3-7 and the discussion in Chapter 2.

24. On the payment of taxes and the management of tax arrears generally, see Singer, *Palestinian peasants*, 64–88.

25. TSAD-3643/3, TSAE-3643/4, which refer to 961–62, although dated in 963.

26. TSAE-7301/2 and TSAD-10609.

27. TSAD-3643/6/p. 3, right.

28. TSAD-3643/2 (Evahir Rebiülevvel 963/4–14 March 1556) gives the details of accounts from the tenure of 'Ali *kethüda* (end of 959 to mid-961), and then records how Ferhad collected 95 percent of the revenues outstanding.

29. TSAD-3643/6/p. 3, right.

30. TSAD-6482/p. 3b; TSAE-2536.

31. Rhoads Murphey, *Ottoman Warfare, 1500–1700* (London: University College London Press, 1999), 62.

32. Title deed TSAE-7816/7; TSAD-961/p. 14b. Another example of purchasing comes from the village of Lidd, which became the supplier of honey and cooking fat *(samn)* to the 'imaret. The villagers were troubled, however, when the waqf failed to pay its bills one year. JS-107/p. 352 (29 Rabī' al-Thānī 1033/19 Februrary 1624).

33. TSAD-6482, p. 3b; TSAD-3643/6/p. 4, right.

34. JS-28 1612/p. 403.

35. Ze'evi, *An Ottoman Century*, 28.

36. See Heyd, *Ottoman Documents*. This impression given by his compilation was confirmed by a thorough search in the *mühimme defterleri* at the Başbakanlık Arşivi in Istanbul.

37. TSAD-3643/6, dated the beginning of Ṣafar 963 (16–26 December 1555).

38. For a similar question, see Surarya Faroqhi, *Towns and Townsmen of Ottoman Anatolia: trade, crafts and food production in an urban setting, 1520–1650*, (Cambridge, UK: Cambridge University Press, 1984), 207.

39. *Zikr olan 117 sikke-i altun mezkur Ferhad çelebi bize gönderüb teslim eyledi. Ṣaḥḥ.* TSAD-3643/6.

40. *Bir nöbet* refers to a single serving per day, which seems to have been the initial practice at the 'imaret. *"Ve bu faḳirin zamanında vaḳıfname-i şerif*

*mucibince ṭaʿam iki nöbet pişirüb,"* TSAE-2536. See also TSAD-6483, p. 3b. *Nöbet* basically means a "shift" as in "a turn of action, duty, etc., in rotation with others," Redhouse, *A Turkish-English Lexicon,* s.v.

41. TSAE-7301/2, page a.

42. Twenty baṭmān more (TSAD-3643/12); eighty baṭmān yield 1100 loaves (TSAD-3643/8).

43. TSAD-3643/8 (Evasit Cemazielula 962/3–13 April 1555).

44. Weir and Zysow, *"ṣadaḳa"*, VIII:712.

45. Muṣṭafā b. Ahmet ʿAlī, *Muṣṭafa ʿAlī's Counsel for Sultans,* II:27/144.

46. Ibid., II:28/145–46.

47. TSAD-3643/12.

48. TSAD-3643/8.

49. TSAD-3643/8.

50. TSAE-9297/36.

51. TSAD-6482/p. 3b.

52. See the text at the beginning of the chapter (TSAE-7301/2) as well as TSAD-10609 (13 Muḥarrem 963/28 November 1555).

53. Bayram died late in the year 1562. See Natsheh, "Catalogue of Buildings," 711.

54. TSAE-7301/2, p. (b).

55. JS-31 1448/p. 298, 12 Jumāda II 963/23 April 1556.

56. Cohen and Lewis, *Population and Revenue,* 69.

57. See Martin Dow, *The Islamic Baths of Palestine* (Oxford: Oxford University Press, 1996), 93–95 and Yehoshua Ben-Arieh, *Jerusalem in the 19th Century: The Old City* (Jerusalem: Yad Izhak Ben Zvi, 1984), 167, 168.

58. Jennings, "Pious Foundations," 315, and two further examples, 277, 284.

59. On the bath construction see TSAE-7301/2 p. (c). and JS-31 2508/p. 518. About ongoing water problems see MD-36/374 and Heyd, *Ottoman Documents,* 146–50. And on baths generally, see J. Sourdel-Thomine, *"ḥammām,"* *EI*[2], III:139–44.

60. Auld and Hillenbrand, *Ottoman Jerusalem,* 1018–20.

61. The *ferman* is mentioned in TSAD-1511 (evahir Şaʿban 963/30 June–8 July 1556), p. 10b. The precise dates for the bath construction were 1 Receb 961 to the latter part of Cemaziülahar 963 (2 June 1554 to 12–21 April 1556).

62. *"Ḥamam binası muhim olub akçeye muzayak olmağın Bayram çavuş kendi yanından ṣırf eylemiştir."* (TSAD-3539). See also TSAD-3643/11; TSAD-1511.

63. Al-ʿAsalī, *Wathā'iq,* 313–14, a document from 1065/1655.

64. TSAD-3643/5, p. 3b.

65. TSAD-10609.

66. TSAD-3643/12, p. 4a.

67. TSAD-10609.

68. TSAD-3639.

69. TSAD-1511/p. 3a; the Muslim calendar has 354 days.

70. TSAD-961/p. 14b, p. 15b.

71. MD-2/1120/p. 110, 5 Ramazan 963/July 1556.

72. TSAD-1511/pp. 12b–13a (evahir Şaʿban 963/30 June–8 July 1556).

73. This was in the period before Jericho was exchanged out of the endowment properties. See JS-33/1454/p. 275 (8 Jumada I 964/9 March 1557), where the village leaders come to request the cauldron. Such a cauldron was listed among the miscellaneous expenses of the endowment: "for the price of a cauldron for making indigo in the village of Jericho: one cauldron, 1600 *akçe*." (TSAD-5262).

74. TSAD-3628/20 (evahir Şaʿban 963/30 June–8 July 1556). This request was signed by Ṭurgud during his brief first tenure as manager.

75. The Franciscans had been squeezed out over the course of two decades, being expelled altogether in 1551 (Cohen, "The Expulsion of the Franciscans from Mt. Zion," 154). The sufis received eight and one-half cups of food and thirty-four loaves of bread, hence their portions were comparable to those of other *fuḳara* of all types: two loaves and one-half cup of food per person (TSAD-1511, p. 8a).

76. JS-33/717; JS-33/2834.

77. TSAD-8466. This *defter* is undated but explicitly says that it is from Bayram's time: *"hala mütevelli olan Bayram çavuş."*

78. MD-3/138/p. 58, 15 Şevval 966/21 July 1559.

79. MD-3/746/p. 258, 2 Cemaziülevvel 967/30 January 1560.

80. TSAD-4576, no date but during the tenure of Ṭurgud *ağa*, described as "the new manager," and after the year 965/1557–58 which is covered in the register. Even in the earlier register (TSAD-3643/10) for the year 963/1555–56, which reflected the calculation of revenues for the year of the exchange, Bayram collected far more than the amount projected in the survey register.

81. The figures cited for the villages in the *sancak* of Jerusalem correspond to those given in TTD 289, dating from 952/1545 while those for villages in the *sancak* of Ramle are taken from TTD 265, dating from 955/1548–49.

82. On the comparison between yields projected in the surveys and those actually recorded, see the discussion in Singer, *Palestinian peasants,* 64–88.

83. Compare on grain prices in Konya, see Faroqhi, *Towns and townsmen,* 208.

84. MD-3/12 and 13/p. 4, 14 Ramazan 966/20 June 1559; MD-3/28/p. 9, 15 Ramazan 966/21 June 1559.

85. MD-36/372/p. 133, 23 Muḥarram 987/22 March 1579. On the import of rice from Egypt, see Suraiya Faroqhi, "Crisis and Change," in *An Economic and Social History,* ed. Inalcik and Quataert, 493–94 and Stanford Shaw, *The Financial and Administrative Organization and Development of Ottoman Egypt 1517–1798* (Princeton: Princeton University Press, 1962), 125, 274.

86. MD-3/481/p. 174, 30 Muḥarram 967/1 November 1559.

87. MD-3/486, 3 Ṣafer 967/4 November 1559.

88. Inalcik and Quataert, *An Economic and Social History,* 256–70.

89. TSAD-4576/p. 2b.

90. JS-31/227/p. 49; JS-44/569/p. 94, and see Singer, *Palestinian peasants,* 116.

91. Hütteroth and Abdulfattaḥ, *Historical Geography*, 138.

92. MD-3/483/p. 175–76, 2 Ṣafer 967/3 November 1559.

93. MD-36/373/p. 133, 23 Muḥarrem 987/22 March 1579.

94. Auld and Hillenbrand, *Ottoman Jerusalem*, 1049, JS-39/p. 30–31 (967/1559).

95. MD-33/315/p. 158, 4 Şevval 985/15 December 1577. This mühimme entry also includes the farm of Marfūqa, and the plot of land called al-Qaqar as part of the *ze'amet* properties, though they do not appear in the *muḥasebe* registers, e.g. TSAD-3528/1.

96. These additions date from evaḥir Şevvāl 967/25 July–4 August 1560. For more on them, see Chapter 2. The text of the additional waqfiyya may be found in Al-'Asalī, *Wathā'iq*, 147–50.

97. MD-6/66/p. 32, dispatched on 18 Muḥarrem 972/26 August 1564.

98. For a more extensive discussion of the incorporation of Ṭurgud's *ze'amet* properties and its implications, see Amy Singer, "A Note on Land and Identity: From *Ze'amet to Waqf*," in *New Perspectives on Property and Land in the Middle East*, ed. Roger Owen (Cambridge, MA: Harvard University Press, 2001), 161–73.

99. 'Abdülkerim was appointed no later than 17 Muḥarrem 972/25 August 1564. (MD-6/50/p. 25). On his removal, see MD-7/2367/p. 864, 5 Cemaziülevvel 976/26 October 1568.

100. MD-26/850/p. 293, 15 Receb 982/31 October 1574.

101. See Halil Inalcik, "Adâletnâmeler," *Belgeler* 2, no. 3–4 (1965): 49–145; Heyd, *Ottoman Documents, passim* and Singer, *Palestinian peasants,* Chapter 5, for the complaints lodged against these officials.

102. Muṣtafa b. Aḥmet 'Alī, *Muṣṭafa 'Ali's Counsel for Sultans*, II: 28–29/146–47.

103. Cohen and Lewis, *Population and Revenue*, 89.

104. Success could also be due to popularity; that is, a particular endowment might be perceived as especially successful, thereby attracting other donors, and so be reinforced by their contributions. For this phenomenon in Algiers, see Hoexter, *Endowments, Rulers and Community*, 52–53.

## CHAPTER 5

1. Evliya Çelebi, *Evliya Çelebi Seyahatnamesi, 1. Kitap: İstanbul,* prepared by Orhan Şaik Gökyay (Istanbul: Yapi Kredi Yayınları, 1996), 132(a).

2. Peirce offers a succinct discussion of the role of food in the Ottoman administration, on which see *The Imperial Harem*, 175.

3. Kate Fleet, *European and Islamic Trade in the Early Ottoman State* (Cambridge, UK: Cambridge University Press, 1999), 63–73.

4. Güçer understood the logic of this system as aimed at controlling military supplies, intervening in times of famine and ensuring tax revenues, see Lutfi Güçer, *XVI–XVII. Asırlarda Osmanlı İmparatorluğunda Hububat Meselesi*

*ve Hububattan Alınan Vergiler* (Istanbul: İstanbul Üniversitesi, İktisat Fakültesi, 1964), 38–41. Barkan characterized the Ottoman system as one of "imperial self-sufficiency," creating "a tightly closed economic order," which lasted until the transformations of the later sixteenth century. (Ö. L. Barkan, "The Price Revolution of the Sixteenth Century," *IJMES* 6 (1975): 4–5. On Istanbul as the hub, see Inalcik, *The Ottoman Empire,* 145. The Ottoman regime kept shipping directed toward Istanbul and away from many smaller ports, such as Izmir, in order to isolate them from the market demands of European merchants. The situation changed in the later sixteenth century, with the resulting growth of port towns and the commercialization of littoral agriculture. See Daniel Goffman, *Izmir and the Levantine World, 1550–1650* (Seattle: University of Washington Press, 1990), 10, 139. Murphey emphasizes the supply of food to the entire population of the city, especially to those who ate at the public kitchens. Rhoads Murphey, "Provisioning Istanbul: The State and Subsistence in the Early Modern East," *Food and Foodways* 2 (1988): 217–63.

5. Population figures are, of course, difficult to estimate, and the estimates vary wildly. Inalcik dismisses figures like 700,000 for the sixteenth century as impossibly high, preferring to take the Byzantine and early twentieth-century figures for Istanbul and Galata together to put a ceiling at 400,000. Ottoman documents record some 80,000 households in 942/1535, a figure which could indicate anything between 320,000 and 560,000, depending on what kind of household multiplier is used. Yet these are figures for the *re'aya.* The palace personnel and *kapı kulu* troops in Istanbul added approximately 24,000 people to the city's population in 1526. See Halil Inalcik, "Istanbul," *EI*², IV:242–43.

6. Inalcik and Quataert, *An Economic and Social History,* 50, 181–87. See also Goffman, *Izmir,* 36–49, on the intensified smuggling problems of the late sixteenth and early seventeenth centuries.

7. Inalcik and Quataert, *An Economic and Social History,* 39, and S. Faroqhi, "Camels, Wagons and the Ottoman State in the Sixteenth and Seventeenth Centuries," *IJMES* 14 (1982): 531–33.

8. See Inalcik, "Istanbul," 226; and "Unkapanı" and "Kapanlar" in *İstA.*

9. *Evliya Çelebi Seyahatnamesi, 1. Kitap,* 218 ff.

10. Inalcik and Quataert, *An Economic and Social History,* 179.

11. On bread and bakers, see C. Pellat, *"khubz," EI*², V:41–43 and *Evliya Çelebi Seyahatnamesi, 1. Kitap,* 230. There is a detailed discussion of the provisioning of Istanbul, based in part on Evliya, in Mantran, *Istanbul dans la seconde moitié,* 179–213 and maps 12 & 13.

12. B. Cvetkova, "Les Celep et leur rôle dans la vie économique des Balkans à l'époque Ottomane (XVe–XVIIIe s.)," in *Studies in the Economic History of the Middle East,* ed. M. A. Cook (London: Oxford University Press, 1970), 182–83.

13. Work on the many aspects of consumption in the Ottoman empire is just beginning. For quantities of meat consumed by the Ottoman elites in

Istanbul in the sixteenth century, see Artan, "Aspects of the Ottoman Elite's Food Consumption," 135–37. In general on consumption, see S. Faroqhi, "Research on the History of Ottoman Consumption: A Preliminary Exploration of Sources and Models," in *Consumption Studies and the History of the Ottoman Empire, 1550–1922,* ed. Donald Quataert (Albany: State University of New York Press, 2000), 15–44.

14. On *narh,* see Inalcik and Quataert, *An Economic and Social History,* 46, and Pakalın, 2:654–57.

15. On the imperial kitchen (*maṭbah-i ʿamire*), see Uzunçarşılı, *Osmanlı Devletinin Saray Teşkilatı,* 379–84; H. Inalcik, D. Waines, and J. Burton-Page, "*maṭbakh,*" *EI*², VI:811; and Necipoğlu, *Architecture, Ceremonial and Power,* 70.

16. In the eighteenth century, these daily deliveries represented an important commitment of human and material resoruces, on which see Artan, "Aspects of the Ottoman Elite's Food Consumption."

17. Arslan Terzioğlu, *Helvahane Defteri* (Istanbul: Arkeoloji ve Sanat Yayınları, 1992).

18. Necipoğlu, *Architecture, Ceremonial and Power,* 69–72, 178.

19. Faroqhi, *Towns and townsmen,* 58, and Cohen, *Economic life,* 39.

20. Murphey, "Provisioning Istanbul," 218, and Singer, *Palestinian peasants,* 116.

21. Cohen and Lewis, *Population and Revenue,* 94; Faroqhi, *Towns and townsmen,* Table 1, 303.

22. On manufacturing and production in Jerusalem during this period, see Cohen, *Economic life;* on the guilds, see idem, *The Guilds of Ottoman Jerusalem* (Leiden: Brill, 2001), 5, 13.

23. Cohen and Lewis, *Population and Revenue,* 95.

24. For the *ḳanunname* (regulatory code) of Jerusalem in the sixteenth century, see Ö. L. Barkan, *XV ve XVIıncı asırlarda Osmanlı İmparatorluğunda Ziraî Ekonominin Hukukî ve Malî Esasları: Kanunlar* (Istanbul: Bürhaneddin Matbaası, 1943), 217.

25. Christine Woodhead, "Perspectives on Süleyman," in *Süleyman the Magnificent and His Age: The Ottoman Empire in the Early Modern World,* ed. Metin Kunt and Christine Woodhead (Essex: Longman Group UK, 1995), 168.

26. Murphey, *Ottoman Warfare 1500–1700,* 70–73, 85–103.

27. I. Metin Kunt, *The Sultan's Servants: The Transformation of Ottoman Provincial Goverment, 1550–1650* (New York: Columbia University Press, 1983), 62–68.

28. Inalcik and Quataert, *An Economic and Social History,* 179–81; Gilles Veinstein, "Some Views on Provisioning in the Hungarian Campaigns of Süleyman the Magnificent," in *Osmanistische Studien Zur Wirtschafts- und Socialgeschichte,* ed. H. G. Majer (Wiesbaden: Harrassowitz, 1986), 177–85; Caroline Finkel, *The Administration of Warfare: The Ottoman Military Campaigns in Hungary, 1593–1600.* (Vienna: VWGÖ, 1988), 130–43.

29. Inalcik and Quataert, *An Economic and Social History,* 96; Finkel, *The Administration of Warfare,* 137, 207. On the general attempts to limit abuses of

the peasantry by military-administrative personnel and irregulars, see Inalcik, "Adâletnâmeler," 69–72, 89 ff.

30. Muṣṭafā ʿĀlī, *Muṣṭafā ʿĀli's Counsel for Sultans,* I:33–34, 115–16. See Finkel, *The Administration of Warfare,* 151–61, 308, for a parallel and more successful story on the Hungarian front.

31. Gibb and Bowen, *Islamic Society and the West,* I:319.

32. John Kingsley Birge, *The Bektashi Order of Dervishes* (London: Luzac, 1937), 175–76.

33. Algar, "Food in the Life of the Tekke," 297; Inalcik, et al., *"maṭbakh,"* VI:810; Cemal Kafadar, "Yeniçeriler," in *İstA.*, 472–76. Bozkurt Güvenç, "Introduction: Food, Culture and the Culture of Eating," in Ersu Pekin and Ayşe Sümer, dir., *Timeless Tastes: Turkish Culinary Culture* (Istanbul: Vehbi Koç Vakfı, 1996), 15–16.

34. Inalcik and Quataert, *An Economic and Social History,* 98, and Finkel, *The Administration of Warfare,* 154.

35. Suraiya Faroqhi, *Pilgrims and Sultans: The Hajj Under the Ottomans 1517–1683,* (London: I. B. Tauris, 1994), 46–47; Robert Mantran, ed., *Histoire de l'Empire Ottoman* (Paris: Fayard, 1989), 371.

36. Faroqhi, *Pilgrims and Sultans,* 33–37, 42–45.

37. Ibid., 58–65.

38. ʿAdel Mannaʿ, "The Jerusalem Governors of the Farrukh Family and their relations with the Bedouin," (Hebrew) in *Perakim be-Toldot Yerushalayim: be-Reshit ha-Tekufa ha-Othmanit,* ed. Amnon Cohen (Jerusalem: Yad Izhak Ben Zvi, 1979), 196–232. In his "Revolt of the Naqib al-Ashraf in Jerusalem (1703–1705)" (Hebrew) *Cathedra* 35 (1989): 49–74, Mannaʿ discusses how a commander and his troops might even be removed from the siege they were mounting in order to accompany the caravan as an escort.

39. Faroqhi, *Pilgrims and Sultans,* 80–83; Doris Behrens-Abouseif, "Qāytbāy's Foundation in Medina, the *Madrasah,* the *Ribāṭ* and the *Dashīshah,*" *Mamluk Studies Review* 2 (1998): 65–67.

40. See Faroqhi, *Pilgrims and Sultans,* 82–84, and Hoexter, *Endowments, Rulers and Community.*

41. Necipoğlu, "The Süleymaniye Complex," 96–99; Fleischer, "The Lawgiver as Messiah, 160, 171–74.

42. See for examples and a discussion, Aptullah Kuran, "Architecture: The Classical Ottoman Achievement," in *Süleymân the Second [*Sic*] and His Time,* ed. Halil Inalcik and Cemal Kafadar (Istanbul: Isis Press, 1993), 326–29.

43. Caʿfer Efendi, *Risāle-i Miʿmāriyye,* 107/86v.

44. Hans Wehr, *A Dictionary of Modern Written Arabic (Arabic-English),* 4th ed., ed. J. Milton Cowan (Wiesbaden: Otto Harrassowitz, 1979) s.v. Lane says the modern usage is "a public edifice," in E. W. Lane, *An Arabic-English Lexicon* (London: Williams and Norgate, 1863), 2156. See also Cl. Huart, *"ʿimāret,"* *EI* (1927), II:475.

45. This is especially confusing in the case of this Jerusalem waqf. The other facilities—caravansaray and mosque—are almost never mentioned.

46. Cf. Francisco Mesgnien Meninski, *Lexicon Turcico-Arabico-Persicum*, 2nd edition (Vienna: Joseph de Kurzböck, 1780), III:762; and T. X. Bianchi and J. D. Kieffer, *Dictionnaire Turc-Français*, 2d ed. (Paris: Typographie de Mme Ve Dondey–Dupré, 1850), II:284.

47. Johann Wild, *Neue Reysbeschreibung eines gefangenen Christen* (Nurnbert: B. Scherff, 1613), 190, as quoted in R. Dozy, *Supplément aux Dictionnairies Arabes*, 2d ed, (Leiden: Brill, 1927), II:171. (My translation. A. S.)

48. See Franz Rosenthal, "The Stranger in Medieval Islam," *Arabica* 44 (1997), 41–43; and Miri Shefer, "Hospitals in Three Ottoman Capitals: Bursa, Edirne and Istanbul in the Sixteenth and Seventeenth Centuries." (Hebrew, Ph.D. diss., Tel Aviv University, 2001), 50–53.

49. See Barkan, "Osmanlı İmparatorluğunda İmâret Sitelerinin Kuruluş."

50. Inalcik, "Istanbul: An Islamic City," 10.

51. Ibid., 11.

52. Osman N. Ergin, *Türk Şehirlerinde İmâret Sistemi* (Istanbul: Cumhuriyet Matbaası, 1939), 8–15. Ergin also cites inscriptions of mosques where they say "*banā hadhā'l-jāmiʿ al-jalīl al-shān wa'l-ʿimāra al-rafīʿa al-binyān min fawāḍil ṣadaqāt al-sulṭān . . .*" as opposed to the *aşhane* section where the inscription is Quranic: "*Innamā naṭaʿamkum li-wajh Allah . . .*" (p. 11), (my emphasis, A. S.) For other contributions to the discussion, see İ. H. Uzunçarşılı, "Karamanoğulları Devri Vesikalarında İbrahim Bey'in Karaman İmareti Vakfiyesi," *Belleten* 1 (1937): 92, n.2; Ünver, "Anadolu ve İstanbulda imaretlerin aşhane," 2390–410; Pakalın, II:62. Eyice cites Uzunçarşılı's work on Anatolian inscriptions ("*Afyon, Karahisar . . . 'deki Kitabeler ve Sahıp, Saruhan . . . hakkında malumat*" as demonstrating that the term ʿimaret is used to describe what might otherwise be called a *mescid* (a term which he did not find); according to Eyice, ʿimaret in earlier times had a much broader meaning, which was already narrowed in meaning by the early Ottoman period, where it referred to *zaviyes* or *zaviyeli camis*, and then later to *aşhane*. Eyice, "İlk Osmanlı Devrinin Dini-İctimai Bir Müessesesi," 30–31, and also M. Baha Tanman, "Sinan'ın Mimârîsi İmaretler," *Mimarbaşı Koca Sinan Yaşadığı Çağ ve Eserleri*, Vol. 1 (Istanbul, 1988), 333.

53. Yūsuf Khāṣṣ Ḥājib, *Wisdom of Royal Glory (Ḳutadgu Bilig), A Turko-Islamic Mirror for Princes*, ed. and trans. Robert Dankoff (Chicago: University of Chicago Press, 1983), 177 (l.4219), 178 (l.4275), 181 (l.4350). Dankoff also states that "tuz etmek" is a calque on the Persian "nan nemek," pp. 10–11. On the genre of "mirrors for princes," see the general remarks in R. Stephen Humphreys, *Islamic History*, 2nd ed. (Princteon: Princeton University Press, 1991), 164–65.

54. Evliya Çelebi, *The Intimate Life of an Ottoman Statesman: Melek Ahmed Pasha (1588–1662)*, trans. and ed. Robert Dankoff (Albany: State University of New York Press, 1991), 88.

55. See also Ömer Asım Aksoy, *Atsözleri ve Deyimler Sözlüğü* (Ankara: Türk Dili Kurumu, 1971), I:364.

56. Hājib, *Ḳutadgu Bilig*, 180 and R. R. Arat, ed., *Kutadgu Bilig* (Istanbul: Milli Eğitim Basımevi, 1947), 435, l. 4330. This work is also discussed in Inalcik, *The Ottoman Empire*, 67.

57. Niẓām al-Mulk, *The Book of Government, or Rules for Kings* (London: Routledge and Paul, 1960), 124–25. On the place of the *Siyasat-nama* in the mirrors-for-princes genre, see Humphreys, *Islamic History*, 163–64.

58. Eliyahu Ashtor, *A Social and Economic History of the Near East in the Middle Ages* (London: Collins, 1976), 232 ff; and Angelika Hartmann, "Al-Nāṣir li-Dīn Allāh," *EI*², VII:996–1003.

59. A. K. S. Lambton, "Awqaf in Persia: 6th–8th/12th–14th Centuries," *Islamic Law and Society* 4 (1997): 316–17; W. Barthold, "Ghāzān," *EI*², II:1043.

60. S. A. Arjomand, "Philanthropy, the Law and Public Law in the Islamic World Before the Modern Era," in *Philanthropy in the World's Traditions*, ed. W. Ilchman, et al. (Bloomington: Indiana University Press, 1998), 121–22; Lambton, *Continuity and Change*, 155.

61. Maria Eva Subtelny, "A Timurid Educational and Charitable Foundation: the Ikhlāṣiyya Complex of ʿAli Shīr Navā'ī in 15th-Century Herat and Its Endowment," *JAOS* 111 (1991): 47–48.

62. Inalcik et al, "*maṭbakh*," VI:809 and Artan, "Aspects of the Ottoman Elite's Food Consumption," 133. The *toys* were also called *şölen*. *Toy* originally meant "camp," evolving to signify a large gathering and hence, a feast, on which see Sir Gerard Clauson, *An Etymological Dictionary of Pre-Thirteenth Century Turkish* (Oxford: Clarendon Press, 1972), 566–67.

63. This description appears in different forms many times throughout the text. See Dede Korkut, *The Book of Dede Korkut*, 29, 132, 170, 183.

64. Paula Sanders, *Ritual, Politics, and the City in Fatimid Cairo* (Albany: State University of New York Press, 1994), 28, 52, 75, 79.

65. Ibid., 75–79.

66. Mujīr al-Dīn, *Al-Uns al-Jalīl*, I:59.

67. Nasir-i Khusraw, *Sefer Nameh*, ed. and trans. C. Schefer (Paris: E. Leroux, 1881), 57–58.

68. Behrens-Abouseif, "Qāytbāy's Foundation in Medina," 66.

69. Mujīr al-Dīn, *Al-Uns al-Jalīl*, II:443.

70. Mujīr al-Dīn, *Al-Uns al-Jalīl*, I:58–59.

71. ʿAbd al-Ghanī al-Nābulsī, *Al-Ḥaḍra al-Unsiyya fī al-Riḥla al-Qudsiyya* (Beirut: al-Maṣādir, 1990), 252. Al-Nābulsī was in Jerusalem and Hebron in 1101/1689.

72. Evliya Çelebi, *Seyahatname*, Vol. 9 (1671–72) (Istanbul: Devlet Matbaası, 1935), 510.

73. Boaz Shoshan, *Popular Culture in Medieval Cairo* (Cambridge, UK: Cambridge University Press, 1993), 58–60.

74. Tabbaa, *Constructions of Power and Piety*, 158, 160; Behrens-Abouseif, *Egypt's Adjustment to Ottoman Rule*, 164.

75. Sabra, *Poverty and Charity*, 92.

76. Ibid., 88–93.

77. These institutions were mostly called *zaviye* (Ar. *zāwiya*) in Anatolia and the Balkans, while the terms *ribāṭ* and *khānaqāh* were found more frequently in the Arabic-speaking lands of the empire. Donald P. Little, "The

Nature of *Khānqahs, Ribāṭs,* and *Zāwiyas* Under the Mamlūks," in *Islamic Studies Presented to Charles J. Adams,* ed. Wael B. Hallaq and Donald P. Little (Leiden: Brill, 1991), 103–04 and *passim.* See also Inalcik, et al., *"maṭbakh,"* VI:810, 812.

78. Annemarie Schimmel, *The Triumphal Sun: A Study of the Works of Jalalüddin Rumi* (London: East-West Publications, 1980), 138–52. On the convents as distributors of food, see Algar, "Food in the Life of the Tekke," 302.

79. Wolper, "The Politics of Patronage."

80. M. Fuad Köprülü, *The Origins of the Ottoman Empire,* trans. and ed. Gary Leiser (Albany: State University of New York Press, 1992), 64.

81. On the multiple roles of the sufis in the consolidation of Ottoman society, see Eyice, "İlk Osmanlı Devrinin Dini-İctimai Bir Müessesesi," 23; Ira M. Lapidus, "Sufism and Ottoman Islamic Society," in *The Dervish Lodge,* ed. Raymond Lifchez (Berkeley: University of California Press, 1992) 26–28; and Raymond Lifchez, in ibid., 4.

82. Evliya, *Evliya Çelebi Seyahatnamesi, 1. Kitap,* 132(a).

83. Oktay Aslanapa, *Turkish Art and Architecture* (London: Faber, 1971), 336.

84. Behrens-Abouseif, *Egypt's Adjustment to Ottoman Rule,* 164.

85. Huart, "ʿimāret," *EI,* II:475.

86. M. Baba Tanman, "İmaretler," in *IstA,* 4:164–66. Tanman says many were founded in the 200 years before the conquest of Istanbul, but relatively few of these survive.

87. On canonization see Necipoğlu, "A *Kânûn* for the State, a Canon for the Arts." Tanman reinforces this idea when he identifies the crystallization of the ʿimaret form in the buildings of the sixteenth-century master architect, Sinan. See Tanman, "Sinan'ın Mimârîsi İmaretler," 333.

88. Barkan, "Osmanlı İmparatorluğunda İmâret Sitelerinin Kuruluş," 242–43.

89. Caʿfer Efendi, *Risāle-i Miʿmāriyye,* 107/86v.

90. Tanman, "İmaretler," 166.

91. See Freely, *Blue Guide: Istanbul,* maps; and Taşkıran, *Hasekinin Kitabı,* 49, 114–23.

92. Konyalı, *Âbideleri ve Kitabeleri,* 972–73.

93. Pakalın, II:61–63. Unfortunately, Pakalın gives no date for these figures.

94. Gerber, "The Waqf Institution in Early Ottoman Edirne," 43–44. In his calculations, Gerber implies that only men ate in these ʿimarets. However, the examples of the Haṣṣeki Sultan ʿimaret, the Süleymaniye, and the Jerusalem ʿimaret suggest that this is not a sound assumption.

95. Muṣṭafa ʿAli's writings about the capitals are distorted by his own unhappiness at spending most of his life in provincial service, unable to contrive the combination of patronage and luck to gain a central appointment for his talents. His remarks, however, are based on his own broad experiences and observations and so should be given a guarded hearing. On his life and work, see Cornell Fleischer, *Bureaucrat and Intellectual in the Ottoman Empire, The Historian Mustafa ʿAli, 1541–1600* (Princeton: Princeton University Press, 1986), 40, 101–01, 103.

96. *Evliya Çelebi in Diyarbekir,* trans. and ed. Martin von Bruinessen and Hendrik Boeschoten (Leiden: Brill, 1988), 31–32, 222 n.131. On Konya, see Konyalı, *Âbideleri ve Kitabeleri,* 979.

97. Evliya Çelebi, *Seyahatname,* 9:189. Evliya neglects to name the three ʿimarets in Jerusalem, and thus far only that of Hurrem has been identified. Unfortunately, it is not altogether unheard of that observations in Evliya cannot easily be corroborated by other sources.

98. Evliya, *Evliya Çelebi Seyahatnamesi, 1. Kitap: Istanbul,* 132.

99. ʿAshiqpashazādeh, *ʿAshiqpashazādeh Taʾrīkhī,* 42.

100. Niẓām al-Mulk, *The Book of Government,* 143–44.

101. Konstantin Mihailovic, *Memoirs of a Janissary,* trans. B. Stolz (Ann Arbor: University of Michigan, 1975), 31.

102. Necipoğlu, *Architecture, Ceremonial and Power,* 55.

103. Mottahedeh, *Loyalty and Leadership,* 72–77.

104. Note the expression *"ve Saruhan sancağını yirdi,"* Mehmed Neşrî, *Kitâb-ı Cihan-Nümâ. Neşrî Tarihi,* Faik Reşit Unat and Mehmed A. Köymen, eds. (Ankara: Türk Tarih Kurumu Yayınları, 1987), I:348–49.

105. As quoted in Kunt, *The Sultan's Servants,* 41–42. Contrast this with the threat issued by a Serb policeman to an Albanian in Peç: "you will never eat Serbia's bread again," as quoted by Jeffrey Smith, "Thousands Flee as Lawlessness Spreads in Kosovo," *The Washington Post,* 20 July 1998, p. A12.

106. Rhoads Murphey, ed. and trans., *Kanûn-nâme-i Sultânî Li ʿAzîz Efendi: Aziz Efendi's Book of Sultanic Laws and Regulations: An Agenda for Reform by a Seventeenth-Century Ottoman Statesman* (Cambridge, MA: Harvard University, 1985), 24, 42.

107. Mottahedeh, *Loyalty and Leadership,* 75.

108. Muṣṭafā ʿAlī, *Muṣṭafā ʿĀli's Counsel for Sultans,* I:32/113.

109. Ibid., I:46/135.

110. Murphey remarks that this is akin to the modern English saying, "biting the hand that feeds one." See Murphey, *Kanûn-nâme-i Sultânî,* 52, n.58.

111. Murphey, "Provisioning Istanbul," 217–19.

## CONCLUSION

1. Cahit Uçuk, *Bir İmparatorluk Çökerken* (Istanbul: Yapı Kredi Yayınları, 1995), 51. This memoir about the last years of the Ottoman empire was written by one of Turkey's prominent women writers, well-known beginning from the 1930s.

2. Cited in Cohen, *Economic life,* 120 (JS-55/p. 495).

3. JS-64/367, 16 Rabīʿ al-Awwal 993/18 March 1585, as cited in Auld and Hillenbrand, *Ottoman Jerusalem,* 1015, 1048.

4. See registers TSAD-1527/1 for the years 995–98/1586–90 and TSAD-3643/16 dated 995/1586–87.

5. JS-112/476, as cited in Auld and Hillenbrand, *Ottoman Jerusalem,* 1015–16, 1046–47.

6. Adele Lindenmeyr, "Public Life, Private Virtues: Women in Russian Charity, 1762–1914," *Signs* (1993): 562–91.

7. Cavallo, *Charity and power*, 153–82.

8. Ginzberg, *Women and the Work of Benevolence*, 50–51.

9. Kristin Ohlson, "Deep Pocketbooks: Women, Money, and Power," *MS Magazine*, September/October 1998, 58–63.

10. For a cogent articulation of the dynamic of provincial Ottomanization, although for the eighteenth and nineteenth centuries, see Dina Rizk Khoury, *State and provincial society in the Ottoman Empire: Mosul, 1540–1834* (Cambridge: UK: Cambridge University Press, 1998), 213–14.

11. Behrens-Abouseif, *Egypt's Adjustment to Ottoman Rule*, 157.

12. For difference articulations of this idea, see Fyzee, *Outline of Muhammadan Law*, 230; and Richard van Leeuwen, *Waqfs and Urban Structures: The Case of Ottoman Damascus* (Leiden: Brill, 1999).

13. Mottahedeh, *Loyalty and Leadership*, 77, and see also 72–77.

14. Gerber, "The Waqf Institution in Early Ottoman Edirne," 43; I. Metin Kunt, "The Waqf as an Instrument of Public Policy: Notes on the Köprülü Family Endowments," in *Studies in Ottoman History in Honour of Professor V. L. Ménage*, ed. Colin Heywood and Colin Imber (Istanbul: Isis Press, 1994), 189–90, 198; and Hoexter, *"Ḥuqūq Allāh and Ḥuqūq al-ʿIbād."*

15. Stillman, "Waqf and the Ideology of Charity," 358–59.

16. Imber, *Ebus's-suʿud: The Islamic Legal Tradition*, 82, 139.

17. Caʿfer Efendi, *Risāle-i Miʿmāriyye*, 42.

18. Uçuk, *Bir İmparatorluk Çökerken*, 51.

19. Evliya Çelebi, *Evliya Çelebi in Bitlis*, trans. Robert Dankoff (Leiden: Brill, 1990), 147.

20. Artan, "Aspects of the Ottoman Elite's Food Consumption," 143.

21. Imber, *Ebu's-suʿud*, 139.

22. This is clearly reminiscent of potlatch, yet lacks the destructive component. Here, nothing is destroyed or wasted, only redistributed, pehaps several times over, in a chain of entangled beneficence and patronage.

# Bibliography

## Documentary Sources


Başbakanlık Arşivi (Prime Minister's Archives), Istanbul

Ahkam defterleri

Kamil Kepeci

Mühimme defterleri

Nezaret Sonrası Evkaf Defterleri (EV)

Tapu Tahrir defterleri

Topkapı Saray Arşivi, Istanbul

Defter series

Evrak series

Topkapı Saray Kütüphanesi, Istanbul

Koğuşlar 888

Türk ve İslam Eserleri Müzesi, Istanbul

#2192, waqfiyya

Tapu ve Kadastro Umum Müdürlüğü

Tapu Tahrir defterleri

Sijillāt al-Maḥkama al-Sharʿiyya, al-Quds (Microfilm collection at Haifa University Library)

## Published Sources

Abbott, Nabia. *Two Queens of Baghdad.* Chicago: University of Chicago Press, 1946.

"Adiabene" in *Encyclopaedia Britannica Micropedia,* 15th ed. (1974).

Agulhon, M., and Pierre Bonte. *Marianne. Les Visages de la République.* Paris: Gallimard, 1992.

Aksoy, Ömer Asım. *Atsözleri ve Deyimler Sözlüğü.* Ankara: Türk Dili Kurumu, 1971.

Algar, Ayla. "Food in the Life of the Tekke." In *The Dervish Lodge: Architecture, Art, and Sufism in Ottoman Turkey,* edited by Raymond Lifchez, 296–303. Berkeley: University of California Press, 1992.

Anderson, J. N. D. *Law Reform in the Muslim World.* London: Athlone Press, 1976.

———. "Recent Developments in Sharīʿa Law IX: The Waqf System." *Muslim World* 42 (1952): 257–76.

———. "The Religious Element in Waqf Endowments." *Journal of the Royal Central Asian Society* 38 (1951): 292–99.

———. "The Sharia and Civil Law: The Debt Owed by the New Civil Codes of Egypt and Syria to the Sharia." *Islamic Quarterly* 1 (1954): 29–46.

Arat, R. R., ed. *Kutadgu Bilig.* Istanbul: Milli Eğitim Basımevi, 1947.

Arberry, A. J. *The Koran Interpreted.* Oxford: Oxford University Press, 1983.

Arjomand, S. A. "Philanthropy, the Law and Public Law in the Islamic World Before the Modern Era." In *Philanthropy in the World's Traditions,* edited by W. Ilchman, S. N. Katz, and E. L. Queen, 109–32. Bloomington: Indiana University Press, 1998.

Artan, Tülay. "Aspects of the Ottoman Elite's Food Consumption: Looking for 'Staples,' 'Luxuries,' and 'Delicacies,' in a Changing Century." In *Consumption Studies and the History of the Ottoman Empire, 1550–1922. An Introduction,* edited by Donald Quataert, 107–200. Albany: State University of New York Press, 2000.

———. "From Charismatic Leadership to Collective Rule: Introducing Materials on the Wealth and Power of Ottoman Princesses in the Eighteenth Century." *Dünkü ve Bugünüyle Toplum ve Ekonomi* 4 (1993): 53–94.

———. "Noble Women Who Changed the Face of the Bosphorus and the Palaces of the Sultanas." *Istanbul (Biannual)* 1 (1993): 87–97.

Al-ʿAsalī, K. J. *Wathāʾiq Maqdisiyya Taʾrīkhiyya.* Amman: al-Jāmiʿa al-Urdunniyya, 1983.

ʿĀshiqpashazādeh. *ʿĀshiqpashazādeh Ta'rīkhī. A History of the Ottoman Empire to A.H. 883 (A.D. 1478).* Edited by ʿAlī Bey. Istanbul: Matbaa-i Amire, 1332/1914.

Ashtor, Eliyahu. *A Social and Economic History of the Near East in the Middle Ages.* London: Collins, 1976.

Aslanapa, Oktay. *Turkish Art and Architecture.* London: Faber, 1971.

Atıl, Esin. "Islamic Women as Rulers and Patrons." *Asian Art* 6 (1993): 3–12.

Auld, S., and R. Hillenbrand. *Ottoman Jerusalem. The Living City: 1517–1917.* London: Altajir World of Islam Trust, 2000.

Baer, G. "The Dismemberment of *Awqâf* in Early Nineteenth-Century Jerusalem." In *Ottoman Palestine 1800–1914: Studies in Economic and Social History,* edited by Gad G. Gilbar, 299–319. Leiden: Brill, 1990.

———. "The Muslim Waqf and Similar Institutions in Other Civilizations." Unpublished paper, presented at the Workshop on Economic and Social Aspects of the Muslim Waqf, Jerusalem, 1981.

———. "The Waqf as a Prop for the Social System, 16th–20th Centuries." *Islamic Law and Society* 4 (1997): 264–97.

———. "Waqf Reform in Egypt." *Middle Eastern Affairs* 1 (1958): 61–76.

———. "Women and Waqf: An Analysis of the Istanbul Tahrîr of 1546." *Asian and African Studies* 17 (1983): 9–27.

Bakhit, M. A. *Kashshāf iḥṣā'ī zamanī li-sijillāt al-maḥākim al-sharʿiyya wa'l-awqāf al-islāmiyya fī bilād al-Shām.* Amman: Markaz al-Wathā'iq wa'l Makhṭūṭāt, 1984.

Barkan, Ö. L. "İstanbul Saraylarına ait Muhasebe Defterleri." *Belgeler* 9 (1979): 1–380.

———. *XV ve XVIıncı asırlarda Osmanlı İmparatorluğunda Ziraî Ekonominin Hukukî ve Malî Esasları: Kanunlar.* Istanbul: Bürhaneddin Matbaası, 1943.

———. "Osmanlı İmparatorluğunda Bir İskân ve Kolonizasyon Metodu Olarak Vakıflar ve Temlikler." *Vakıflar Dergisi* 2 (1942): 279–386.

———. "Osmanlı İmparatorluğunda İmâret Sitelerinin Kuruluş ve İşleyiş Tarzına âit Araştırmalar." *İstanbul Üniversitesi İktisat Fakültesi Mecmuası* 23 (1962–63): 239–96.

———. "The Price Revolution of the Sixteenth Century." *International Journal of Middle East Studies* 6 (1975): 3–28.

———. *Süleymaniye Camii ve İmareti İnşaatı (1550–1557).* 2 vols. Ankara: Türk Tarih Kurumu, 1972–79.

———. "Süleymaniye Camii ve İmareti Tesislerine ait Yıllık Bir Muhasebe Bilânçosu 993–994 (1585–1586)," *Vakıflar Dergisi* 9 (1971): 109–62.

Barkey, Karen. *Bandits and Bureaucrats: The Ottoman Route to State Centralization.* Ithaca: Cornell University Press, 1994.

Barnai, Yakov. *Historiography and Nationalism: Trends in the Study of Eretz Israel and Its Jewish Settlement, 634–1881.* Jerusalem: Magnes Press, 1995.

Barnes, John Robert. *An Introduction to Religious Foundations in the Ottoman Empire.* Leiden: Brill, 1987.

Barron, J. B. *Mohammedan Wakfs in Palestine.* Jerusalem: Printed at the Greek Convent Press, 1922.

Barthold, W. "Ghāzān." In *EI*², II: 1043.

Bartlett, W. H. *Jerusalem Revisited.* London: A. Hall, Virtue and Co., 1855.

Bates, Ülkü Ü. "The Architectural Patronage of Ottoman Women." *Asian Art* 6 (1993): 50–65.

———. "Women as Patrons of Architecture in Turkey." In *Women in the Muslim World,* edited by Lois Beck and Nikki Keddie, 245–60. Cambridge, MA: Harvard University Press, 1978.

Behrens-Abouseif, Doris. *Egypt's Adjustments to Ottoman Rule: Institutions, Waqf and Architecture in Cairo (16th & 17th Centuries).* Leiden: Brill, 1994.

———. "Qāytbāy's Foundation in Medina, the *Madrasah,* the *Ribāṭ* and the *Dashīshah.*" *Mamluk Studies Review* 2 (1998): 60–71.

———. "The *Maḥmal* Legend and the Pilgrimage of the Ladies of the Mamluk Court." *Mamluk Studies Review* 1 (1997): 87–96.

Ben-Arieh, Yehoshua. *Jerusalem in the 19th Century: The Old City.* Jerusalem: Yad Izhak Ben Zvi, 1984.

Berchem, M. van. *Matériaux pour un corpus inscriptionum arabicarum. Deuxième partie: Syrie du Sud II. Jérusalem 'Ville.'* Cairo: Institut Français d'archaeologie Orientale, 1922–23.

Berger, M. *"khayr."* In *EI*², IV: 1151–53.

Berkey, Jonathan P. *The Transmission of Knowledge in Medieval Cairo: A Social History of Islamic Education.* Princeton: Princeton University Press, 1992.

Bianchi, T. X., and J. D. Kieffer. *Dictionnaire Turc-Français.* 2d ed. Paris: Typographie de Mme Ve Dondey–Dupré, 1850.

Bilici, Faruk, ed. *Le Waqf dans le monde musulman contemporain (XIXe–XXe siècles): Fonctions sociales, économiques et politiques.* Istanbul: Institut Français d'Etudes Anatoliennes, 1994.

Birge, John Kingsley. *The Bektashi Order of Dervishes.* London: Luzac, 1937.

Bonner, Michael. "Definitions of Poverty and the Rise of the Muslim Urban Poor." *Journal of the Royal Asiatic Society* 6, 3rd series (1996): 335–344.

Boyle, Robert. *The Tragedy of Mustapha, the Son of Solyman the Magnificent.* In *Five Heroic Plays,* edited by Bonamy Dobrée. London: Oxford University Press, 1960.

Bryer, Anthony. "Greek Historians on the Turks: The Case of the First Byzantine-Ottoman Marriage." In *The Writing of History in the Middle Ages. Essays Presented to R. W. Southern,* edited by R. H. C. Davis and J. M. Wallace-Hadrill, 471–93. Oxford: Clarendon Press, 1981.

———. "Rural Society in Matzouka." In *Continuity and Change in Late Byzantine and Early Ottoman Society,* edited by Anthony Bryer and Heath Lowry.

Bryer, Anthony, and Heath Lowry. *Continuity and Change in Late Byzantine and Early Ottoman Society.* Birmingham, UK: Centre for Byzantine Studies and Dumbarton Oaks, 1986.

Burgoyne, Michael H. *Mamluk Jerusalem: An Architectural Study.* London: World of Islam Festival Trust, 1987.

Caʿfer Efendi. *Risāle-i Miʿmāriyye. An Early-Seventeenth-Century Ottoman Treatise on Architecture.* Facsimile with translation and notes. Edited by Howard Crane. Leiden: Brill, 1987.

Cahen, Claude. "Réflexions sur le *Waqf* Ancien." *Studia Islamica* 14 (1961): 37–56.

Cattan, Henry. "The Law of Waqf." In *Law in the Middle East,* edited by M. Khadduri and Herbert J. Liebseny, 203–22. Washington, D.C., 1955.

Cavallo, Sandra. *Charity and power in early modern Italy: Benefactors and their motives in Turin, 1541–1789.* Cambridge, UK: Cambridge University Press, 1995.

Chabbi, J. *"khānḳāh."* In *EI*², IV: 1025–26.

Chamberlain, Michael. *Knowledge and social practice in medieval Damascus, 1190–1350.* Cambridge, UK: Cambridge University Press, 1994.

Çizakça, Murat. *A History of Philanthropic Foundations. The Islamic World From the Seventh Century to the Present,* Istanbul: Boğaziçi University Press, 2000.

———. "Cash Waqfs in Bursa, 1555–1823." *JESHO Special Issue on Waqfs* and Other Institutions of Religious/Philanthropic Endowment in Comparative Perspective 38(1995): 313–54.

Clauson, Sir Gerard. *An Etymological Dictionary of Pre-Thirteenth Century Turkish.* Oxford: Clarendon Press, 1972.

Cohen, Amnon. *Economic life in Ottoman Jerusalem.* Cambridge, UK: Cambridge University Press, 1989.

———. "The Expulsion of the Franciscans from Mt. Zion." *Turcica* 18 (1986): 147–57.

———. *The Guilds of Ottoman Jerusalem.* Leiden: Brill, 2001.

———. "The Walls of Jerusalem." In *The Islamic World: From Classical to Modern Times. Essays in Honor of Bernard Lewis,* edited by C. E. Bosworth and Charles Issawi, 467–77. Princeton: The Darwin Press, Inc. 1989.

Cohen, Amnon, and Bernard Lewis. *Population and Revenue in the Towns of Palestine in the Sixteenth Century.* Princeton: Princeton University Press, 1978.

Cohen, Amnon, and Elisheva Simon-Pikali, eds. and trans. *Jews in the Moslem Religious Court: Society, Economy and Communal Organization in the XVIth Century, Documents from Ottoman Jerusalem.* Jerusalem: Yad Izhak Ben-Zvi, 1993.

Cohen, Mark R. "Poverty as Reflected in the Genizah Documents." *Proceedings of the Seventh International Conference of the Society for Judaeo-Arabic Studies,* edited by Paul Fenton. Forthcoming.

Conrad, Lawrence I., and Barbara Kellner-Heinkele. "Ottoman Resources in the Khalidi Library in Jerusalem." In *Aspects of Ottoman History. Papers from CIEPO IX, Jerusalem,* edited by A. Singer and A. Cohen, 280–93. Jerusalem: The Magnes Press, 1994.

Constantelos, Demetrios J. *Byzantine Philanthropy and Social Welfare.* New Brunswick: Rutgers University Press, 1968.

———. *Poverty, Society and Philanthropy in the Late Medieval Greek World.* New Rochelle, NY: Aristide D. Caratzas, 1992.

Crane, Howard. "Notes on Saldjūq Architectural Patronage in Thirteenth Century Anatolia." *JESHO* 36 (1993): 1–57.

Crecelius, Daniel N. "The Waqf of Muḥammad Bey Abū al-Dhahab in Historial Perspective." Paper presented at the conference on Social and Economic Aspects of the Muslim Waqf, Jerusalem, 1979.

Crouch, N. *A Journey to Jerusalem: Or, A Relation of the Travels of Fourteen Englishmen in the Year 1669.* London: printed by T. M. for N. Crouch in Exchang-Alley, 1672.

Cvetkova, B. "Les Celep et leur rôle dans la vie économique des Balkans à l'époque Ottomane (XVe–XVIIIe s.)." In *Studies in the Economic History of the Middle East*, edited by M. A. Cook, 172–92. London: Oxford University Press, 1970.

Darwish, Linda. "Images of Muslim Women: 'A'isha, Fatima, and Zaynab Bint 'Ali in Contemporary Gender Discourse." *McGill Journal of Middle East Studies* 4 (1996): 93–132.

Davis, Natalie Zemon. *The Gift in Sixteenth-Century France*. Madison: University of Wisconsin Press, 2000.

Dede Korkut. *The Book of Dede Korkut*. Translated by Geoffrey Lewis. Harmondsworth: Penguin Books Ltd, 1974.

Deguilhem, Randi, ed. *Le Waqf dans l'espace islamique. Outil de pouvoir socio-politique*. Damas: Institut Français de Damas, 1995.

Dols, Michael. *Majnūn: The Madman in Medieval Islamic Society*. Oxford: Oxford University Press, 1992.

Dow, Martin. *The Islamic Baths of Palestine*. Oxford: Oxford University Press, 1996.

Dozy, R. *Supplément aux Dictionnaries Arabes*, 2e ed. Leiden: Brill, 1927.

Duff, P. W. "The Charitable Foundations of Byzantium." In *Cambridge Legal Essays*, 83–99. Cambridge, MA: Harvard University Press, 1926.

Duran, Tülay, ed. *Tarihimizde Vakıf Kuran Kadınlar. Hanım Sultan Vakfiyyeleri*. Istanbul: Tarihi Araştırmalar ve Dokümentasyon Merkezleri kuruma ve Geliştirme Vakfı, 1990.

Ergin, Osman N. *Türk Şehirlerinde İmâret Sistemi*. Istanbul: Cumhuriyet Matbaası, 1939.

Evliya Çelebi. *Evliya Çelebi in Bitlis*. Translated and edited by Robert Dankoff. Leiden: Brill, 1990.

———. *Evliya Çelebi in Diyarbekir*. Translated and edited by Martin von Bruinessen and Hendrik Boeschoten. Leiden: Brill, 1988.

———. *Evliya Çelebi Seyahatnamesi, 1. Kitap: Istanbul*. Prepared by Orhan Şaik Gökyay. Istanbul: Yapi Kredi Yayınları, 1996.

———. *The Intimate Life of an Ottoman Statesman: Melek Ahmed Pasha (1588–1662)*. Translated and edited by Robert Dankoff. Albany: State University of New York Press, 1991.

———. *Seyahatname*. Vol. 9 (1671–72). Istanbul: Devlet Matbaası 1935.

Eyice, Semavi. "İlk Osmanlı Devrinin Dini-İctimai Bir Müessesesi: Zâviyeler ve Zâviyeli-Camiler." *İstanbul Üniversitesi İktisat Fakültesi Mecmuası* 23 (1962–63): 1–80.

Faroqhi, Suraiya. "A Great Foundation in Difficulties: Or Some Evidence on Economic Contraction in the Ottoman Empire of the Mid-Seventeenth Century." In *Mélanges Professeur Robert Mantran*, edited by A. Temimi, 109–21. Zaghouan: CEROMDE, 1988.

———. *Approaching Ottoman History: An Introduction to the Sources.* Cambridge, UK: Cambridge University Press, 1999.

———. "Camels, Wagons and the Ottoman State in the Sixteenth and Seventeenth Centuries." *IJMES* 14 (1982): 523–39.

———. "Crisis and Change." In *An Economic and Social History*, edited by H. Inalcik and D. Quataert, 413–636.

———. *Pilgrims and Sultans: The Hajj Under the Ottomans 1517–1683.* London: I. B. Tauris, 1994.

———. "Research on the History of Ottoman Consumption: A Preliminary Exploration of Sources and Models." In *Consumption Studies and the History of the Ottoman Empire, 1550–1922. An Introduction*, edited by Donald Quataert, 15–44. Albany: State University of New York Press, 2000.

———. "Seyyid Gazi Revisited: The Foundation as Seen Through Sixteenth and Seventeenth Century Documents." *Turcica* 13 (1981): 90–122.

———. "The Tekke of Haci Bektaş: Social Position and Economic Activities." *IJMES* 7 (1976): 183–208.

———. *Towns and townsmen of Ottoman Anatolia: trade, crafts and food production in an urban setting, 1520–1650.* Cambridge, UK: Cambridge University Press, 1984.

———. "Vakıf Administration in Sixteenth Century Konya: The *Zaviye* of Sadreddin-i Konevî." *JESHO* 17 (1974): 145–72.

Farquhar, George. *The Beaux' Strategem. 1707. In Three Restoration Comedies*, edited by Norman Marshall, 181–254. London: Pan Books Ltd., 1953.

Fay, Mary Ann. "Women and *Waqf*: Property, Power, and the Domain of Gender in Eighteenth-Century Egypt." In *Women in the Ottoman Empire: Middle Eastern Women in the Early Modern Era*, edited by Madeline C. Zilfi, 28–47. Leiden: Brill, 1997.

Fernandes, Leonor. "Mamluk Architecture and the Question of Patronage." *Mamluk Studies Review* 1 (1997): 107–20.

Findley, Carter Vaughn. "Social Dimensions of Dervish Life as Seen in the Memoirs of Aşçı Dede İbrahim Halil." In *The Dervish Lodge: Architecture, Art, and Sufism in Ottoman Turkey*, edited by Raymond Lifchez, 175–86. Berkeley: University of California Press, 1992.

Finkel, Caroline. *The Administration of Warfare: The Ottoman Military Campaigns in Hungary, 1593–1600.* Vienna: VWGÖ, 1988.

Fleet, Kate. *European and Islamic Trade in the Early Ottoman State.* Cambridge, UK: Cambridge University Press, 1999.

Fleischer, Cornell. *Bureaucrat and Intellectual in the Ottoman Empire, The Historian Mustafa ʿAli, 1541–1600.* Princeton: Princeton University Press, 1986.

———. "The Lawgiver as Messiah: The Making of the Imperial Image in the Reign of Süleyman." In *Soliman le Magnifique et Son Temps,* edited by Gilles Veinstein, 159–77. Paris: Documentation Française, 1992.

Freely, John. *Blue Guide: Istanbul.* London: Ernest Benn, 1983.

Fyzee, A. A. A. *Outline of Muhammadan Law.* 3d ed. London: Oxford University Press, 1964.

Gabriel, Albert. *Les monuments turcs d'anatolie.* Paris: E. de Boccard, 1934.

Gerber, H. "The Waqf Institution in Early Ottoman Edirne." *Asian and African Studies* 17 (1983): 29–45.

Gibb, H. A. R., and Harold Bowen. *Islamic Society and the West. Vol. 1: Islamic Society in the Eighteenth Century.* London: Oxford University Press, 1950.

Gil, Moshe. *Documents of the Jewish Pious Foundations from the Cairo Geniza.* Leiden: Brill, 1976.

Ginzberg, Lori D. *Women and the Work of Benevolence: Morality, Politics, and Class in the Nineteenth-Century United States.* New Haven: Yale University Press, 1990.

Goffman, Daniel. *Izmir and the Levantine World, 1550–1650.* Seattle: University of Washington Press, 1990.

Goitein, S. D. *A Mediterranean Society.* Vol. 2. Berkeley: University of California Press, 1971.

———. *Muslim Law in the State of Israel.* (Hebrew) Jerusalem, 1957.

Gökbilgin, M. Tayyib. "Hurrem Sultan." In *İA,* V:593–96.

Goodwin, Godfrey. *A History of Ottoman Architecture.* Baltimore: Johns Hopkins University Press, 1971.

Güçer, Lütfi. *XVI–XVII. Asırlarda Osmanlı İmparatorluğunda Hububat Meselesi ve Hububattan Alınan Vergiler.* Istanbul: İstanbul Üniversitesi, İktisat Fakültesi, 1964.

Güvenç, Bozkurt. "Introduction: Food, Culture and the Culture of Eating." In *Timeless Tastes: Turkish Culinary Culture.* Directed by Ersu Pekin and Ayşe Sümer. Istanbul, 1996.

Haarmann, U. "Islamic Duties in History." *Muslim World* 68 (1978): 1–24.

Ḥājib, Yūsuf Khāṣṣ. *Wisdom of Royal Glory (Ḳutadgu Bilig), A Turko-Islamic Mirror for Princes.* Translated by Robert Dankoff. Chicago: University of Chicago Press, 1983.

Halbwachs, Maurice. *La Topographie légendaire des évangiles en Terre Sainte: Étude de mémoire collective.* Paris: Presses Universitaires de France, 1941.

Hambly, Gavin R. G. "Becoming Visible: Medieval Islamic Women in Historiography and History." In *Women in the Medieval Islamic World: Power, Patronage and Piety,* edited by Gavin R. G. Hambly, 3–27. New York: St. Martin's Press, 1998.

Hambly, Gavin R. G., ed *Women in the Medieval Islamic World: Power, Patronage and Piety.* New York: St. Martin's Press, 1998.

Hands, A. R. *Charities and Social Aid in Greece and Rome: Aspects of Greek and Roman Life.* Ithaca: Cornell University Press, 1968.

Hartmann, Angelika. "Al-Nāṣir li-Dīn Allāh." In *EI*[2], VII: 996–1003.

Heffening, W. *"wakf."* In *EI,* IV:1096–103.

———. *"wakf."* In SEI, 624–28.

Heffening, W., and J. Schacht. *"ḥanafiyya."* In *EI*[2], III:162–64.

Hennigan, Peter Charles. "The Birth of a Legal Institution: The Formation of the Waqf in the Third Century A. H. Ḥanafī Legal Discourse." Ph.d. diss., Cornell University, 1999.

Herrin, Judith. "From Bread and Circuses to Soup and Salvation: The Origins of Byzantine Charity." Davis Center Paper, Princeton, 1985.

———. "Ideals of Charity, Realities of Welfare: The Philanthropic Activity of the Byzantine Church." In *Church and People in Byzantium,* edited by Rosemary Morris, 151–64. Birmingham: Center for Byzantine, Ottoman and Modern Greek Studies, University of Birmingham, 1990.

———. "Public and Private Forms of Religious Commitment Among Byzantine Women." In *Women in Ancient Societies,* edited by J. Léonie Archer, et al., 181–203. London: Macmillan, 1994.

Heyd, Uriel. *Ottoman Documents on Palestine 1552–1615.* Oxford: Oxford University Press, 1960.

Hillenbrand, Robert, *Islamic Architecture: Form, Function, and Meaning.* New York: Columbia University Press, 1994.

Hodgson, Marshall G. S. *The Venture of Islam.* Chicago: University of Chicago Press, 1974.

Hoexter, Miriam. *Endowments, Rulers and Community: Waqf al-Ḥaramayn in Ottoman Algiers.* Leiden: Brill, 1998.

———. "*Ḥuqūq Allāh* and *Ḥuqūq al-ʿIbād* as Reflected in the Waqf Institution." *Jerusalem Studies in Arabic and Islam* 19 (1995): 133–56.

———. "*Waqf* Studies in the Twentieth Century: The State of the Art." *JESHO* 41(1998): 474–95.

Holum, Kenneth G. *Theodosian Empresses: Women and Imperial Dominion in Late Antiquity.* Berkeley: University of California Press, 1982.

Huart, Cl. "*ʿimāret.*" In *EI,* II:475.

Humphreys, R. Stephen. *Islamic History,* 2nd ed. Princeton: Princeton University Press, 1991.

———. "Politics and Architectural Patronage in Ayyubid Damascus." In *The Islamic World: From Classical to Modern Times,* edited by C. E. Bosworth and Charles Issawi, 151–74. Princeton: The Darwin Press, Inc., 1989.

———. "Women as Patrons of Religious Architecture in Ayyubid Damascus." *Muqarnas* 11 (1994): 35–54.

Al-Ḥusaynī, Shaykh Asʿad al-Imām. *Al-Manhal al-Ṣāfī fī'l-Waqf wa-Aḥkāmihi.* Jerusalem, 1982.

Hütteroth, Wolf D., and Kamal Abdulfattah. *Historical Geography of Palestine, Transjordan and Southern Syria.* Erlangen: Frankische Geographische Gesellschaft, 1977.

Ibn 'Imād, 'Abd al-Ḥayy b. Aḥmad. *Shadharāt al-Dhahab fi akhbar man dhahab.* Beirut: Dar Ibn Kathir, 1986–93.

Ibn Khallikān. *Wafayāt al-A'yān wa-anba' abna' al-zaman.* Beirut: Dār al-Thaqāfa, 1968–72.

Ilchman, W., S. N. Katz, and E. L. Queen, eds. *Philanthropy in the World's Traditions.* Bloomington: Indiana University Press, 1998.

Imber, Colin. *Ebu's-suʿud. The Islamic Legal Tradition.* Stanford: Stanford University Press, 1997.

———. "Süleymân as Caliph of the Muslims: Ebû's-Suʿûd's Formulation of Ottoman Dynastic Ideology." In *Soliman le magnifique,* edited by Gilles Veinstein, 179–84. Paris: Documentation Française, 1992.

Inalcik, Halil. "Adâletnâmeler," *Belgeler* 2, no. 3–4 (1965): 49–145.

———. "Istanbul." In *EI*², IV:224–48.

———. "Istanbul: An Islamic City." *Journal of Islamic Studies* 1 (1990): 1–23.

———. *The Ottoman Empire: The Classical Age 1300–1600.* London: Weidenfeld and Nicolson, 1973.

Inalcik, Halil, and Donald Quataert, eds. *An Economic and Social History of the Ottoman Empire, 1300–1914.* Cambridge UK: Cambridge University Press, 1994.

Inalcik, H., D. Waines, and J. Burton-Page. "*maṭbakh.*" In *EI*², VI:807–15.

Jennings, Ronald C. *Christians and Muslims in Ottoman Cyprus and the Mediterranean World, 1571–1640.* New York: New York University Press, 1993.

———. "The Development of Awqaf in a New Ottoman Province: Cyprus, 1571–1640." Presented at the conference on "Social and Economic Aspects of the Muslim Waqf." Jerusalem, 1979.

———. "Pious Foundations in the Society and Economy of the Ottoman Trabzon, 1565–1640. A Study Based on the Judicial Registers *(Şer'i Mahkeme Sicilleri)* of Trabzon." *JESHO* 33 (1990): 271–336.

Jütte, Robert. "Diets in Welfare Institutions and in Outdoor Poor Relief in Early Modern Western Europe." *Ethnologia Europaea* 16, no. 2 (1986): 117–36.

Kafadar, Cemal. *Between Two Worlds: The Construction of the Ottoman State.* Berkeley: University of California Press, 1995.

———. "Yeniçeriler." In *İstA*, VIII:472–76.

Kafescioğlu, Çiğdem. "The Ottoman Capital in the Making: The Reconstruction of Constantinople in the Fifteenth Century." Ph.D. diss., Harvard University, 1996.

Kallner-Amiran, D. H. "A Revised Earthquake Catalogue of Palestine." *Israel Exploration Journal* 1, 2 (1950–51): 223–46, 48–65.

Kazancıgil, Ratip. *Edirne İmaretleri.* Istanbul: Türk Kütüphaneciler Derneği Edirne Şübesi Yayınevi, 1991.

Kermeli, Eugenia. "Ebū Suʿūd's Definitions of Church *Vaḳfs*: Theory and Practice in Ottoman Law." In *Islamic Law: Theory and Practice,* edited by Robert Gleave and Eugenia Kermeli, 141–56. London: I. B. Tauris, 1997.

Khadduri, Majid. "*maṣlaḥa.*" In *EI*², VI:738–40.

Khoury, Dina Rizk, *State and provincial society in the Ottoman Empire: Mosul, 1540–1834.* Cambridge, UK: Cambridge University Press, 1997.

Kiel, Machiel. "The Vakifnâme of Raḳḳas Sinân Beg in Karnobat (Ḳarîn-âbâd) and the Ottoman Colonization of Bulgarian Thrace (14th–15th Century)." *Osmanlı Araştırmaları/Journal of Ottoman Studies* 1 (1980): 15–32.

Kiple, Kenneth F., and Kriemhild Coneè Ornelas, eds. *The Cambridge World History of Food.* Cambridge, UK: Cambridge University Press, 2000.

Koçi Bey, *Koçi Bey Risalesi.* Edited by Ali Kemal Aksüt. 1630. Istanbul: Vakit Kütüphane, 1939.

Konyalı, İbrahim Hakki. *ʿÂbideleri ve Kitabeleri ile Konya Tarihi.* Konya: Yeni Kitap Basımevi, 1964.

———. "Kanunî Sultan Süleyman'ın Annesi Hafsa Sultan'ın Vakfiyesi ve Manisa'daki Hayır Eserleri." *Vakıflar Dergisi* 8 (1969): 47–56.

Köprülü, M. Fuad. *The Origins of the Ottoman Empire.* Translated and edited by Gary Leiser. 1935. Albany: State University of New York Press, 1992.

Kozlowski, Gregory C. *Muslim Endowments and Society in British India.* Cambridge, UK: Cambridge University Press, 1985.

Küçükdağ, Yusuf. *Karapınar Sultan Selim Külliyesi.* Konya: Karapınar Belediyesi Kültür Yayını, 1997.

Kunt, I. Metin. *The Sultan's Servants: The Transformation of Ottoman Provincial Government, 1550–1650.* New York: Columbia University Press, 1983.

———. "The Waqf as an Instrument of Public Policy: Notes on the Köprülü Family Endowments." In *Studies in Ottoman History in Honour of Professor V. L. Ménage,* edited by Colin Heywood and Colin Imber, 189–98. Istanbul: Isis Press, 1994.

Kuran, Aptullah. "Architecture: The Classical Ottoman Achievement." In *Süleymân the Second [Sic] and His Time,* edited by Halil Inalcık and Cemal Kafadar, 317–32. Istanbul: Isis Press, 1993.

Kürkçüoğlu, Kemal Edib. *Süleymaniye Vakfiyesi.* Ankara: Resimli Posta Matbaası, 1962.

Lambton, A. K. S. "Awqaf in Persia: 6th–8th/12th–14th Centuries." *Islamic Law and Society* 4 (1997): 298–351.

———. *Continuity and Change in Medieval Persia: Aspects of Administrative, Economic and Social History, 11th–14th Century.* New York: Bibliotheca Persica, 1988.

Lane, E. W. *An Arabic-English Lexicon.* London: Williams and Norgate, 1863.

Lapidus, Ira M. *A History of Islamic Societies.* Cambridge, UK: Cambridge University Press, 1988.

———. "Sufism and Ottoman Islamic Society." In *The Dervish Lodge: Architecture, Art, and Sufism in Ottoman Turkey,* edited by Raymond Lifchez, 15–32. Berkeley: University of California Press, 1992.

Layish, Aharon. "The Muslim Waqf in Israel." *Asian and African Studies* 2 (1966): 41–76.

———. "Waqfs and Sûfî Monasteries in the Ottoman Policy of Colonization: Sultân Selîm I's Waqf of 1516 in Favor of Dayr al-Asad." *Bulletin of the Society of Oriental and African Studies* 50 (1987): 61–69.

Leiser, Gary. "The Endowment of the al-Zahariyya in Damascus." *JESHO* 27 (1984): 33–55.

Lewis, Geoffrey. "Heroines and Others in the Heroic Age of the Turks." In *Women in the Medieval Islamic World: Power, Patronage and Piety,* edited by Gavin R. G. Hambly, 147–60. New York: St. Martin's Press, 1998.

Lewis, Raphaela. *Everyday Life in Ottoman Turkey.* New York: Dorset Press, 1971.

Lifchez, Raymond, ed. *The Dervish Lodge: Architecture, Art, and Sufism in Ottoman Turkey.* Berkeley: University of California Press, 1992.

Linant de Bellefonds, Y. "*hiba.*" In *EI*², III:350–51.

Lindenmeyr, Adele. *Poverty is Not a Vice: Charity, Society, and the State in Imperial Russia.* Princeton: Princeton University Press, 1996.

———. "Public Life, Private Virtues: Women in Russian Charity, 1762–1914." *Signs* 18 (1993): 562–91.

Little, Donald P. "The Nature of *Khānqahs, Ribāṭs,* and *Zāwiyas* Under the Mamlūks." In *Islamic Studies Presented to Charles J. Adams,* edited by Wael B. Hallaq and Donald P. Little, 91–105. Leiden: Brill, 1991.

Makdisi, George. *The Rise of Colleges.* Edinburgh: Edinburgh University Press, 1981.

Mandaville, J. "Usurious Piety: The Cash Waqf Controversy in the Ottoman Empire." *IJMES* 10 (1979): 289–308.

Manna', 'Adel. "The Revolt of the Naqib al-Ashraf in Jerusalem (1703–1705)." (Hebrew) *Cathedra* 35 (1989): 49–74.

———. "The Jerusalem Governors of the Farrukh Family and their Relations with the Bedouin." (Hebrew) In *Perakim be-Toldot Yerushalayim: Be-Reshit ha-Tekufa ha-Othmanit,* edited by Amnon Cohen, 196–232. Jerusalem: Yad Yitzhak Ben Zvi, 1979.

Mantran, Robert, ed. *Histoire de l'empire Ottoman.* Paris: Fayard, 1989.

———. *Istanbul dans la seconde moitié du XVIIe siècle. Essai d'histoire institutionnelle, économique et sociale.* Paris: Maisonneuve, 1962.

Mauss, Marcel. *The Gift: The Form and Reason for Exchange in Archaic Societies.* Translated by W. D. Halls, foreword by Mary Douglas. London: Routledge, 1990.

McCarthy, Kathleen. "Parallel Power Structures: Women and the Voluntary Space." In *Lady Bountiful Revisited: Women, Philanthropy, and Power,* edited by Kathleen McCarthy, 1–31. New Brunswick: Rutgers University Press, 1990.

McChesney, Robert D. *Charity and Philanthropy in Islam: Institutionalizing the Call to Do Good.* Indianapolis: Indiana University Center on Philanthropy, 1995.

———. *Waqf in Central Asia: Four Hundred Years in the History of a Muslim Shrine, 1480–1889.* Princeton: Princeton University Press, 1991.

Meninski, Francisco Mesgnien. *Lexicon Turcico-Arabico-Persicum.* Second edition. Vienna: Joseph de Kurzböck, 1780.

Meriwether, Margaret L. "Women and *Waqf* Revisited: The Case of Aleppo, 1770–1840." In *Women in the Ottoman Empire: Middle Eastern Women in the Early Modern Era,* edited by Madeline C. Zilfi, 128–52. Leiden: Brill, 1997.

Mihailovic, Konstantin. *Memoirs of a Janissary.* Translated by B. Stolz, historical commentary S. Soucek. Ann Arbor: University of Michigan, 1975.

Miller, Timothy S. *The Birth of the Hospital in the Byzantine Empire.* Baltimore: Johns Hopkins University Press, 1985.

Morison, Antoine. *Relation historique d'un voyage nouvellement fait au Mont de Sinaï et à Jérusalem.* Paris: Antoine Dezallier, 1705.

Mottahedeh, Roy P. *Loyalty and Leadership in an Early Islamic Society.* Princeton: Princeton University Press, 1980.

Mujīr al-Dīn al-Ḥanbalī. *Al-Uns al-jalīl bi-ta'rīkh al-Quds wa'l-Khalīl.* Amman: Maktabat al-Muḥtasib, 1973.

Murphey, Rhoads, ed. and trans. *Kanûn-nâme-i Sultânî li 'Azîz Efendi: Aziz Efendi's Book of Sultanic Laws and Regulations: An Agenda for Reform by a Seventeenth-Century Ottoman Statesman.* Cambridge, MA: Harvard University, 1985.

———. *Ottoman Warfare 1500–1700.* London: University College London Press, 1999.

———. "Provisioning Istanbul: The State and Subsistence in the Early Modern East." *Food and Foodways* 2 (1988): 217–63.

Muṣṭafā b. Aḥmet ʿĀlī. *Muṣṭafā ʿĀlī's Counsel for Sultans of 1581.* Edited and translated by Andreas Tietze. Vienna: Österreichische Akademie der Wissenschaften, 1979.

Myres, David. "Al-ʿImara al-ʿAmira: the Charitable Foundation of Khassaki Sultan (959/1552)." In *Ottoman Jerusalem. The Living City: 1517–1917,* edited by S. Auld and R. Hillenbrand, 539–82. London: Altajir World of Islam Trust, 2000.

Al-Nābulsī, 'Abd al-Ghanī, *Al-Ḥaḍra al-Unsiyya fī al-Riḥla al-Qudsiyya.* Beirut: al-Maṣādir, 1990.

Najm, Ra'if Yusuf et al. *Kunūz al-Quds.* Milan: Matabi Brughiriyu, 1983.

Nasir-i Khusraw. *Sefer Nameh.* Edited and translated by C. Schefer. Paris: E. Leroux, 1881.

Natshe, Yusuf Sa'id. "My Memories of Khassaki Sultan or 'The Flourishing Edifice.' " *Jerusalem Quarterly File* 7 (2000).

Natsheh, Yusuf. "Al-ʿImara al-'Amira: the Charitable Foundation of Khassaki Sultan (959/1552)." In *Ottoman Jerusalem. The Living City: 1517–1917,* edited by S. Auld and R. Hillenbrand, 747–90. London: Altajir World of Islam Trust, 2000.

———. "Catalogue of Buildings." In *Ottoman Jerusalem. The Living City 1517–1917,* edited by S. Auld and R. Hillenbrand, 657–1012. London: Altajir World of Islam Trust, 2000.

Necipoğlu, Gülru. "A *Kânûn* for the State, a Canon for the Arts: Conceptualizing the Classical Synthesis of Ottoman Arts and Architecture." In *Soliman le Magnifique et Son Temps,* edited by Gilles Veinstein, 195–216. Paris: Documentation Française, 1992.

———. *Architecture, Ceremonial and Power, The Topkapı Palace.* Cambridge, MA: M.I.T. Press, 1992.

———. "The Süleymaniye Complex in Istanbul: An Interpretation." *Muqarnas* 3 (1985): 92–117.

Neşrî, Mehmed. *Kitâb-ı Cihan-Nümâ. Neşrî Tarihi.* Edited by Faik Reşit Unat and Mehmed A. Köymen. 1949. Ankara: Türk Tarih Kurumu Yayınları, 1987.

Niẓām al-Mulk, *The Book of Government, or Rules for Kings: the Siyasatnama or Siyar al-muluk.* Translated by Hubert Darke. London: Routledge and Paul, 1960.

Ohlson, Kristin. "Deep Pocketbooks: Women, Money, and Power." *MS Magazine,* September/October 1998, 58–63.

Pakalın, Z. *Osmanlı Tarih Deyimleri ve Terimleri Sözlüğü.* Istanbul: Milli Eğitim Basımevi, 1946–56.

Pascual, J. P. *Damas à la fin du XVIe siècle d'après trois actes de waqf ottoman.* Damas: IFAED, 1983.

Patlagean, Evelyne. *Pauvreté économique et pauvreté sociale à byzance 4e–7e siècles.* Paris: Mouton, 1977.

Peçevi, Ibrahim. *Tarīḫ-i Peçevi.* Constantinople: Matbaa-i Amire, 1281–83.

Peirce, Leslie P. "Gender and Sexual Propriety in Ottoman Royal Women's Patronage." In *Women, Patronage, and Self-Representation in Islamic Societies,* edited by D. Fairchild Ruggles, 53–68. Albany: State University of New York Press, 2000.

———. *The Imperial Harem: Women and Sovereignty in the Ottoman Empire.* New York: Oxford University Press, 1993.

Pellat, C. "*khubz.*" In *EI*², V:41–43.

Peri, Oded. "The Ottoman State and the Question of the Christian Holy Places in Jerusalem and Its Vicinity During the Latter Half of the Seventeenth Century" (Hebrew), Ph.D. diss., Hebrew University of Jerusalem, 1995.

———. "Political Trends and Their Consequences as Factors Affecting the Founding of Waqfs in Jerusalem at the End of the Eighteenth Century." (Hebrew) *Cathedra* 21 (1981): 73–88.

Perikhanian, A. G. "Iranian Society and Law." In *Cambridge History of Iran, Vol. 3(2),* edited by Ehsan Yarshatar, 627–80. Cambridge, UK: Cambridge University Press, 1983.

Peters, Rudolph. "waḳf." In *EI*², XI:59–63.

Petry, Carl F. "A Geniza for Mamluk Studies? Charitable Trust (*Waqf*) Documents as a Source for Economic and Social History." *Mamluk Studies Review* 2 (1998): 51–60.

———. "A Paradox of Patronage During the Later Mamluk Period." *Muslim World* 73 (1983): 182–207.

———. "Class Solidarity vs. Gender Gain: Women as Custodians of Property in Later Medieval Egypt." In *Women in Middle Eastern History: Shifting Boundaries in Sex and Gender,* edited by Nikki R. Keddie and Beth Baron, 122–42. New Haven: Yale University Press, 1991.

———. *Protectors or Praetorians? The Last Mamlūk Sultans and Egypt's Waning as a Great Power.* Albany: State University of New York Press, 1994.

Pierotti, Ermete. *Jerusalem Explored, Being a Description of the Ancient and Modern City, with Numerous Illustrations Consisting of Views, Ground Plans, and Sections.* Translated by Th. Geo. Bonney. London: Bell and Daldy, 1864.

Powers, D. S. "Orientalism, Colonialism and Legal History: The Attack on Muslim Family Endowments in Algeria and India." *Comparative Studies in Society and History* 31 (1989): 535–71.

Qadrī Pāshā, Muḥammad. *Qānūn al-ʿadl wa'l-inṣāf li'l-qaḍā ʿalā mushiklat al-awqāf,* 5th ed. Cairo: Maktabat al-Ahram, 1928.

Quataert, Donald, ed. *Consumption Studies and the History of the Ottoman Empire, 1550–1922. An Introduction.* Albany: State University of New York Press, 2000.

al-Qushayri, Muslim b. al-Hajjāj *Ṣaḥīḥ Muslim.* Cairo: Dar al-Ghad al-ʿArabi, 1987–1990.

Rabie, Hassanein. "Some Financial Aspects of the Waqf System in Medieval Egypt." *Al-Majalla al-Ta'rīkhiyya al-Miṣriyya* 18 (1971): 1–24.

Raymond, A. "The Ottoman Conquest and the Development of the Great Arab Towns." *International Journal of Turkish Studies* 1, no. 1 (1979–80): 84–101.

Redhouse, James. *A Turkish-English Lexicon.* Constantinople: A. H. Boyajian, 1890.

Reiter, Yitzhak. *Waqf in Jerusalem 1948–1990.* Jerusalem: Jerusalem Institute for Israel Studies, 1991.

Rivlin, H. A. B. *The Agricultural Policy of Muḥammad ʿAlī in Egypt.* Cambridge, MA: Harvard University Press, 1961.

Rizvi, Kishwar. "Gendered Patronage: Women and Benevolence During the Early Safavid Empire." In *Women, Patronage, and Self-Representation in Islamic Societies,* edited by D. Fairchild Ruggles, 123–53. Albany: State University of New York Press, 2000.

Roded, Ruth. *Women in Islamic Biographical Collections: From Ibn Sa'd to Who's Who.* Boulder: Lynne Rienner Publishers, 1994.

Rosen-Ayalon, Myriam. "On Suleiman's *Sabīls* in Jerusalem." In *The Islamic World: From Classical to Modern Times. Essays in Honor of Bernard Lewis,* edited by C. E. Bosworth and Charles Issawi, 589–607. Princeton: The Darwin Press, Inc., 1989.

Rosenthal, Franz. "Ṣedaḳa, Charity." *Hebrew Union College Annual* 23 (1950–51): 411–30.

———. "The Stranger in Medieval Islam." *Arabica* 44 (1997): 35–75.

Rosenthal, Franz, et al. "*hiba.*" In *EI*², III:342–50.

Rossabi, Morris. "Khubilai Khan and the Women in His Family." *Studia Sino-Mongolica: Festschrift für Herbert Franke,* 153–80. Weisbaden: Steiner, 1979.

Ruggles, D. Fairchild, ed. *Women, Patronage, and Self-Representation in Islamic Societies.* Albany: State University of New York Press, 2000.

Sabra, Adam. *Poverty and charity in medieval Islam: Mamluk Egypt 1250–1517.* Cambridge, UK: Cambridge University Press, 2000.

Saintine, P. Gérardy (Xavier Boniface). *Trois Ans en Judée.* Paris: Hachette, 1860.

Salama, O., and Y. Zilberman. "The Supply of Water to Jerusalem in the 16th and 17th Centuries." (Hebrew) *Cathedra* 41 (1986): 91–106.

Sanders, Paula. *Ritual, Politics, and the City in Fatimid Cairo.* Albany: State University of New York Press, 1994.

de Saulcy, F. *Jérusalem.* Paris: Vve A. Morel et Cie., 1882.

Sauvan, Yvette. "Une Liste de Fondations Pieuses (Waqfiyya) Au Temps de Selim II." *Bulletin d'études orientales* 28 (1975): 231–58.

Schacht, J. "Early Doctrines on Waqf." In *Fuad Köprülü Armağanı,* 443–52. Istanbul: Osman Yalçın Matbaası, 1953.

———. "*zakāt.*" SEI. 654–56.

Schacht, J. and A. Layish. "*mīrāth.*" *EI*², VII:106–13.

Schimmel, Annemarie. *The Triumphal Sun: A Study of the Works of Jalalüddin Rumi.* London: East-West Publications, 1980.

Shaw, Stanford. *The Financial and Administrative Organization and Development of Ottoman Egypt 1517–1798.* Princeton: Princeton University Press, 1962.

Shefer, Miri. "Hospitals in Three Ottoman Capitals: Bursa, Edirne and Istanbul in the Sixteenth and Seventeenth Centuries." (Hebrew) Ph.D. diss., Tel Aviv University, 2001.

Shoshan, Boaz. *Popular culture in medieval Cairo.* Cambridge, UK: Cambridge University Press, 1993.

Silverman, Rachel Emma. "Rich and Richer." *The Wall Street Journal,* 11 January, 1999, B6.

Simsar, M. A. *The Waqfiyah of 'Aḥmed Pāšā.* Philadelphia: University of Pennsylvania Press, 1940.

Singer, Amy. "A Note on Land and Identity: From *Ze'amet to Waqf.*" In *New Perspectives on Property and Land in the Middle East,* edited by Roger Owen, 161–73. Cambridge, MA: Harvard University Press, 2001.

———. "The Mülknāmes of Hürrem Sultan's Waqf in Jerusalem." *Muqarnas* 14 (1997): 96–102.

———. "Ottoman Jerusalem: Conquering the Urban Frontier." Paper presented at the Middle East Center of the University of Utah, October 2000.

———. *Palestinian peasants and Ottoman officials.* Cambridge, UK: Cambridge University Press, 1994.

———. "*Tapu Taḥrir Defterleri* and *Kadı Sicilleri:* A Happy Marriage of Sources." *Tārīḫ* 1 (1990): 95–125.

Smith, Margaret, and C. Pellat. "Rābiʿa al-ʿAdawiyya." *EI*², VIII:354–56.

Smith, Jeffrey. "Thousands Flee as Lawlessness Spreads in Kosovo." *The Washington Post,* 20 July 1998, A12.

Sourdel-Thomine, J. "*ḥammām*." In *EI*², III:139–44.

Spellberg, D. A. *Politics, Gender and the Islamic Past: The Legacy of 'A'isha Bint Abi Bakr.* New York: Columbia University Press, 1994.

Steingass, F. *Persian-English Dictionary.* New Delhi: Cosmo Publications, 1977.

Stephan, St. H. "An Endowment Deed of Khâsseki Sultân, Dated 24th May 1552." *Quarterly of the Department of Antiquities in Palestine* 10 (1944): 170–94.

———. "Three Firmans Granted to the Armenian Catholic Community." *Journal of the Palestine Oriental Society* 13 (1933): 238–46.

Stillman, Norman A. "Charity and Social Service in Medieval Islam." *Societas* 5 (1975): 105–15.

———. "Waqf and the Ideology of Charity in Medieval Islam." In *Hunter of the East: Studies in Honor of Clifford Edmund Bosworth. Vol. 1: Arabic and Semitic Studies,* edited by I. R. Netton, 357–72. Leiden: Brill, 2000.

Stowasser, Barbara F. *Women in the Qur'an, Traditions, and Interpretation.* New York: Oxford University Press, 1994.

Streck, M. "*ḳaysāriyya*." In *EI*², IV:840–41.

Subtelny, Maria Eva. "A Timurid Educational and Charitable Foundation: The Ikhlāṣiyya Complex of 'Alī Shīr Navā'ī in 15th-Century Herat and Its Endowment." *JAOS* 111 (1991): 38–61.

Süreyya, Mehmed. *Sicill-i Osmanî.* Istanbul: Matbaa-i Âmire, 1308–11/1891–93.

Szuppe, Maria. "La Participation des femmes de la famille royale à l'exercice du pouvoir en Iran safavide au XVI siècle." *Studia Iranica* 23, 24 (1994): 211–58; 61–122.

Tabbaa, Yasser. *Construction of Power and Piety in Medieval Aleppo.* University Park, PA: Penn State Press, 1997.

Tanman, M. Baha. "İmaretler." In *İstA,* IV:164–66.

———. "Sinan Mimârîsi İmaretler." *Mimarbaşı Koca Sinan Yaşadığı Çağı ve Eserleri* 1 (1988): 333–53.

Taşkıran, Nimet. *Hasekinin Kitabı.* Istanbul: Yenilik Basımevi, 1972.

Tekindağ, M. C. Şihabeddin. "Çanakkale." In *İA,* III:345.

Terzioğlu, Arslan. *Helvahane Defteri.* Istanbul: Arkeoloji ve Sanat Yayınları, 1992.

Tezcan, Semih. *Bir Ziyafet Defteri.* Istanbul: Simurg, 1998.

Thys-Şenocak, Lucienne. "The Yeni Valide Mosque Complex at Eminönü." *Muqarnas* 15 (1998): 58–70.

———. "The Yeni Valide Mosque Complex at Eminönü, Istanbul (1597–1665): Gender and Vision in Ottoman Architecture." In *Women, Patronage, and Self-Representation in Islamic Societies,* edited by D. Fairchild Ruggles, 69–90. Albany: State University of New York Press, 2000.

Tolmacheva, M. "Female Piety and Patronage in the Medieval 'Ḥajj'." In *Women in the Medieval Islamic World,* edited by Gavin R. G. Hambly, 161–79. New York: St. Martin's Press, 1998.

Tuğlacı, Pars. *Osmanlı Şehirleri.* Istanbul: Milliyet Yayınları, 1985.

Uçuk, Cahit. *Bir İmparatorluk Çökerken.* Istanbul: Yapı Kredi Yayınları, 1995.

Uluçay, M. Cağatay. "Kanuni Sultan Süleyman ve Ailesi ile İlgili Bazı Notlar ve Vesikalar." In *Kanuni Armağanı,* 227–58. Ankara: Türk Tarih Kurumu, 1970.

———. *Padişahların Kadınları ve Kızları.* Ankara: Türk Tarih Kurumu, 1980.

Ünver, A. Süheyl. "Anadolu ve İstanbulda imaretlerin aşhane, tabhane ve misafirhanelerine ve müessislerinin ruhî kemâllerine dair." *Tıb Fakültesi Mecmuası* 4 (1941): 2390–410.

———. *Fâtih Aşhânesi Tevzî'nâmesi.* Ankara: Istanbul Fethi Derneği, 1953.

Uzunçarşılı, İ. H. "Çandarlı Zade Ali Paşa Vakfiyesi." *Belleten* 5 (1941): 550–75.

———. "Karamanoğulları Devri Vesikalarında İbrahim Bey'in Karaman İmareti Vakfiyesi." *Belleten* 1 (1937): 56–164.

———. *Osmanlı Devletinin Saray Teşkilatı.* Ankara: Türk Tarih Kurumu, 1945.

Vacca, V. "Zainab bint Djaḥsh." In *EI,* IV:1200.

van Leeuwen, Richard. *Notables and Clergy in Mount Lebanon: The Khāzin Sheiks and the Maronite Church (1736–1840).* Amsterdam: Institute for Near Eastern and Islamic Studies, 1992.

———. "The Maronite Waqf of Dayr Sayyidat Bkirkī in Mount Lebanon During the 18th Century." In *Le Waqf dans l'espace islamique: Outil de pouvoir socio-politique,* edited by Randi Deguilhem, 259–75. Damas: Institut Français de Damas, 1995.

———. *Waqfs and Urban Structures: The Case of Ottoman Damascus.* Leiden: Brill, 1999.

Veinstein, Gilles. "Some Views on Provisioning in the Hungarian Campaigns of Süleyman the Magnificent." In *Osmanistische Studien Zur Wirtschafts- und Socialgeschichte,* edited by H. G. Majer, 177–85. Wiesbaden: Harrassowitz, 1986.

Vryonis Jr., Speros. *The Decline of Medieval Hellenism in Asia Minor and the Process of Islamization from the Eleventh Through the Fifteenth Century.* Berkeley: University of California Press, 1971.

Walther, Wiebke. *Women in Islam.* Updated text. Introduction by Guity Nashat. Princeton: Markus Wiener Publishers, 1993.

Warner, Marina. *Alone of All Her Sex. The Myth and the Cult of the Virgin Mary.* London: Weidenfeld & Nicolson, 1976.

Wehr, Hans. *A Dictionary of Modern Written Arabic (Arabic-English).* 4th ed. Edited by J. Milton Cowan. Wiesbaden: Otto Harrassowitz, 1979.

Weir, T. H., and A. Zysow. "*ṣadaḳa.*" In *EI*², VIII:708–16.

Wild, Johann. *Neue Reysbeschreibung eines gefangenen Christen.* Nurnbert: B. Scherff, 1613.

Wolper, Ethel Sara. "Princess Safwat al-Dunyā wa al-Dīn and the Production of Sufi Buildings and Hagiographies in Pre-Ottoman Anatolia." In *Women, Patronage, and Self-Representation in Islamic Societies,* edited by D. Fairchild Ruggles, 35–52. Albany: State University of New York Press, 2000.

———. "The Politics of Patronage: Political Change and the Construction of Dervish Lodges in Sivas." *Muqarnas* 12 (1995): 39–47.

Woodhead, Christine. "Perspectives on Süleyman." In *Süleyman the Magnificent and His Age: The Ottoman Empire in the Early Modern World,* edited by Metin Kunt and Christine Woodhead, 164–90. Essex: Longman Group UK, 1995.

Yazıcı, Tahsin. "Ḳalandariyya. In *EI*², IV:473–74.

Yediyıldız, Bahaeddin. *Institution du vaqf au XVIIIe siècle en Turquie—Étude socio-historique.* Ankara: Imprimerie de la Société d'Histoire Turque, 1985.

———. *"vakıf."* In *İA,* XIII:153–72.

Young, Bette Roth. *Emma Lazarus in Her World: Life and Letters.* Philadelphia: The Jewish Publication Society, 1995.

Ze'evi, Dror. *An Ottoman Century: The District of Jerusalem in the 1600s.* Albany: State University of New York Press, 1996.

Zilfi, Madeline C., ed. *Women in the Ottoman Empire: Middle Eastern Women in the Early Modern Era.* Leiden: Brill, 1997.

# Index


'Abbasids, 5
'Abdul-Raḥman, kadi of Jerusalem, 116
'Abdülkerim, 'imaret manager, 127
'Abdülkerim (imperial envoy), report of, 99–102, 103–130, *passim*
Abraham, tomb of, 105
Abū Dhahab, waqf of (Cairo), 181 n. 4
Abū Ḥanīfa, 20
Abū Yūsuf, 20
accounts registers. See *muḥasebe defterleri*
Aegean Sea, 134
agriculture: crisis, 124; revenues, 111; yields, 122, 124
*ahlī* (also *dhurrī*) waqf, 31, 180 n. 60
Aḥmed I (r. 1603–17), 30
Aḥmed Paşa, *bey* of Damascus, 118
Ahmediye 'imaret (Üsküdar), 172 n. 13
'Āisha (wife of the Prophet Muḥammad), 81, 82
'Akka (Acre), 126
Aksaray, 137
'Alaeddin Kayḳubad I, 87
Aleppo, 27, 87, 95, 136
'Ali Bali, *sipahi*, 117
'Ali *Kethüda*, 105, 108, 109, 110, 117
'Ali Shīr Navā'ī, 147
almonds, 60
alms. See *zakāt*
Amasya, 137, 151, 154
*'amāyir* (pl. of 'imaret), 29
*amir*, 25, 27
*amīr al-ḥajj* (commander of the pilgrimage), 141
Amyūn, 48, 107
'Anāba, 50
Anatolia, 32, 72, 84, 85, 88, 89, 107, 134, 136, 137, 139, 140, 142, 151, 152
apricots, 60
'Aqabat al-Sitt, 3, 46; quarter in Jerusalem, 48, 128, 160
'Aqabat al-Sūq. *See* 'Aqabat al-Sitt
'Aqabat al-Takiyya. *See* 'Aqabat al-Sitt
*'āqil* (of sound mind), 18
al-Aqṣā mosque, 3, 37, 66
aqueduct, 106, 112
Arab provinces, 84, 142, 152
Arabia, 23
Arabs, 80
archival sources, 172 n. 12
Armenian Catholics, 118
Arslan Khatun, 87
Arwa, 83
*aş* (gruel, soup), 146, 173 n. 17
*aşcı* (cook), 140
*aşevi* (kitchen), 140, 143
*aşhane* (public kitchen), 19, 143